# The Rise of China and a Changing East Asian Order

The Japan Center for International Exchange wishes to thank

Asia Pacific Agenda Project

# The Rise of China and a Changing East Asian Order

*Edited by*

Kokubun Ryosei

*and*

Wang Jisi

## JCIE

Japan Center for International Exchange
*Tokyo • New York*

The surnames of the authors and other persons mentioned in this book are
positioned according to country practice.

Copyediting by Micheline Tusenius and Pamela J. Noda.
Cover design, typographic design, and typesetting by Patrick Ishiyama.
Printed in Japan.
ISBN4-88907-069-9

Distributed outside Japan by Brookings Institution Press (1775 Massachu-
setts Avenue, N.W., Washington, D.C. 20036-2188 U.S.A.) and Kinokuniya
Company Ltd. (5-38-1 Sakuragaoka, Setagaya-ku, Tokyo 156-8691).

Japan Center for International Exchange
9-7 Minami Azabu 4-chome, Minato-ku, Tokyo 106-0047 Japan
www.jcie.or.jp

Japan Center for International Exchange, Inc. (JCIE/USA)
274 Madison Avenue, Suite 1102, New York, N.Y. 10016 U.S.A.
www.jcie.org

# Contents

Foreword      vii

## INTEGRATIVE PAPERS ON THE RISE OF CHINA

1. China's Changing Role in Asia      3
   WANG JISI

2. Globalizing China: The Challenges and the Opportunities      23
   KOKUBUN RYOSEI

3. China and Asia Pacific Regionalism      37
   JUSUF WANANDI

4. The Rise of China and Emergent East Asian Regionalism      49
   CHIA SIOW YUE

5. The Cultural Implications of the Rise of China on the Region      77
   WANG GUNGWU

## CHINESE PERSPECTIVES

6. Political Developments in the Rise of China      91
   YANG GUANGBIN

7. A Sustainable Chinese Economy?      103
   MEN HONGHUA

8. China's Foreign Trade Policy after WTO Accession      119
   WANG RONGJUN

9. The Shaping of China's Foreign Policy      139
   NI FENG

Perspectives from Other Asia Pacific Nations

10. Japan's Political Response to the Rise of China          157
    Takahara Akio

11. The Impact of China's Rise on Sino-Japanese          175
    Economic Relations
    Ohashi Hideo

12. The Rise of China and Korea's China Policy          195
    Lee Geun

13. The Rise of China's Economy: Opportunities and          205
    Threats to China-Korea Economic Relations
    Jwa Sung-Hee *and* Yoon Yong

14. ASEAN and the Rise of China: Engaging, While          229
    Fearing, an Emerging Regional Power
    Noel M. Morada

15. China's Economic Rise and the Responses of ASEAN          241
    Mari Pangestu

16. Reactions in Australia and New Zealand to a          265
    Rising China
    Greg Austin


About the Contributors          276

# Foreword

THE PROSPECT OF a new, rapidly rising China poses both opportunities and challenges for the task of regional community building in Asia Pacific. As the rise and growth of China became eminent and realistic in recent years, it seemed extremely important for a consortium of policy research institutions such as the Asia Pacific Agenda Project (APAP) to examine the nature of China's development in the Asia Pacific region as a whole. With this conviction, the APAP steering committee requested Wang Jisi and Kokubun Ryosei to direct a multilateral research project on the theme of "The Rise of China and the Governance of the Asia Pacific Region." Following the APAP tradition of joint research projects, a study group was formed under the guidance of both directors by recruiting younger scholars from China, Japan, South Korea, the ASEAN countries, and Australia and New Zealand as paper writers. A few senior intellectual leaders from the region worked with the study group and contributed the integrative papers for this project.

The study group met for a planning meeting in Singapore in November 2002, and draft papers were submitted to the APAP Plenary Meeting in Kunming, China, in March 2003. Comments and suggestions offered during the conference were incorporated by the authors as they finalized their respective papers for submission for this publication.

China, with its robust economic performance in recent years, is providing an expanding market for many countries in the region and is increasingly serving as a production base for the corporations of these countries, as seen in the sharp increase in inward investment in China. This obviously contributes to a more dynamic and stronger regional economy in Asia. Yet, the Chinese economy also poses a threat to other countries in the region; its growing competitive strength can result in the decline of certain economic sectors or the hollowing out of industries in these countries. In the political and security arena, the economic development of China, with the largest population in the world, can mean a reduction of the tensions between developed and developing countries that have plagued the region. There is, however, an increasing concern among the Asia Pacific countries about the possibility of China becoming a dominant power with growing political influence and rapidly expanding military capabilities. This feeling is particularly acute at a time when many countries in the region are preoccupied with domestic political and economic concerns and are suffering from weak political leadership.

Another critical concern from the point of view of community building in the region, particularly with respect to a shared interest in human and social development, is the fact that the phenomenal rise of China has occurred under conditions of uncertainty in the political and social arenas. Such uncertainty accompanying the rise of China has led to ambivalent reactions from countries in a region that is still struggling to establish a viable arrangement for regional governance for the sake of economic development and political and security stability. The reactions of the countries in the region, as is the case with the rest of the world, can generally be regarded as either excessive in evaluating China's economic and political/security strength or categorical in pointing to serious problems that China will face domestically or that China can cause in its external relationships. Likewise, China is disturbed by what it would regard as emotional and irresponsible analyses about its own future course, and by the seeming unwillingness of some others to welcome it to joint efforts to build a stable regional order.

I firmly believe that the discussions and examinations presented in this volume constitute significant contributions to the continuous discussion on the theme of China's multidimensional developments in the Asia Pacific region.

I wish to take this opportunity to express our deepest and sincere gratitude to Dr. Wang and Dr. Kokubun and all the authors who took up this challenging task. Congratulations to them for having successfully completed the task. I also wish to thank various funding organizations, most notably the Japanese government, whose generous grant to APAP made it possible to conduct this project.

Tadashi Yamamoto
President
Japan Center for International Exchange
Secretariat
Asia Pacific Agenda Project

# Integrative Papers on the Rise of China

# *I*

# China's Changing Role in Asia

## WANG JISI

This chapter provides a Chinese perspective on the role of the People's Republic of China in Asia and its strategy toward its Asian neighbors. It does this by examining China's response to the widely shared perception in recent years of its "rise" and by discussing the principal concerns that shape China's strategy toward Asia. Finally, China's strategy toward the region is considered in terms of its relations with the United States.

## THE RISE OF CHINA

Even though many are preoccupied with the aftermath of the September 11, 2001, terrorist attacks in the United States and the war in Iraq, China's ascendance continues to attract international attention. While some pessimists point to the "coming collapse of China,"[1] most observers appear deeply impressed with China's economic achievements and social progress.[2] The leadership transition of 2002–2003 proceeded smoothly, with both President Hu Jintao, the new general secretary of the Communist Party, and Premier Wen Jiabao projecting moderate, confident, and competent leadership. Few analysts predict political upheaval in China in the foreseeable future. For at least the next couple of years, it appears there will be more continuity than change in Chinese foreign and domestic policies.

The international discourse on the regional and global impact of the "rise of China" has, of course, caught the Chinese leadership's attention. Chinese leaders and ordinary citizens alike are obviously happy to hear praise of China's successes, and such commentary arouses national pride. Official speeches, reports, and domestic media are also inundated with success stories suggesting the competence of the Communist Party and the correctness of its policies. These sources call too for Chinese people to unite and work together to realize the "great revival" of their nation by the middle of this century. They urge everyone to help build an "all-round, well-off society," a goal that the Sixteenth Party Congress of the Chinese Communist Party set for itself in November 2002.

In contrast to commentary in the international arena, China's leadership is, however, rather restrained in promulgating the notion of the "rise" or "revival" of China. Despite the progress made so far, Chinese are aware that the gap—in terms of national wealth, standard of living, education, and science and technology—between China and developed nations, the United States in particular, is enormous. They know that it will take China decades to catch up, at least, with the Western world. In the interim, there are also formidable impediments that might derail modernization programs.[3] An example of such an obstacle is the impact of the Severe Acute Respiratory Syndrome (SARS) epidemic, which sharply reduced tourism and international commercial activities in China in spring 2003 and damaged China's image abroad.

Beijing has responded in a muted way to the international attention on "China's rise." The Chinese leadership is conscious of ambivalent feelings in neighboring countries, as well as in the United States and Europe, about the growth in Chinese power. Chinese leaders are following comments on the "China threat," "China's coming collapse," and such opinions in the international media, but they have not overreacted to them. Vice Premier Qian Qichen, China's foreign policy architect, has suggested that Gordon Chang gave his book *The Coming Collapse of China* its "sensational" title because he wanted to promote sales (*Study Times*[4] 14 October 2002). Qian added that the "China threat" and "China collapse" theories appear to contradict each other, but "they are in fact two sides of the same coin. They both reflect the views of anti-China elements in the world . . . They are not worth refuting anyway." Qian also commented that if China's comprehensive power were at the same level today that it was decades ago, there would be no loud voices about the "China threat." He also felt that there would not be a market for this theory in a few decades, when China had developed further. Chinese leaders also appear to have concluded that exaggerations of China's economic achievements, either by foreigners or by Chinese, might have undesirable practical results. These might include reductions in foreign aid, pressure for China to reevaluate its currency, and calls for China to use more of its foreign trade surplus.

The general consensus among Chinese political analysts is that the media, including China's own official media, do not overrate China's comprehensive national strength, and that the projection of Chinese power abroad will remain very limited in coming years. Yet there are diverse views among Chinese political analysts regarding how China should respond to perceptions of its growing power and influence in the world. Some feel that U.S. domination of world affairs will constrain the rise of China in that the United States will not allow a strategic challenger and competitor as large as China to rise in Asia. The rhetoric of the "offensive realists"[5] and neo-conservatives in the Bush administration and American think tanks has given ammunition to this pessimism. Some Chinese thinkers are concerned, for instance, that China's increasing dependence on oil and natural gas supplies from the Middle East and Central Asia make it vulnerable to newly gained U.S. influence there. It is thought that the United States might try to impede these supplies if it felt it were necessary to contain China.

However, mainstream thinking seems more sanguine. An earlier comprehensive report on the international environment for the rise of China (Yan et al. 1998) suggested that both international political and economic circumstances were generally conducive for China. A more recent assessment (Huang 2002) stresses domestic reform and balanced development as top priorities for China to enhance its international stature. Promoting economic integration and common security in Asia, establishing constructive cooperation and partnerships with other great powers, and strengthening crisis management capabilities were also raised as prerequisites for China becoming more powerful in world affairs. Many Chinese observers emphasize China's "soft power"—its strategic vision and cultural cohesion, for example—for expanding Chinese influence in international affairs. They also contend that the growth of Chinese power today is contingent on economic globalization, making its situation vastly different to the emergence of the Soviet Union whose development occurred separately from the industrialized world. Unlike Japan and Germany before and between the two World Wars, they also suggest that China today is far from being militarized. Although these arguments may not sound convincing to some international observers, they nonetheless reflect serious Chinese thinking about their nation's path of development and its projection of a peaceful international image.

The Sixteenth Party Congress of the Chinese Communist Party endorsed moderate views of China's international surroundings. It suggested a

"20-year period of strategic opportunities" (Jiang 2002, 19) that China should grasp. The international environment provided the foundation for a moderate and pragmatic Chinese international strategy while allowing China to concentrate on domestic priorities. This pronounced optimism was based on the confident forecast that strategic confrontation between China and the United States or other major powers could be avoided.

Lacking, though, in Chinese deliberations on the "rise of China" is clear realization of the need to promote an institutionalized regional or global order in which China would play a major role—in cooperation with other great powers—and in which China would assume more international obligations. A 2001 report to the Trilateral Commission (Morrison 2001, 9) notes, "China's rapid rise is occurring in a region that lacks firmly established, integrating institutions like the European Union that help build trust. Asia has no security community in the transatlantic sense of peace in which resort to violence has become virtually unimaginable."

Subtle changes in China's approach, for example, to the North Atlantic Treaty Organization (NATO) can be detected. The Chinese press is now less critical of this Western alliance, and the Chinese Foreign Ministry is even exploring possibly establishing some relationship with it. The Chinese have also shown some interest in participating in meetings of the Group of Eight industrialized countries. However, these sporadic indications do not appear to be a systematic approach to dealing with the existing "U.S.-led" world order. The pronounced principles and goals of Chinese foreign policy remain abstractions, such as "establishing a new international political and economic order," "promoting world peace and common development," "accelerating multipolarization," and "opposing hegemonism and power politics."

## Defining China's Strategy toward Asia

As shown in its official attitude toward the Iraq war in March–April 2003, China is likely to take a largely detached position to international events that do not directly affect core Chinese interests. Some Chinese have expressed private reservations about Beijing's reaction to the Kosovo conflict in 1999. During the crisis and the war in Yugoslavia, the Chinese sided staunchly with Slobodan Milosevic, the Yugoslav president, against the NATO alliance. Tensions there did not involve core Chinese interests.

Nevertheless, Milosevic's defeat and the NATO bombing of the Chinese embassy in Belgrade harmed China's relations with the West, delayed China's entry into the World Trade Organization (WTO), and stimulated nationalistic sentiments that were not helpful to the Chinese leadership. Since then, Beijing has been more prudent about involving itself in European and Middle Eastern affairs.

Meanwhile, Chinese strategists have proposed active Chinese engagement in affairs on China's periphery. A difficulty in delineating China's Asia strategy lies in a perception gap between Chinese and many international observers. For the majority of international observers, Asia means East Asia, and Asia Pacific refers to East Asia plus probably Australia, Canada, New Zealand, and the United States. In contrast, references in Chinese publications to China's *zhoubian guojia* (surrounding countries) are taken to comprise East Asian states and neighboring countries like the Central Asian states, India, Mongolia, Pakistan, and Russia. This definitional difference has important policy implications. It reflects the fact that Chinese look beyond East Asia in formulating a regional strategy. China's regional strategy in Asia has to focus on a complex matrix of geopolitical and geo-economic factors, such as Russia, terrorism and the conflicts in Southwest and South Asia, and oil and natural gas supplies from Central Asia. This perception gap between China and other East Asian countries reflects the historical reality that China is a continental power, whereas most other East Asian countries are maritime or semi-maritime powers.

A cluster of overlapping issue areas circumscribes China's regional strategy. These issues include the momentum of East Asian economic cooperation; the regional security environment, especially on the Korean peninsula; arms control regimes and regional reaction to China's growing military capabilities, against the backdrop of existing regional security arrangements; the Taiwan issue; China's special relationship with Japan; and Chinese-U.S. relations, the most relevant independent variable. Given the importance of Chinese relations with the United States, they will be discussed separately.

## REGIONAL ECONOMIC COOPERATION

In the early 1990s, China was not very enthusiastic about formal, structured regional trade arrangements, partly because it was not yet ready for rapid trade and investment liberalization at home, and partly because it was skeptical about Japan playing a leading role in the regional economy. Strong objections from the United States to the forming of an East Asian economic grouping—such as the East Asia Economic Caucus proposed by Malaysia—also revealed political complications to new regional economic initiatives. China's participation in the Asia-Pacific Economic Cooperation (APEC) initiative was largely circumstantial, and it went along with an insistence that APEC remain a "forum."

China has now reached the stage of economic development where it can open up further to international competition, and integrate itself regionally and globally for long-term gain. China's WTO accession and its increased economic ties with its neighbors will greatly impact the region, as well as China itself. WTO membership is compelling faster liberalization of the Chinese economy, and it is providing Chinese policymakers with a clear mandate to implement reforms in the face of inevitable resistance from entrenched domestic interests. In terms of the ratio of trade to gross domestic product, a simple indicator of openness, China already has an open economy. The ratio is currently near 40 percent, compared to roughly 20 percent for India, Japan, and the United States. Likewise, in recent years, foreign direct investment in China's economy has equaled about 18 percent of total investment, which compares with a level of 6 percent in the United States (Shin 2002). China is perceived as having taken foreign investment away from other countries, but it is also rapidly becoming the region's main engine for economic growth. It could even become a net exporter of capital to East and Southeast Asian countries.

As the largest exporter among developing economies, China is being called on to represent the interests of Asian and other developing economies. China could possibly also lead efforts to better balance the interests of developing and developed countries in multilateral trading arrangements. A study by Asian economists showed that a free trade area between China and the Association of Southeast Asian Nations (ASEAN) would bring mutual wealth, partially by diverting ASEAN's trade away from Western economies to China (*People's Daily* 13 February 2003). Some have already predicted that a free trade arrangement (FTA) between China and ASEAN would rival the European Union and the North American Free Trade Agreement (*Express China News* November/December 2001).

However, China must guard against trade challenges from Asia resulting in developed countries abandoning the WTO framework in favor of more limited multilateral arrangements. This would surely be detrimental to the economic prospects of developed and developing countries alike. It is also unfortunate that U.S. reaction to various ideas and institutions for East Asian regional economic cooperation has overshadowed their merits.

China should also guard against viewing its nascent FTA with ASEAN as a counterbalance to Japan's efforts to establish its own FTA with ASEAN. A Chinese economist (Li 2003, 208) notes that "while Japan was trying, on the one hand, to sign an [FTA] with ASEAN to exclude China from the East Asian free trade zone, it was also trying to sign the first bilateral [FTAs] with South Korea and Singapore." The FTA which China and ASEAN began considering in November 2001 is a "type of South-South regional economic cooperation arrangement that has a ten-year transitional period [which prohibits attaching] too much short-term significance to it" (Li 2003). Too many political considerations could encumber the long process of meaningful successes in East Asian economic cooperation.

Since sustaining economic growth remains China's top priority, promoting East Asian economic cooperation will be an integral part of China's regional strategy. Yet it is still unclear whether China harbors a strategic vision of an East Asian economic bloc comparable to that of the European Union, or whether it believes that Chinese FTAs with ASEAN, Japan, and South Korea could provide more desirable opportunities for China's economic integration.

## THE REGIONAL SECURITY ENVIRONMENT

Undoubtedly the most difficult security problem China faces today is the North Korean nuclear issue, and China cannot afford to lose the influence it does have over events on the Korean peninsula. Vital interests are at stake. Two painful historical memories for Chinese are that the Sino-Japanese war over Korea in 1894 resulted in the cession of Taiwan, and that the outbreak of the Korean War in 1950 deprived China of the capability and opportunity to take over Taiwan, with China remaining divided ever since.

Current tensions over the North Korean nuclear issue have aroused a great deal of attention in Beijing. Unlike earlier occasions when problems around North Korea were treated with great discretion and sensitivity in the Chinese media, since December 2002, the Chinese public has been provided with more detailed information and commentary. For example, an official news report on January 10, 2003, revealed that former President Jiang Zemin told U.S. President George W. Bush that China did not endorse North Korea's decision to withdraw from the Nuclear Nonproliferation Treaty. The message here was that Beijing and Washington share more common ground than Beijing and Pyongyang do. In April 2003, Beijing hosted a three-party meeting between China, North Korea, and the United States, suggesting once again its distance from Pyongyang on the nuclear issue. In August 2003, China hosted six-party talks in Beijing, involving itself, Japan, the two Koreas, Russia, and the United States.

There are at least two priorities in Beijing's strategic objectives toward the Korean peninsula. First, it is definitely in China's best long-term interest to maintain a nuclear-free Korea. No country is as concerned as China about nuclear threats as it already shares borders with three nuclear powers—India, Pakistan, and Russia (the United States previously threatened China with its nuclear arsenal). In addition to creating a huge problem for Chinese national security, an additional nuclear power in the region could also provide the rationale for other players, notably Japan and even Taiwan, to develop nuclear arms. Suggestions along these lines, and how such a development would affront Chinese sensitivities, have reportedly already been made in Japan. U.S. apprehensions about possible North Korean nuclear proliferation to countries or terrorist groups outside the region also make sense to China.

Preventing North Korea from going nuclear is a sufficient priority for Beijing to cooperate with Washington and the international community in seeking a viable solution to the problem. Beijing does not regard the problem as a bilateral issue between the United States and North Korea, with China being a bystander. China and the United States share strong concerns to keep other Northeast Asian players from acquiring nuclear arms capabilities. Beijing's hesitation to act more vigorously on the North Korean issue is related to what it sees as uncertainties in U.S. strategic plans.

China's influence on North Korea is undeniable but limited. The most frequently suggested way of using Chinese influence is for Beijing to join others in imposing economic sanctions. Aside from questions about the feasibility, legitimacy, and desirability of such a coordinated effort, the effectiveness of possible economic sanctions against the North is doubtful at this stage. Past instances of the use of sanctions, notably vis-à-vis Cuba, Iraq, and China itself in the 1950s, pose questions about whether economic punishment of a people can change the behavior of its political leadership. Yet China's economic instruments could be used, in certain circumstances.

Another way of exerting China's influence is through a multilateral framework for an international solution, even though Pyongyang has insisted in the past that the issue is a bilateral one between it and Washington. A United Nations Security Council resolution, coordinated with the International Atomic Energy Agency, could, however, be effective if the international community mobilized the instruments to implement it.

The second priority in China's strategic calculation for the Korean peninsula is the preservation of peace and stability. Chinese and U.S. perceptions of North Korea's domestic stability do diverge. Chinese analysts believe their predictions of North Korea's survivability in the 1990s were validated, in contrast to many U.S. forecasts of an imminent North Korean collapse. Today the Chinese continue to believe in North Korea's likely survivability. The Chinese certainly have a larger stake in maintaining stability in the North than any other country, except (arguably) for South Korea. This is so because of geographic, demographic, and economic realities in China's northeast, not because of any ideological or political affinity.

To Beijing, either a nuclear Korea or a military conflict there would be disastrous.[6] China's maneuverability over North Korea is definitely circumscribed, particularly with both the United States and North Korea sticking firmly to their respective positions. While the Bush administration is preoccupied with the Middle East and terrorism, it is unlikely that the United States will react decisively to North Korea's prodding, and the North Koreans could proceed with military maneuvers and move further toward reactivating its nuclear program. Things may become worse before they get better; it is urgent to find a way now to stop the dangerous escalation of tensions.

There should be a third priority in dealing with the situation: assisting North Korea's economic recovery. Pyongyang's poor economic performance and the widening gap between the living standards in North Korea and those of its neighbors exacerbate its siege mentality. The Chinese government already supplies a sizeable amount of energy, food aid, and other emergency assistance to the North, and it also has to deal, in a humanitarian way, with the matter of North Korean refugees residing in China.

Another potential flash point in China's regional security environment is the India-Pakistan confrontation. While maintaining its traditionally cordial relationship with Pakistan, Beijing has been sensitive to anxieties in New Delhi and Washington about alleged Chinese sales of nuclear and missile technologies to Pakistan. The Chinese government is committed to tightened control of such sales in accordance with the Missile Technology Control Regime, and bilateral agreements between Beijing and Washington. The two governments have committed themselves to preventing the export of equipment, materials, or technologies that might help India or Pakistan in their plans to develop nuclear weapons or ballistic missiles for carrying such weapons (Gu 2002, 82).

Meanwhile, Chinese-Indian relations are greatly improving, having overcome difficulties resulting from India's nuclear tests in 1998. Border disputes between the two countries remain unsettled though, with the psychological wounds from the 1962 border war needing still more time to heal. The United States has reportedly reached out to India for security consultations and cooperation, partly aimed at the perceived "China threat." Russian politicians and strategists have also proposed some kind of Chinese-Indian-Russian trilateral strategic cooperation to offset U.S. influence in the region.

Other problems for China in its regional security outlook are international terrorism, domestic turbulence in Indonesia and elsewhere, refugees and illegal immigration from China's neighboring countries, and crime and drug trafficking across China's borders. Judging from its behavior since Chinese policy thinking has moderated, China would involve itself very reluctantly in regional crises and other countries' domestic disturbances, even though it might have to cope with resulting human security problems. For instance, although Chinese were incensed by the victimization of ethnic Chinese during turmoil in Indonesia, Beijing's official position remained that the vast majority of the ethnic Chinese were Indonesian rather than Chinese citizens, so Indonesians had to solve this internal problem. To this extent, China will continue to be a conservative or status quo power in the region. At the same time, Beijing has indicated its concerns about terrorist and pirate activities in Southeast Asia that have caused casualties or suffering to Chinese citizens.

Since the 1990s, Beijing has downplayed the significance of territorial disputes with Southeast Asian countries in the South China Sea. In retrospect, the disputes did not enhance China's influence in the region, but gave rise to regional suspicions about China's long-term strategic intentions. From China's perspective, the United States could also try to drive a wedge between China and ASEAN countries by taking advantage of the territorial problems between them. In recent years, more urgent external and internal issues—including the Asian financial crisis, separatist tendencies in Taiwan, and the North Korean quagmire—have eclipsed the strategic and economic importance of the tiny Spratly and Paracel islets.


## ARMS CONTROL REGIMES AND REGIONAL REACTION TO CHINA'S MILITARY MODERNIZATION

A number of regional arms control issues, such as the planned U.S. missile defense systems, Japan's willingness to participate in them, the nuclearization of South Asia, and the consequences of a North Korea possibly armed with nuclear weapons, are contributing to a defensiveness in China's strategic thinking. The natural response to these developments would be to continue, if not speed up, the modernization of China's armed forces. Yet improved Chinese defense capabilities may, in turn, stimulate regional concerns. China has to convince its regional partners, particularly those with which China still has territorial disputes, that a stronger Chinese military power will not threaten them. Failure to do so may push such states further into the U.S. orbit. The best ways to reduce regional suspicions and misunderstandings about China are, first, to increase the transparency of China's strategic thinking, planning, and defense capabilities, and, second, to strengthen regional security dialogues.

China's strategic plans and arms control policies in Asia are directed mostly at the United States. Some Chinese specialists have proposed that the United States and China should engage in strategic dialogue to discuss whether and to what extent China would be allowed to obtain a reliable nuclear deterrent by adding more heads and missiles to its nuclear arsenal (Gu 2002, 82–83). The Chinese have also considered redeploying some of China's missiles aimed across the Taiwan Strait as a gesture to reducing tension with Taiwan and the United States. The hope here was for some reciprocal U.S. gesture that would reduce Chinese anxieties over U.S. military cooperation with Taiwan. However, neither proposal has received any substantive or positive response from the U.S. side. Failure to address these issues properly is detrimental to Asian regional security.

# The Taiwan Issue

The Taiwan issue features in China's regional strategy in several ways. Many Chinese feel that China's revival would be meaningless and unreal if the mainland failed to reunify with Taiwan. So China's regional policies need to be geared toward fulfilling this national goal. Taiwan's leaders also spare no efforts in trying to have certain types of experiences by Taiwan's leadership, such as tours through Japan or Southeast Asia, viewed as failures of Chinese diplomacy. The Chinese also always find it awkward to deal with Taiwan's participation in regional organizations like APEC. While much of China's military modernization is designed to deter Taiwan from adventurous moves toward de jure independence, it has unfavorable regional repercussions, and a hardened Chinese posture toward Taiwan will disserve China's image as a benign power seeking harmonious relations with its neighbors.

Since 2001, there have been two subtle modifications in Beijing's conceptualization of the Taiwan issue. First, it is more apparent to Chinese that, despite conspicuous U.S. political support of Taiwan and its democratization, Washington's policy toward the island is not intended to encourage or endorse Taiwan's de jure independence. The Bush administration's consistent statements not supporting Taiwan independence have assured Beijing that Washington understands China's "red line." Namely, that a provocative Taiwanese action to change Taiwan's legal status would trigger a major confrontation between Beijing and Taipei, which could engage the United States in a deadly military conflict with the Chinese mainland. Washington, therefore, prefers the status quo of "no reunification, no separation" in cross-Strait relations (Wang and Li 2002). This interpretation contrasts with earlier mainstream Chinese perceptions that the U.S. strategy toward Taiwan was to separate Taiwan from China permanently, in order to contain China.

The other modification in Beijing's posture is based on the assessment that time is on the mainland's side. The mainland's economy is growing much faster than Taiwan's, and the strategic balance of power is changing increasingly in the mainland's favor. Beijing is hoping that deepening socioeconomic interdependence between the two sides will pave the way for ultimate political integration. This new Chinese confidence bodes well for more accommodating and manageable relations between the mainland and Taiwan, and also for reduced international tensions in East Asia.

## Japan—Partner or Competitor?

The relationship with Japan remains a centerpiece of China's regional strategy and deserves special attention. As new generations of Chinese elites with no personal experience of the Second World War emerge, the historical imprint in China's policy toward Japan will hopefully fade. This process is likely to take more than a few years, and, hopefully, reduced unfavorable Japanese feelings about China should facilitate this too. Chinese perceptions of Japan definitely add an element of uncertainty to China's long-term strategy toward Japan. At the same time, there are also enormous reservoirs of realistic and sensible thinking, as well as interests, in both societies that favor a more productive, friendly China-Japan relationship.

Recent developments in East Asia offer opportunities for Japan and China to become better partners, rather than long-term competitors. First is the ongoing momentum of regional economic cooperation, highlighted by regular meetings of ASEAN + 3, namely, ASEAN members and the countries of China, Japan, and South Korea.[7] The recovery of Japan's economy will paradoxically help construct a more solid foundation for strategic as well as economic cooperation between the two Asian giants. Second is the North Korea nuclear issue. China and Japan have many common interests on the Korean peninsula. Both of them have huge stakes in preventing the nuclearization of North Korea, and in maintaining peace and stability there. Both would benefit from any North Korean economic opening up. Nonetheless, there are few indications that these opportunities have been adequately grasped. Both Beijing and Tokyo seem to be paying attention to other policy issues, and are not injecting enough energy into bilateral cooperation.

## The China-U.S. Relationship: A Dominant Factor

China's Asia strategy 20–25 years ago was preoccupied with Soviet encirclement of China, a perception that the Soviet-Vietnamese alliance reinforced. As recently as ten years ago, China's regional strategy was focused on an assertive United States that proposed establishing a "New Pacific Community." This notion, which alarmed Beijing, was vaguely put forward by then President Bill Clinton at the 1993 Seattle meeting of APEC. At the time, Beijing was under severe pressure to change its domestic policies after Tiananmen, while it was also making painstaking efforts to keep its most-favored-nation status with the United States. China was also about to resume diplomatic relations with Indonesia, and establish them with South Korea. No comprehensive regional strategy was possible then without marked improvement in China's bilateral relations with the United States as well as its Asian neighbors.

China's regional concerns today still focus strongly on the United States, albeit to a lesser extent. Some Chinese strategists are apprehensive, for example, that the expanded U.S. military presence in Afghanistan, Pakistan, and Central Asia since the attacks of September 11, 2001, along with enhanced U.S-Indian strategic understanding, will once again result in China's strategic encirclement. Most Chinese policy advisors, however, remain unperturbed by these new security circumstances. Instead, they point to greatly improved bilateral ties with China's neighbors, contending that few, if any, Asian powers would join a U.S.-led coalition to contain China. Increased Chinese vigilance against separatists, terrorists, and religious extremists in China's northwest national minority areas since September 2001 seems to have reduced Chinese interest in viewing the Shanghai Cooperation Organization (SCO) as a counterweight to U.S. influence in the region. The SCO is a regional grouping formed by China to improve cooperation on nontraditional security issues between itself, Russia, and the Central Asian republics of Kazakhstan, Kyrgyzstan, Tajikistan, and Uzbekistan.

Having experienced many ups and downs in relations since the end of the cold war, Beijing's policy toward the United States is now increasingly temperate and mature. With China needing a peaceful environment to sustain economic growth and social progress, Beijing has been developing a long-term strategy based on some fundamental assumptions. These assumptions are independent variables, subject to reassessment and readjustment by Chinese leaders.

The first assumption is that the global strategic structure is seriously unbalanced in favor of the United States. In the first post–cold war years, the rise of the United States to global primacy was debatable. There is little doubt today though that a unipolar world is the reality with which China must cope. China's projection of the "inevitability of multipolarity" does not prevent it from noting, at least privately, that the United States will remain the global hegemonic power for decades to come.[8] Being realists, Chinese policy analysts also have few illusions about the feasibility of a lasting international coalition to counter U.S. power. China has neither the capability nor the desire to take the lead in formulating such a coalition, let alone an interest in confronting the U.S. hegemon by itself.

In the diplomatic showdown at the United Nations prior to the 2003 war in Iraq, China generally sided with France, Germany, and Russia in the efforts to stall a military solution, but it did not incur the wrath of the Bush administration in doing so. The result of the major military campaign of the war in Iraq once again illustrated the preponderance of U.S. military and political power, and Washington's willingness to use it unilaterally. Unofficial public polling in China prior to the outbreak of the war showed that over 80 percent of Chinese citizens opposed the use of force in Iraq. The bulk of them also supported the Chinese government's moderation in dealing with the crisis.

Even without active Chinese resistance, hegemonic U.S. behavior will not go unchecked in the international arena. Chinese firmly believe this, especially when they look at Asia Pacific where few countries, if any, would give unequivocal support to a possible U.S. policy intended to isolate or contain China. This strategic situation will give China enough breathing space for enhancing its stature and influence. ASEAN, Japan, Russia, South Korea, and other regional powers will increasingly strengthen their economic ties with China as China's economy, markets, and capital grow. More political understanding will then follow. The general trend in Asia, therefore, is conducive for China's aspirations to integrate itself more extensively into the region and the world. It will be difficult for the United States to reverse the direction of this trend.

The second Chinese assumption about the longer term is that different views and interests regarding China will continue to exist within the United States. Hardliners, centered on the so-called Blue Team, within and without the Bush administration are balanced by moderate realists, some of whom are respected China specialists with political experience. U.S. military views that see China as a threat are in conflict with, but balanced against, commercial interests. U.S. corporate giants like Boeing, Citibank, Motorola, and Wal-Mart have an increasingly large stake in the China market. Engagement between China and the United States is so extensive today that the Bush administration would not easily be able to conduct a China policy similar to U.S. policy toward the Soviet Union during the cold war.

The Chinese calculation is that, for a considerable time at least, U.S. national security strategy will mainly be directed at what Americans define as international terrorism. Although it is politically sensitive to link terrorism to any religious belief or group, the "9/11 syndrome" will focus the U.S. strategy of suppressing terrorist elements and the proliferation of weapons of massive destruction (WMD) on the Middle East, Central Asia, and South Asia. China has no interest either in allying itself strategically with countries seen as hostile to the United States or in proliferating WMD, so it is unlikely that the United States will regard China as its principal strategic adversary in coming years.

In the final analysis, a policy of avoiding confrontation with the United States is consistent with China's domestic political agenda. To be sure, many Americans look at China's political system with distaste, and the United States provides sanctuary to representatives of virtually all groups regarded as being against the present Chinese government. Political conflict with the United States would worsen the situation. As China's reform agenda emphasizes the rule of law, democratic practices, and a market economy, and the Chinese government has accepted the concept of human rights, many political issues between the two nations can be discussed through dialogue. Also, excessive nationalistic feelings among Chinese, most of which are directed against the United States and some against Japan, are not helpful in enhancing the authority of the Chinese leadership. A stable political situation in China is partly contingent on successful diplomacy that better manages China's relationship with the world's only superpower.

This strategy toward the United States, of course, is not without problems and difficulties. The contrast between media coverage of international affairs on the one hand, which may inflame undesirable, unnecessary nationalistic tendencies, and actual policy thinking and practice on the other hand, is a serious challenge. Interagency coordination within the Chinese government is also proving to be a daunting task, especially in crisis management. The nature of the Chinese political structure preconditions the difficulty of engaging the United States, whose political strength lies largely in its pluralist society rather than the concentration of power.

In general, reduced mutual suspicions and mistrust between China and the United States would help pave the way for more creative and proactive Chinese approaches to regional security and economic cooperation. China's leading strategists also perceive the "rise" of China as needing to be accompanied by the rise of Asia as a whole. A structural change in the global balance of power along these lines would better position China vis-à-vis the United States.

## CONCLUSION

Certain trends in China's relations with other Asian powers help define China's role in Asia. These include improved bilateral relationships with all China's neighboring states; more active participation in multilateral security and economic arrangements; cautious support for new forms of regional economic cooperation; and serious consideration of U.S. influence and interests in the region, and how these interests concur with China's own strategic concerns.

Overall, an excessively assertive Chinese posture toward the Asia Pacific region is unlikely. This is precluded because of Beijing's desire to concentrate on domestic development, Chinese consciousness of international sensitivities to the perceived and actual "rise of China," and successful pragmatism in China's international behavior in the post–cold war era.

Meanwhile, a few questions remain with regard to China's future role in Asia. First, although China has become a full-fledged regional player, its relationships with the other two major players—the United States and Japan—are still in flux, and the recent improvement in relations with each is not yet irreversible. Second, and related to China-U.S. and China-Japan relations, the Taiwan problem lingers, and how Beijing manages it will strongly impact countries' perceptions of China. Third, China's relative political underdevelopment contrasts with most of its Asian neighbors, who are generally content with the market-oriented reforms China is carrying out, but are cautious about China's longer-term future. Finally, the kind of value system China presently upholds at home and internationally, and will uphold in future as its power has grown further, is a perplexing question.

## NOTES

1. See Chang (2002) for the best-known writing on this theme.
2. For a recent discussion of the emergence of China's power, see Overholt (2002).
3. For an official description of the gap between China and the developed world, and of difficulties in socioeconomic development, see Jiang (2002, 18–19).
4. *Study Times* is a weekly published by China's Central Party School.

5. For a representative view of "offensive realism," see Mearsheimer (2001).
6. Chinese analysts differ over whether China should prioritize one over the other. Shi Yinhong (2003) argues that "China's supreme strategic interest or primary strategic goal is to insulate North Korea from nuclearization." In contrast, Jin Xide (2003) contends that China should not prioritize denuclearization over peace, and should never abandon North Korea as a friendly neighbor.
7. Chinese analysts share the view that China and Japan are competing about which country plays the leadership role in East Asia's regional economy. See Jiang (2003, 52–53).
8. For a recent Chinese assessment of U.S. power and influence, see Men (2003).

## BIBLIOGRAPHY

Chang, Gordon G. 2002. *The Coming Collapse of China.* New York: Random House.
Gu Guoliang. 2002. "Zhongguo de junkong yingdui celue: Jianlun xiao Bushi zhengu junkong sixiang yu zhengce de tiaozheng ji bianhua" (China's arms control tactics and the changes in the Bush administration's arms control thinking and policy). *Zhanlue Yu Guanli* (Strategy and Management) 4(53): 77–84.
Huang Renwei. 2002. *Zhongguo jueqi de shijian he kongjian* (The timeframe and space for China to rise up). Shanghai: The Shanghai Academy of Social Sciences Press.
Jiang Ruiping. 2003. "Dongya FTA re zhong de leng sikao" (Cold thinking in the FTA fever in East Asia). *Shijie Zhishi* (World Affairs) 6: 62–53.
Jiang Zemin. 2002. *Zai zhongguo gongchandang di shiliu ci quanguo daibiao dahui shang de baogao* (Report to the Sixteenth National Congress of the Communist Party of China). Beijing: The People's Press.
Jin Xide. 2003. "Zhongguo hui di'er ci kang mei yuan chao ma?" (Would China wage a second war of "resisting America and aiding Korea"?). *Shijie Zhishi* (World Affairs), no. 6: 14–15.
Li Xiangyang. 2003. "Quanqiu quyu jingji hezuo de fazhan qushi" (Global trends in regional economic cooperation). In Wang Luolin and Yu Yongding, eds. *Shijie jingji huangpishu 2002–2003* (Yellow book of in-

ternational economy 2002–2003). Beijing: Social Sciences Documentation Publishing House.

Mearsheimer, John J. 2001. *The Tragedy of Great Power Politics.* New York: W. W. Norton.

Men Honghua. 2003. "Lengzhan hou meiguo da zhanlue de zhengming jiqi yiyi (The debate on post–cold war U.S. grand strategy and its implications). In Hu Angang and Men Honghua, eds. *Jiedu meiguo da zhanlue* (Decoding U.S. grand strategy). Hangzhou: The Zhejiang People's Press.

Morrison, Charles E., coordinator. 2001. *East Asia and the International System: Report of a Special Study Group.* New York: The Trilateral Commission.

Overholt, William. 2002. *The Rise of China.* New York: W. W. Norton.

Shi Yinhong. 2003. "Chaoxian he weiju yu Zhongguo de zhanlue anquan" (North Korean nuclear crisis and China's strategic security). *21 Shiji Huanqiu Baodao* (21st Century World Herald). (20 January).

Shin Myoung-Ho. 2002. "Asian Economic Cooperation in the New Millennium: China's Economic Presence." Speech to the Asian Development Bank. <http://www.adb.org/Documents/Speeches/2002/ms2002060.asp> (April 2003).

Wang Jisi and Li Xiaogang. 2002. "Meiguo de shijie zhanlue yu Taiwan wenti" (America's world strategy and the Taiwan issue). In Lu Xiaoheng, ed. *Zhongguo duiwai guanxi zhong de Taiwan wenti* (The Taiwan issue in China's foreign relations). Beijing: Economic Management Publishing House.

Yan Xuetong, Wang Zaibang, Li Zhongcheng, and Hou Ruoshi. 1998. *Zhongguo Jueqi–guoji huanjing pinggu* (The international environment for China's rise). Tianjin: Tianjin People's Press.

# 2

## Globalizing China:
## The Challenges and the Opportunities

### KOKUBUN RYOSEI

#### GLOBALIZATION AND SYSTEM TRANSFORMATION

Globalization has been greatly debated in China in recent years, particularly since China became interested in joining the World Trade Organization (WTO), and then started preparing for entry to the world trading body. Cadres of all ranks, farmers, laborers, intellectuals, and students—all segments of society have become interested in the phenomenon of globalization, and the international organization called the WTO. This interest stems from the possibilities they represent of reconstructing China's very foundation.

The WTO is distinctly different from the multilateral trading body, the General Agreement on Tariffs and Trade, which it succeeded in 1995. Once a country becomes a WTO member, it has no choice but to change its domestic economic system in accordance with WTO rules. In other words, once it is admitted as a member of the WTO, a country is obliged to reform its economy to conform with market mechanisms. All features of an economic system, such as taxation, business practices, and property and intellectual property rights, have to be addressed. It is for this reason—that there are so many aspects and instruments of the Chinese economic system that will have to be reformed, and that China will not be able to avoid reforming them—that interest in China in globalization and the WTO is so high.

As a result of it formally becoming a WTO member in December 2001, China has particular obligations that it must meet. For example, average tariffs for mining and manufacturing products must be lowered to 9.4 percent by 2005, from their current rate of 24.6 percent; major agricultural products must be reduced to 14.5 percent, from their present 31.5 percent; and tariffs on automobiles must drop to 25 percent by 2006, from the current 80 percent–100 percent. Also, two years after China joined the WTO, foreign-affiliated banks and securities companies must be able to do business in renminbi with Chinese companies, and five years after WTO accession, they must be able to do business with individuals. As a WTO member, and by opening its markets to the world, China will increasingly be directly affected by the international economic system. Yet WTO accession also means that inexpensive but relatively high-quality Chinese products can be easily marketed, and that production of Chinese textile products—which already dominate world markets—can be accelerated. Exports of more technology-intensive tools, machinery, household appliances, and other basic industrial products are also expanding. Overall, increased interdependence between the Chinese market and world markets, and closer economic cooperation also mean increased potential for economic conflict of various types.

The essential reason that China wanted to become a WTO member lies in the hard reality of its economic situation. China kicked off the next phase of economic reform in 1992, with Deng Xiaoping's tour through southern China, and the subsequent declaration of the "socialist market" economy. China's economy grew 14.2 percent in 1992 and 10.5 percent in 1995, and the driving force behind this remarkable economic growth was increased trade and foreign direct investment (FDI). China's economic growth then slowed—to 9.6 percent in 1996, and 7.1 percent in 1999— due to the 1997 Asian financial crisis, and a resulting decline in FDI. In terms of contracts, there were 7,273 cases of FDI in 1990, amounting to approximately US$6.6 billion; 8,347 cases in 1993, amounting to roughly US$111.4 billion; and 16,918 cases in 1999, totaling roughly US$41.2 billion (Mitsubishi Research Institute 2000, 343 and 506).

In 1990, 29.8 percent of China's gross domestic product was dependent on trade; in 2000, this trade dependence was 43.9 percent. Half of China's economic growth depends on trade, foreign corporations contribute 50 percent to exports, and close to 18 percent of state tax revenue is from foreign corporations (Hosokawa 2002, 68–69). In short, China's economic growth depends greatly on foreign capital, specifically on FDI. So the Chinese government pushed for WTO membership in order to accelerate the marketization of China's economy through "forceful" opening.

In its history, China has always been very "Sino-centric" and very cautious about the penetration of external influences. Late Qing Dynasty reformists tried to introduce science and technology from the West as a means to modernize the nation (*zhongti xiyong*) without really changing the system. However, through exposure to scientific and technological principles, people became interested in Western values, so, sensing danger, the government suspended the reforms.

Since 1978, socialist China has pursued modernization under the slogan of "reform and opening," with the idea being to use Western science and technology to complement and complete socialist rule. In the 1980s, when "planning" was regarded as primary and "the market" as secondary, China was considering internal reform premised on the maintenance of socialism. After the Tiananmen Square incident and the collapse of the Soviet Union, China recognized the limits of "planning," and decided to introduce a "socialist market economy." Although many aspects of a market economy were to be implemented, the point was definitely the maintenance of socialism, and the principles of public ownership and the leadership of the Chinese Communist Party (CCP).

Some actions that the Chinese have taken in order to join the WTO have, however, caused contradictions in the basic principles of public ownership and CCP leadership. Indeed, the very act of reforming its domestic system using external sources—an unusual phenomenon in China's history—may be considered an encroachment on China's spirit and Chinese values.

"The economic substructure alters the superstructure of politics and other arenas" was the proposition of Karl Marx. In China, too, many considered that basing economic reorganization on collectivization would transform politics and the social superstructure into socialism. The "uninterrupted revolution" of Mao Zedong's Cultural Revolution is a powerful example of attempts to radically transform politics and society. In the end, however, the superstructure could not change the substructure. Only later, with the economic reforms introduced by Deng, did transformations of the economic substructure start to affect the superstructure. In this regard, Marx's view appears to have been correct.

So the issue arises of state power and the political regime that supports it, and, more specifically, the type of political regime that accords with a market-based system. The market mechanism definitely functions best with a small government that supports the principles of competitiveness, liberalization, and freedom of information. In the case of China, the CCP is unable to really implement these principles, as it cannot allow changes that threaten its control and that create pressures for a multiple-party system. CCP leaders have, however, been attracted by the principle of corporatism. By co-opting actors to give the suggestion of pluralizing, the CCP might be able to maintain its power. Jiang Zemin's theory of the "Three Represents" is an attempt to provide the theoretical underpinning of the CCP's new corporatist strategy.

By joining the WTO, China has chosen to proceed with marketization. Various government departments are attempting to reduce their size in the interests of "small government," and market forces will become more determining. Yet conflicts will arise, especially if the CCP intervenes too much. Given the experience of the collapse of the Soviet Union, and the fact that the CCP is the core of the Chinese political regime, discussing the direction of the CCP is urgent (Dickson 2000–2001).

## THE "THREE REPRESENTS": A THEORETICAL BREAKTHROUGH?

In a parallel with Deng's 1992 visit to southern China that reinvigorated China's reform drive, Jiang first mentioned the "Three Represents" early in 2000 during a visit to Guangzhou. He declared that, "The practices of our 70 some years tell us that one very important factor is the cause of overwhelming support of people at different stages of the revolution, construction, and reform. It is the fact that our Party has represented a need for the development of advanced productive forces of China; it has represented the direction for China's advanced culture; and it has represented the fundamental interests of the masses of the people. Furthermore, the Party is constantly fighting for the fundamental interests of the state and people through the establishment of correct lines, directions, and policies" (Jiang 2001, 2).

In other words, the CCP was seen as representing three factors; advanced productive forces, advanced culture, and the people. The seemingly simple reference to "the people" is very revealing. According to Marxist-Leninist principles, the CCP is supposed to represent a certain class of people, namely, the "proletariat." The nonchalant switching to "the people" could be perceived as suggesting that the CCP was moving away from being a class-based party. At the same time, numerous cases of political corruption within the CCP were exposed, and, given the reference to the CCP representing "the people," harsh criticisms were directed against it.

"Since China adopted the reform and opening policy, the composition of China's social strata has changed to some extent. There are, among others, entrepreneurs and engineers employed by scientific and technological enterprises of the nonpublic sector, managers and technocrats employed by foreign-funded enterprises, self-employed, private entrepreneurs, employees in intermediaries, and freelance professionals. Moreover, many people frequently move from one ownership, sector, or place to another, changing their jobs or capacity from time to time. This trend of developments will continue. Under the leadership of the Party line, principles, and policies, most of these people in the new social strata have contributed to the development of productive forces and other undertakings in a socialist society through honest labor and work or lawful business operations. They work, together with workers, farmers, intellectuals, cadres, and the officers and men of the People's Liberation Army. They are also working for building socialism with Chinese characteristics" (Jiang 2001, 169).

With these words at celebrations for the eightieth anniversary of the founding of the CCP, Jiang reemphasized his earlier suggestion that the CCP should admit private entrepreneurs into its ranks, to reflect the rapid expansion of the private sector, and the scaled-back state sector. The reality is that many CCP members became entrepreneurs while maintaining their CCP membership, and that many private entrepreneurs were CCP members. Jiang also proposed admitting "newly emerging private entrepreneurs" into the CCP.

As private ownership has not been approved, private entrepreneurs are only responsible for management, thus they are not "capitalists" who own "private property." Yet the concept of "private property rights" was officially acknowledged at the Third Plenum of the Sixteenth Central Committee in October 2003, and it is to be included in the newly revised constitution to be adopted by the National People's Congress in the spring of 2004. The CCP will then no longer be a "communist party" in the Marxian sense. Chinese intellectuals have, in fact, already been discussing changing the CCP's name. The "People's Party of China," the "Social Democratic Party of China," and the "Liberal Democratic Party of China" are some of the suggestions. Introducing a change of such magnitude will, however, take time.

The "Three Represents" can also be interpreted as part of the theoretical preparations for China shifting toward a market economy before entering the WTO. Taken as a cornerstone for the regime shift to allowing the markets greater market leeway, it aroused harsh criticism from conservatives. According to *Zhenli de Zhuiqiu* (The Pursuit of Truth), published by the Chinese Academy of Social Sciences, conservatives worried that, if private entrepreneurs were admitted to the CCP based on the "Three Represents," the CCP would then become a bourgeois party. A July 2001 editorial in *Zhongliu* (Middle) magazine, a group connected with *Guangming Ribao*(Guangming Daily), suggested that entrepreneurs were not the class that formed the base support of the Party. Subsequently, in the build-up to the Sixth Plenum of the Fifteenth CCP Central Committee meeting in the summer of 2001, both publications were ordered to stop publishing (Ohe 2002, 16).

On May 31, 2002, in a graduation speech for provincial-level cadres at the Central Party School, Jiang stated, "The 'Three Represents' is the underlying spirit of the formation of the Chinese Communist Party, the foundation of the administration, and the source of energy. And it is the greatest theoretical weapon to reinforce and advance Party building, and to enhance self-reforms and the development of our socialism" (*Renmin Ribao* [People's Daily] 6 June 2002). The concept of the "Three Represents" was formally included in the newly adopted CCP charter at the CCP's Sixteenth Party Congress in November 2002. The new leadership of Hu Jintao and Wen Jiabao has inherited this official guiding theory, the theoretical preparation for corporatism with Chinese characteristics.

## THE ISSUE OF POLITICS: CORPORATISM WITH CHINESE CHARACTERISTICS

After the 1989 experience in Tiananmen Square, and the collapse of the Soviet Union, China is extremely cautious about political reform. Political reform in recent years has encompassed allowing villagers to elect mayors directly, while the CCP has concentrated on justifying its political control by enhancing economic growth. In the late 1980s, reforms were going to be introduced to separate the functioning of the CCP and the government. But the Tiananmen Square incident and the implosion of the Soviet Union intervened, and any reforms that could potentially dilute the CCP's leadership were avoided. In particular, any thoughts about separating the CCP and the government were set aside. Indeed, the socialist market economy is premised on the CCP's leadership.

Yet China must address the need for political reform. Serious corruption is one of the reasons. Thousands of corruption cases are exposed annually, which are, in a way, the unwanted product and unavoidable consequence of the socialist market economy being under CCP leadership. The political mechanisms necessary to expose corruption need to be examined. Under a political regime that does not sanction freedom of speech and expression, there are no other means but to expect the CCP to purge corrupt officials. The Commission for Inspecting Discipline is in place at every level. But, without outside supervision, it is difficult to determine how this self-cleansing mechanism is really functioning. It may be able to eliminate small evils successfully, but it is failing to eliminate heinous evils.

Then there are questions relating to the widening economic disparities in China, and the ironic issue of whose interests the CCP represents. Does it represent the interests of the newly coopted private entrepreneurs, or does it represent those of the workers and peasants who used to be the CCP's core, many of whom may be now slighted by globalization?

The fundamental principle of socialism is the fair distribution of wealth. However, inequality is spreading rapidly in China. Affluent coastal regions and lagging inland regions, especially poverty-ridden farming villages spread out in rural areas; the super-wealthy urban elite in their new homes; and the so-called *waidiren* (outsiders) in the urban metropoles, barely surviving in overfilled collective living quarters—these are some of the diverging contrasts. Addressing the uneven distribution of wealth is a definite political issue. In the past, the CCP tried to reach a balance by transferring surpluses from the wealthy regions to the poorer regions. However, the wealthy regions are solely concerned with their own prosperity, and they demand that the central government aid the poor regions. In terms of the loyal competition principle, they feel they cannot afford the luxury of caring for others. The CCP is positioned to show political leadership, but it does not have sufficient financial resources. Thus, it is seeking foreign capital to help bolster China's economic growth. If its efforts are not successful, those now on the margins will remain on the periphery.

Attention is being devoted these days to peasants and rural villages. Agricultural issues were extensively mentioned in government work reports by Prime Minister Zhu Rongji at the Fifth Meeting of the Ninth National People's Congress in 2002 and at the First Meeting of the Tenth National People's Congress in 2003. In the revolutionary period, most top CCP leaders came from farming villages, and, given their direct connections with farming society, they made sure the rural regions benefited. Yet, nowadays, most pivotal CCP leaders and their families are urbanized.

They may hear and speak of rural poverty, but they have little direct experience of it. Their promotion is mainly related to the strength of their ties to top leaders. Although village-level elections exist, these elections do not seem to influence the central government directly, and they are unable to produce politicians who can represent the interests of peasants at the central level.

In Japanese national elections, votes from farming villages play a very important role, and politicians who ignore them cannot win. In Japan, contrary to China, farmers are a minority interest group, yet their interests are reflected in national government—to an exaggerated degree, in fact. China and Japan have something in common in this regard, namely, that the interests of the majority of people are not necessarily reflected in national politics.

At this stage in China, progressive democratization may not be possible. The focus of political reform in China should then be reforming the CCP. And this will not be an easy task, as the vested interests of close to 70 million people are at stake. An important element could be democratizing the CCP internally. The CCP should clarify and systematize the process whereby it selects leaders so that this occurs in accordance with well-defined and established rules. Also, systemized rules and instituting a supervisory agency outside the CCP would help expose and control political corruption. Some Chinese researchers have begun to address this point, although it is not a position on which there is consensus (see, for example, Lin 2002).

State or authoritarian corporatism was one of the transitional stages in Taiwan's democratization process. China seems to be groping for a similar course. As seen in the "Three Represents" theory, the CCP seems to be trying to stabilize its governing ability by co-opting private entrepreneurs, a particular group with vested interests as part of the newly emerging elite. The major pitfall for state or authoritarian corporatism to work in China is how to co-opt or involve workers and peasants, who are the vast majority of people. The premise of homogenous development for the unity of a huge nation like China is absent.

A Chinese Academy of Social Sciences survey on China's divergent social strata highlighted the extent of the challenge (Lu 2002). It showed the upper social strata, consisting of party and state administrative personnel, managers, private entrepreneurs, experts, and technocrats, and the lower social strata, comprising industrial workers, peasants, and the unemployed. This view of China's social reality shows that the road to corporatism with Chinese characteristics has not been leveled. In order to minimize this contradiction, and to help pave the way for a successful corporatist strategy, the CCP's response is maintaining its focus on attaining rapid economic growth.

## China and Japan in the Global Contexts

News on China appears frequently under sensational headlines, with readers' images of China never settling but constantly shifting. This has been true for much of its recent history. Sometimes, a discussion on China has been filled with romantic descriptions of its grand history or culture. At other times, China has been discussed in idealistic tones, with a focus perhaps on its utopian socialist goals. It has also been examined through pessimistic lenses, as perhaps when its harsh political power struggles have been noted. Whether it was glorifying China at the birth of the People's Republic, agonizing over the Cultural Revolution, or simplistically suggesting China's breakup at the time of the 1989 Tiananmen incident, rarely have views on China been presented logically or objectively, allowing more realistic images of China to be formed. Debate about China has so often been tinged with emotion and subjective value judgments.

These days, much discussion in Japan is about the rise of China. Even this topic seems to reflect more on Japan's self-awareness about its recent dismal economic performance than objective analysis of the real situation.

The circumstances of Japan and China are incomparable. Japan is suffering now from problems stemming from years of successful high economic growth, while China is trying to remain on a growth track. In 1964, Tokyo hosted the Summer Olympic Games after years of high Japanese economic growth; in 2008, China is going to host the Olympic Games in Beijing. Incidentally, Seoul hosted the Olympics in 1988 after South Korea successfully accomplished economic growth and democratization. It will be very difficult for China to accomplish both by 2008. Comparisons are also misleading, because China is 25–26 times larger in area than Japan, and it has ten times Japan's population. Also, China's "rise" is particularly evident in the eastern and southern coastal cities and provinces, but much of the rest of China's vast interior is relatively untouched by the coast's successes.

Even in China, many experts are convinced that Japan will emerge from its present economic recession and will, one day, be a politically and militarily significant nation. Yet, in many cases, Chinese views of Japan remain stuck in the late 1930s or early 1940s, not reflecting at all the changes in Japan's politics and social status. Objectively speaking, both countries have many problems and issues to deal with, and neither party can afford to be envious of the other.

At this point, China has no choice but to concentrate on economic growth. Ongoing growth gives the CCP its political legitimacy, and, for this growth, China relies heavily on foreign trade and foreign direct investment as mentioned. Due to this economic logic and to its domestic needs, China can no longer function without fully participating in and cooperating with the world market (see Medeiros and Fravel 2003).

In this regard, China's relations with the United States are crucial. It must have smooth, cooperative relations with the United States in order to survive and thrive. China's leaders were remarkably silent regarding the U.S. war in Iraq, with their criticisms being very vague and low key. China has also been very active as a host of, and an intermediary in, the six-party-talks process on the North Korean nuclear problem. This is an area where the United States has been greatly appreciative of Chinese help. Yet stable U.S.-China relations are not a given. There are apprehensions in the United States about China, specifically about China's military profile, and its posture toward Taiwan. Indeed, despite increasing economic integration between China and Taiwan, the Taiwan issue is the most serious problem in the U.S.-China relationship.

China has also maintained a low-key attitude toward Japan. The Japanese media widely reported on the May 2002 incident involving North Korean refugees at the Japanese Consulate-General in Shenyang; this was not at all the case in China. When Japan insisted on salvaging a sunken North Korean ship suspected of having been on a spy mission, China agreed. News coverage in China remained relatively muted on Lee Teng-hui's visit to Japan in 2001, a series of problems on Japanese history textbooks, and Prime Minister Koizumi Jun'ichiro's visits to Yasukuni Shrine. China's calm reaction to these types of issues has continued under the leadership of Hu and Wen.

Japan is economically quite important to China, particularly for its generous official development assistance. China is well aware that "anti-China" sentiment is deep-rooted in Japan, and that it would strengthen if China overreacted to historical issues. Moreover, China is very aware of the present close relations between Japan and the United States, and it is keen to avoid unnecessary conflict. As Deng stated, it is essential for China to secure a peaceful and stable international environment for the sake of economic growth.

In recent years, China has also shown a positive interest in Asian regional cooperation. Perhaps its aim is to help China's economy by integrating it with East Asia to secure economic growth. In so doing, China would establish a vast economic bloc centered on the Chinese market, with Taiwan presumably being part of it too. Its decision to pursue a free trade area (FTA) with the Association of Southeast Asian Nations (ASEAN) also reflects its interest in allaying ASEAN fears about its increasing economic muscle.

For China, the Korean peninsula is a sensitive area. China would certainly like to strengthen its relationship with South Korea, given deepening economic ties between the two, yet it cannot neglect relations with North Korea. North Korea's participation in the ASEAN Regional Forum (ARF) has facilitated China's involvement in multinational conferences and frameworks. China would undoubtedly support North Korea's "reform and opening" policy, especially if it would improve their relations with the United States. Any problems in North Korea impact China very negatively, as evidenced by the North Korean refugee flows into China because of the North's dire economic circumstances. And any tension between the United States and North Korea—such as the crisis over North Korea's development of nuclear weapons—has a huge effect on China too. Although China feels the implications of any North Korean action more directly than the United States, it is a mistake to overestimate China's influence on North Korea.

Concerning Japan, after it entered into an FTA with Singapore, FTAs with South Korea and ASEAN may be next. Yet, in order to pursue these arrangements, various complex national issues will have to be confronted, starting with domestic agricultural issues. Globalizing pressures and its serious economic slump may force Japan to open its markets, while manufacturers simultaneously move increasingly overseas, especially to China, in their quest for cheap labor. Specialization and division of work are making headway in securing less expensive but skilled labor, and efficient production. Supporting such private enterprise activities could lead to the revitalization of Japan, and could benefit not only Japan but, ultimately, Asia and the rest of the world. Japan cannot remain internationally competitive by protecting its domestic market; indeed, such an attitude hinders Japan's revitalization in the long run. Compared to the relative openness of the Chinese market, the Japanese market and society continue to be somewhat closed, with a "quasi-socialist" system. Although Japan should adopt and execute reform and opening policies immediately, Japan's political leadership is fragile. Yet, if nothing is done, Japan will remain debilitated and not competitive.

At this point, Japan must think seriously about proposing the establishment of an FTA in East Asia. Discussions on FTAs between Japan and South Korea, Japan and ASEAN, China and ASEAN, and so forth should be geared to covering all of East Asia. An East Asia–wide FTA should not be viewed as being a zero-sum exercise, but instead as being plus-sum, and as bringing mutual benefits for all. Including Taiwan in an East Asian FTA would presumably benefit China's economy, based on current expansive economic relations between the two.

Gradually relieving the tension among East Asian nations through regional economic integration is the way forward. As Japan has to play an important role in such cooperation, given its overwhelming economic power, an economic recovery in Japan is absolutely essential at this time. China's ongoing economic growth and its success in further opening are equally important. As interdependence between Japan and China is actually increasing, it is desirable to build up a relationship of mutual trust between the governments and leaders of both nations, in order to avoid or minimize possible friction. All in East Asia are in the same boat, and the fate of the Titanic should be avoided at all cost.

## Bibliography

Dickson, Bruce J. 2000–2001. "Co-optation and Corporatism in China: The Logic of Party Adaptation." *Political Science Quarterly* 115(4): 517–540.

Hosokawa Mihoko. 2002. "WTO ni kameisita Chugoku keizai no genjo" (The current situation of the Chinese economy since joining the WTO). *Kokusaikinyu* (International Finance) 1078 (January).

Jiang Zemin. 2001. *Lun "Sange Daibiao"* (Discussion of the "Three Represents"). Beijing: Zhongyang Wenjian Chubanshe (Central Documents Publishing House).

Lin Shangli. 2002. *Dangnei minzhu: Zhongguo gongchangdangde lilun yu shijian* (Party democracy: The Chinese Communist Party's theory and practice). Shanghai: Shanghai Shehuikexue Chubanshe (Shanghai Social Sciences Publishing House).

Lu Xueyi, ed. 2002. *Dangdai Zhongguo shehuijiecheng yanjiubaogao* (A research report on contemporary China's social strata). Beijing: Shehuikexue Wenjian Chubanshe (Social Sciences Documents Publishing House).

Medeiros, Evan S., and M. Taylor Fravel. 2003. "China's New Diplomacy." *Foreign Affairs* 82(6) 22–35.

Mitsubishi Research Institute. 2000. *Chugoku joho handbook 2000 (Handbook of China information 2000)*. Tokyo: Soso-sha.

Ohe Shinobu. 2002. "Kotakuminshoshoki saigono toso: 'Mittsu no daihyo' ron to Chugoku kyosantotaikai" (A final battle for General Secretary Jiang Zemin: The "Three Represents" and the Party Congress of the CCP). *Choken Quarterly* 3 (March). Yomiuri Shimbun Research Department.

# 3

## China and Asia Pacific Regionalism

### Jusuf Wanandi

Two questions have to be answered before one can properly assess the significance and impact of China's participation in Asia Pacific regionalism. First is whether China's foreign policy, as laid down by Jiang Zemin's third generation of leaders, is going to be maintained by the fourth generation of leaders under Hu Jintao, who took over the leadership in November 2002. Second, and most important, is the nature of China's policies and relations with the United States. The relationship with the United States has been China's main foreign policy preoccupation since its opening in 1979, and it is considered vital to China's modernization efforts.

China's foreign policy, as it evolved under Jiang's third generation, is well established, and is considered to be balanced, centrist, and based on China's national interest. It is, therefore, likely that it will be maintained, especially as Jiang remains influential in China's primary decision-making bodies. He is still chairman of the Central Military Commission, and his allies are in the majority in the highest policymaking body, the Standing Committee of the Politburo. A substantial change of policy could only occur if there was a split in the Politburo. Some Western journalists and analysts have speculated about this possibility.

The chances of such a split appear to be remote, as the main domestic and foreign policies have been agreed on by the third and fourth generation of leaders together. Of course there are nuances between them, and new challenges could arise in the economy (a dramatic slowdown or some other crisis) or politically (some kind of social unrest due to rising unemployment, discrepancies in income between the coast and the interior, or the like). But, at present, the leadership does seem to be unified and there seems to be consensus on future policies. The fourth generation of leaders under Hu is first and foremost a collective leadership, they have worked together under Jiang for a decade, and they know that their success or failure depends on the unity of the top leadership.

The experience of the leadership splits under Mao Zedong and Deng Xiaoping definitely weighs on their minds, and will be prevented at all cost. But human folly should never be underestimated. Greater openness, flexibility, and accountability in the political system would help prevent future havoc caused by human frailties.

Relations with the United States are most important for China for strategic, political, as well as economic reasons. Only the United States could really hamper China's modernization by constraining it militarily, politically, and economically. Although it would be counterproductive to the United States if China was perceived to be its next adversary, China would suffer more, since she is the weaker party.

China's foreign policy decision-makers have now achieved some sophistication. Earlier, they were still overburdened by history, which placed so many chips on their shoulders regarding relations with the region and the world, especially the West. Western Europe and Japan were colonizers and imperialists, and they tried to subjugate China from the mid-nineteenth century. The subsequent 150 years were particularly hurtful and humiliating for China. The psychological complexities stemming from this historical burden have made the Chinese very defensive and reactive to even the smallest things that impact their national interest.

China has now achieved dramatic economic growth rates, overcome the isolation following the tragedy of Tiananmen in 1989, become a member of the World Trade Organization (WTO), and will host the Summer Olympics in Beijing in 2008. It is now recognized in the region and the world as a great power in its own right. And so it has become much more self-confident and relaxed in its foreign relations. This has happened gradually, only in the last few years under the leadership of Jiang and the third generation. The rhetoric that used to be so shrill has now become more measured. The Chinese have become much more positive on existing rules, norms, and institutions, even those that were established when they were isolated and were not party to their formation.

Following a realistic assessment of its national interest, the changes in the world environment, and the fact that the United States has become the only superpower, China has also tried to adjust its policies and relations, especially with the United States. Its international relations have become more positive, consistent, and stable, despite problems in areas such as the Taiwan question, arms proliferation and sales, human rights, and trade imbalances. Overall, relations with the United States have improved, and a certain stability has been achieved in the relationship, including in cooperation against global terrorism. It is encouraging that both China and the United States, especially the Bush administration that was initially so skeptical about dealing and cooperating with China, have started to understand and appreciate each other, and are willing to cooperate.

Yet complete trust and confidence in each other have not been achieved. The main problem for the United States is how to deal with ascendant China over the longer term. Indeed, for the region as a whole, securing a more stable and peaceful Asia Pacific in the face of emergent China is the primary concern. Economic regionalism and cooperation, intertwined with security cooperation in Asia Pacific, is the key regional response.

## China and Regionalism in East Asia and Asia Pacific

Before deliberating on China's participation in region building in East Asia and Asia Pacific, it is useful to look first at China's efforts in multilateral cooperation. Although this is not easy for China due to its complex history with other countries, it seems that China is gradually becoming involved in existing international norms and institutions, especially where its national interests are clear and obvious. Its active involvement in East Asia is very important for regional stability and peace, which in turn facilitates its ability to pursue reform and modernization.

China was the historical center of the world for a long time. This ended when the Qing dynasty began crumbling in the mid-nineteenth century due to domestic uprisings and incursions from Western and Japanese imperialism. China has never really known how to have allies or be allied to other powers, except for one decade in the 1960s when it was allied with the USSR.

Since the beginning of the twentieth century, when the Qing dynasty collapsed and was replaced with a republic, China did not have a period of stability and peace in order to be able to develop and modernize. Only in 1979, when Deng introduced reforms and the push for modernization, did China gradually develop a full-fledged foreign policy.

Participation in regionalism and multilateralism in general has no precedents in Chinese history. Encroachments on its sovereignty by colonialist and imperialist powers for over a century produced a China that wants to assert itself with absolute state sovereignty, as did European countries after signing the Peace of Westphalia in 1648.

The extent of China's willingness to participate in international institutions and abide by multilateral rules in such a short time is noteworthy. On a global level, China is a member of both the United Nations and the World Trade Organization (WTO). At the regional level, China is active in the Pacific Economic Cooperation Council (PECC) and the Asia-Pacific Economic Cooperation (APEC) initiative. It also participates in the ASEAN (Association of Southeast Asian Nations) Regional Forum (ARF) and the Council for Security Cooperation in Asia Pacific (CSCAP).

Why has China been willing to participate in these forums? Its participation in the UN system is confined to furthering specific national interests, not to promoting big ideas or concepts internationally—although it does appear to be interested in disarmament and arms control issues. Its original involvement in the UN system was primarily to displace Taiwan in the international institution.

China has participated fully in arms control and disarmament efforts, and has endorsed both the Comprehensive Test Ban Treaty (CTBT) and the Nonproliferation Treaty (NPT). It has invested in international security institutions in order to develop expertise in its various national institutions dealing with security. It has also been willing to pay some costs for acceding to existing norms, for example, in the cases of the CTBT and the NPT. China negotiated for more than 13 years to accede to the WTO, membership of which was regarded as very important for its domestic reform and modernization drive. While giving China domestic benefits, its participation in all these international forums and norms also strengthens the international system.

Even on the sacred principle of absolute sovereignty, China is proving to be somewhat flexible. Examples here include UN intervention in Cambodia in 1993, and in East Timor in 1999. In other situations, China has started to accept multilateral principles, such as in developing a regional code of conduct with ASEAN on the South China Sea. Regarding the Korean peninsula, China is cooperating with the Japan, Russia, South Korea, and the United States to find a diplomatic and peaceful resolution to the threat of the proliferation of nuclear weapons. However, these situations are special, because of their proximity to China, and the possibility of them becoming security problems or sources of instability for China.

On the question of global terrorism, China has been a full participant, given its own problems on this issue in its northwestern province of Xinjiang. China supported UN Security Council Resolution 1441 that suggested consequences would result if Iraq failed to disclose fully its weapons of mass destruction.

China also has a "mutual security" agreement on the threat of global terrorism with Russia and other central Asian states under the so-called Shanghai Security Cooperation arrangement. In addition, China has initiated some other common security efforts with neighbors such as Russia and some central Asian countries.

In the early 1990s, when there was great uncertainty about how the post–cold war international system would develop, China seems to have accepted multilateralism as the strategy that accorded with its national interest. Contrarily, the United States and western Europe became more inward-looking and preoccupied with domestic change and other problems closer to home.

The United States is now the only superpower, but it nonetheless needs friends and allies to help implement its strategies. This is especially so after September 11, 2001, when global terrorism and its state supporters showed themselves to be the main threat to international peace and stability. A limited version of multilateralism is still valid, although not based on absolute multipolarity, as China had thought earlier. The new multilateralism looks likely to be based on a concert of big powers acting under the leadership of the United States.

The United States seems to expect that cooperation with powers— such as China, the European Union, India, Japan, and Russia—acting under U.S. leadership could be the basis for a new world order. The United States would of course be more than a *primus inter pares*, especially on critical issues. Whether this idealistic new U.S. system would work is questionable. It would depend partly on how much the United States is willing to involve other great powers in decision-making processes, as well as which institutions would be used, and how other countries could participate.

After the war in Iraq, the situation between China and the United States might be more fluid due to China's opposition to the use of force against Iraq. China has, however, been very subdued in its reactions, and has not been very public in opposing the United States, even since the start of the war.

In the aftermath of the war and as reconstruction in Iraq proceeds, if the United States again acts so unilaterally, or becomes heavy handed—in the case, for example, of nuclear proliferation on the Korean peninsula—China-U.S. relations would suffer.

It must be hoped that the United States learned the right lessons from the Iraq war. Namely that, even as the only superpower, it cannot do everything alone. Particularly in dealing with global terrorism, the United States needs the assistance and cooperation of friends and allies.

## China in East Asia and Asia Pacific

China has always loomed large in the history of East Asia, except in the nineteenth century and the first half of the twentieth century.

Since Deng successfully laid the basis for China's modernization, its economy has grown 7 percent–8 percent annually for the last 30 years, and China has become a big economic power in its own right in the East Asian region. This is also true politically and, to some extent, militarily. China is again seen as a main challenge to the region. The challenge this time does not stem from it being a revolutionary and anti–status quo power, as from the 1950s to the 1970s. The challenge now is how to deal with China as a big power, with the long-term potential to become a superpower.

The region has the opportunity in the next decade or two to incorporate and constructively engage China, and to support its efforts to become a status quo power. The main strategy of the region is to involve China in as many regional economic and security institutions as possible. There is an overlap between Asia Pacific and East Asia, the two regions that are referred to, with the latter being part of the wider former region.

There are also two types of organizations active in the region: "first track" and "second track." First track includes government or state entities, while second track refers to organizations in which government officials participate in their private capacities. First-track entities cooperate with second-track regional organizations to test new ideas or help work out new programs. PECC, which China joined in the mid-1980s, is a second-track or nongovernmental APEC. Some second-track activities are formed through ad-hoc arrangements with academics and business groups, such as ABAC, the APEC Business Advisory Council.

It is in China's national interest to participate in these institutions. And China has been willing to allow Taiwan to participate, as an economic entity, in these forums. Hong Kong joined PECC in the same way. Similarly, Hong Kong and Taiwan are both members of APEC. When U.S. President Bill Clinton proposed a summit of APEC leaders in Seattle in 1993, complications arose over the question of whom to invite from Taiwan. In the end, the U.S. president appointed someone proposed by Taiwan who was acceptable to both China and Taiwan. Overall, a practical limitation for Taiwan is that no PECC or APEC meeting will be held in Taiwan, due to Chinese fears that the Taiwanese government might use such meetings for political purposes.

China is active in both PECC and APEC. It has hosted meetings for each forum in various parts of China, and Taiwanese representatives have attended these. It hosted a very successful PECC general meeting in the early 1990s in Beijing, and the APEC Leaders' Summit in Shanghai in 2001. China has also contributed substantively, especially on issues regarding technical cooperation, and small and medium-sized enterprises. Chinese academics and members of the private sector have participated in PECC and APEC activities. China's national PECC has actively cultivated local participation in its activities and that of the international PECC. The Chinese government has established good inter-agency coordination between its representatives to APEC and PECC.

Regional cooperation on security matters is a different story. As noted, other than an alliance with the USSR that lasted from 1960 to 1970, China has never had alliances with other countries. During Mao's leadership, China was isolated and very defensive of its interests in the face of U.S. containment. Only in 1979, after Deng introduced reforms and started to open China, did China begin to develop an appreciation for multilateralism. Initially, China was very suspicious of regional security cooperation, because such cooperation had existed prior to its participation and it was worried that its special concerns would be ignored.

Toward the end of the cold war, China cooperated in a limited fashion with the United States against the Soviet Union. Then the Tiananmen tragedy of 1989 led to a policy in the West, especially in the United States, of isolating China. This forced China to look for friends elsewhere to overcome its isolation from the West.

During that period in the early 1990s, ASEAN was actively looking for new regional strategies in East Asia, not to replace the U.S. role in the region, but to complement its presence with new ideas about comprehensive and cooperative strategies. Although ASEAN no longer had an obvious adversary, confidence building and security cooperation were regarded as important, especially if there were to be a vacuum in leadership from the United States.

Another factor was how to cope with the new big power rising in East Asia, namely China. Containment would be counterproductive, because China was changing. Besides, it did not have the ambition to become an antithesis to the West in all activities, as did the USSR during the cold war. Confrontation between China and the United States would nevertheless have dramatic negative effects on the region, economically as well as in terms of peace and stability. This lead ASEAN to propose establishing the ARF in 1994, and CSCAP, ARF's second-track counterpart, in 1993.

Due to divisions stemming from the cold war, ARF was meant primarily for confidence-building measures. China agreed to become involved as participation in forums like this coincided with its new strategy of multipolarity based on multilateralism. China's participation was made easy too by the consensus-based "ASEAN way" of decision-making, where every participant has to feel comfortable with any decision.

The Taiwan issue is not included in the agendas of the ARF or CSCAP. However, China's preoccupation with absolute sovereignty has hindered the ARF's development of preventive diplomacy and conflict resolution mechanisms to address issues such as nuclear proliferation on the Korean peninsula. It is unclear whether China is ready for—and, indeed, would like to see—the ARF develop from a "talking shop" into an institution that "does something" about regional tensions and conflicts.

In terms of confidence-building measures, China has performed very well. It has participated in exchanges of military officers and students at military universities and academies, attended joint military exercises, and involved itself in search-and-rescue and peacekeeping efforts. China has also issued defense white papers, which have helped to enhance transparency.

Nontraditional security issues—such as money laundering and terrorism, drug and human trafficking, piracy, environmental and health matters—lend themselves to greater regional cooperation. It is likely that China would be willing to enhance ARF cooperation on such matters, especially responding to global terrorism. Successful cooperation on such issues could open the way for China's future involvement in preventive diplomacy efforts. However, given its sensitivities about matters involving national sovereignty, it will be some time before China is completely on board in transforming the ARF into a more "intrusive" instrument for solving potential conflicts in the region.

Studies and deliberations form the backbone of CSCAP activities, and scholars from China and Taiwan participate in its working groups. Chinese participants have also been very active in exchanges on security developments in the region, and have willingly helped with confidence-building mechanisms, such as developing a code of conduct for the South China Sea with ASEAN. Regarding the Korean peninsula, China is taking the initiative to put diplomatic pressure on North Korea, together with Japan, Russia, South Korea, and the United States in the so-called six-party talks, to give up its existing nuclear capacities and refrain from producing further nuclear weapons.

The regional institution with the greatest potential for deeper Chinese involvement and cooperation is the ASEAN + 3 mechanism, which includes the ten ASEAN member countries and China, Japan, and South Korea. There are several reasons why ASEAN + 3 could evolve—with significant Chinese participation—into an East Asian Community over the longer term. First, it is a more or less institutionalized process involving ASEAN, China, Japan, and South Korea. From the moment ASEAN + 3 was established, it has been a channel in which China has been able to express its interests and priorities. Second, its affairs are conducted in the "ASEAN way," which is informal, consensual, personal, and step by step. This is a style with which China feels quite comfortable. Third, there is a need for East Asia to have a global voice, alongside the voices of the European Union and the United States. China would benefit too from being able to express itself forcefully through the medium of a regional institution.

Establishing a good-neighborly policy in the region and its implications of a peaceful environment would also help China pursue its modernization programs. In addition, solid regional relations would be a sort of insurance policy in case of a severe rupture in China's relations with the United States, an admittedly remote possibility at this stage.

East Asian regionalism also received momentum from the Asian financial crisis in 1997, when East Asian countries found out how important it was to be able to depend on each other—and not on others from outside the region—in a crisis.

Yet there still are real constraints to establishing an East Asian Community. For historical reasons, China and Japan are not completely trustful of each other. There is also underlying competition for regional leadership, which is similar to the situation in Europe between France and Germany. The key is having the political willingness to cooperate in the economic field, which is important, and also in the political and security fields, as well as in the areas of culture, education, the environment, and health.

ASEAN would also benefit from such regional cooperation, with its strong desire for peace, stability, and development in the region. ASEAN countries would be especially keen to benefit from China's economic dynamism, and they would hope to cooperate with China to attract foreign investment and technology. This is why the ASEAN-China free trade area (FTA), which China proposed two years ago, also has such appeal for ASEAN member countries.

East Asian regionalism could assist China in finding its own way of becoming a great power without creating regional apprehensions and tensions. A China grounded in East Asia would also assist China in its relations with the United States. It would suggest that China was a more status quo–oriented power, and that China supported the United States remaining involved in the region to help maintain peace and stability. By being involved in an East Asian regional institution with ASEAN, Japan, and South Korea—all considered allies or friends of the United States—China would show the United States that it was a responsible and peaceful partner.

Involvement in ASEAN + 3 (or any other East Asian regional mechanism) would also help Japan become a more "normal" country, and help alleviate the region's apprehensions about Japan due to its history.

East Asian cooperation would give South Korea the opportunity to feel fully part of the region, and not feel left alone between China and Japan in Northeast Asia.

## Conclusion

Starting with economic institutions such as PECC and later APEC, China has actively participated in and contributed to regional institutions for the last 15 years or so. Since economic cooperation is so important for China's modernization programs, it could be said that it was easy for China to participate in these particular institutions. Participating in regional economic institutions first also helped China prepare itself for involvement in and negotiations with global institutions, such as the WTO.

Now that China is a much bigger and more successful economy, it will surely be expected to do more for the region and its institutions. This is especially true in the wake of the financial crisis of 1997. China was relatively unaffected and in fact experienced phenomenal economic growth, while the rest of the region was greatly stressed. China is aware of these expectations and even pressures. Hence its proposal for an ASEAN-China

Comprehensive Economic Cooperation agreement, including the establishment of an ASEAN-China FTA within the next decade. China has also agreed to an "early harvest" of opening up certain agricultural product sectors to ASEAN countries, particularly to new members, without having completely agreed yet on the full FTA.

ASEAN has responded positively to these developments, because it realizes that China is leaving it behind and out-competing it in many areas. This is true not only in labor-intensive manufacturing, but also in more advanced technological fields, where even Hong Kong, Malaysia, Singapore, South Korea, and Taiwan feel the increased competition. Every East Asian nation faces strong competition from China and is trying to find economic activities it can develop.

All these factors will make the ASEAN + 3 process much more important than previously thought. This new regional institution will have to help manage the strong competition between ASEAN, China, and the other East Asian countries, while also giving East Asia a voice in global forums.

ASEAN + 3 is also the regional institution with which China is most comfortable. This is so because ASEAN + 3 is indigenous to East Asia, it operates in the consensual and nonconfrontational "ASEAN way," and it is less legalistic and formalistic in its approach.

In future, ASEAN + 3 may become even more important as, aside from economic cooperation, it might also have to address political, social, and cultural issues.

Although cooperation in the political-security field will be pursued step by step and as a long-term effort, every member, including China, knows it will have to be considered. Improved relations between the United States and China should also help improve relations between China and Japan, the normalization of which is incomplete though desirable if regional security cooperation is to proceed.

If China could be more forthcoming in ASEAN + 3 on political and security cooperation, this could lead to greater willingness to participate in political and security cooperation in the wider region, such as in the ARF and CSCAP.

China has cooperated in regional security on specific issues in the past. These include helping resolve the Cambodia conflict, supporting and participating in peacekeeping efforts in East Timor, and trying to help further nuclear nonproliferation on the Korean peninsula. China has also initiated an antiterrorism effort in Central Asia through the so-called Shanghai Security Cooperation agreement with Russia and four other central Asian countries. At the second-track level, China participated in the first and second Shangri-La conference of defense ministers in Asia Pacific, initiated by the London-based International Institute for Strategic Studies.

All these developments suggest that China is going to be increasingly involved in East Asia and Asia Pacific regional initiatives. This will be manifest not only in the economic field, but also in the political and security fields. It is quite possible that the ASEAN + 3 process, which could in the future evolve into an East Asian Community, could also play a greater role in regional political and security cooperation. This would need to develop gradually and it would need to be welcomed by China. The region is feeling its way as it deepens relations with China in the economics and political-security realms.

# 4

## The Rise of China and Emergent East Asian Regionalism

### Chia Siow Yue

For two decades until the 1997 financial crisis, East Asia was known as the world's "economic miracle." Rapid economic growth, strong economic fundamentals, and political and social stability characterized the region. East Asian economies benefited from an outward-looking growth strategy and largely pursued multilateralism, eschewing formal regional trading arrangements (RTAs) such as free trade areas, customs unions, or common markets. Growing interregional trade and investment flows were instead in response to market forces, economic complementarities, and the region's economic dynamism.

The scenario began to change in the late 1990s, when East Asia, like the rest of the world, began to embrace regionalism. The General Agreement on Tariffs and Trade (GATT) and its successor, the World Trade Organization (WTO), were notified about some 250 RTAs by December 2002. With the number of RTAs having doubled in the 1990s, it is expected to rise to about 300 by 2005. The vast majority of WTO members are party to one or more RTAs, which suggests that RTAs are a response to unfulfilled needs of multilateralism.

This chapter focuses on the economics of China's rise, particularly its impact on East Asian economic interdependence, and the emergence of East Asian regionalism. It also examines and analyzes some of the key regional initiatives.

# THE RISE OF CHINA

China's "rise" as an economic phenomenon refers to the rapid and sustained growth of the Chinese economy since 1978 when economic reform and open-door policies were first adopted. China's economy has been growing at an average of 10 percent per annum for two decades, and its external trade has been growing even faster, at an annual pace of 15 percent. China has become a major trading partner of Japan, South Korea, and the countries of the Association of Southeast Asian Nations (ASEAN), as well as of the European Union and the United States. It has become the world's second largest recipient of foreign direct investment (FDI) flows, second only to the United States.

In the 1950s and 1960s, Japan was the most dynamic economy in East Asia. It became Asia's first developed economy, and its trade and investment flows had positive spillover effects on the rest of East Asia—in what came to be known as the "flying geese pattern" of East Asian economic development. Japan's rapid development was followed, in the 1970s and 1980s, by that of the newly industrialized economies (NIEs) of Hong Kong, Singapore, South Korea, and Taiwan, and, since the mid-1980s, by the ASEAN-4 economies of Indonesia, Malaysia, the Philippines, and Thailand, and by China and Vietnam.

For most of East Asia, this growth trajectory stopped with the Asian financial crisis that began in mid-1997. Japan remains trapped in a period of economic stagnation that began in the early 1990s, while the other East Asian economies are variously struggling to recover from the crisis. Only China has continued, unscathed, on its dynamic economic growth path.

Table 1 summarizes China's relative economic size and development level, and that of its East Asian neighbors.

— In population, China is overwhelmingly the biggest country in East Asia (and in the world). Its population of 1.3 billion people is six times that of Indonesia, ten times that of Japan, and double that of the ASEAN-10 countries. However, having a large population is not the same as having economic power, although it does signal a huge labor pool and a big potential consumer market. China's huge and cheap labor force does present it with an enormous comparative advantage in labor-intensive production.

— The size of a country's gross national product (GNP) measures its economic power. China's nominal GNP of US$1.1 trillion in 2001 was only a quarter of Japan's GNP. However, when adjusted for purchasing

Table 1. East Asia—Economic Indicators

| | Population | GNP | | GNP-PPP adjusted | | GDP av. annual growth | Merchandise trade | | | Mfg. share of exports | High-tech. share of mfg | Foreign direct investment average ann. inflows | |
|---|---|---|---|---|---|---|---|---|---|---|---|---|---|
| | 2001 | Total 2001 | Per capita 2001 | Total 2001 | Per capita 2001 | 1990–2001 | Exports 2001 | Imports 2001 | Total 2001 | 2000 | 2000 | 1990–95 | 1996–2001 |
| | million | US$billion | US$ | US$billion | US$ | % | US$million | US$million | US$million | % | % | US$million | US$million |
| Japan | 127.1 | 4,574.2 | 35,990 | 3,487 | 27,430 | 1.3 | 404,686 | 350,095 | 754,781 | 94 | 28 | 1,144 | 5,652 |
| China | 1,271.9 | 1,131.0 | 890 | 5,415 | 4,260 | 10.0 | 266,155 | 243,567 | 509,722 | 88 | 19 | 19,360 | 42,684 |
| Hong Kong | 6.9 | 176.2 | 25,920 | 179 | 26,050 | 3.9 | 190,676 | 202,252 | 392,928 | 95 | 23 | 4,859 | 24,328 |
| South Korea | 47.6 | 447.7 | 9,400 | 863 | 18,110 | 5.7 | 150,653 | 141,116 | 291,769 | 91 | 35 | 978 | 5,399 |
| Taiwan | 22.9 | | | | | | 122,902 | 107,243 | 230,145 | | | | |
| Brunei | 0.3 | 5.2 | 15,000 | | | | | | | | | | |
| Indonesia | 213.6 | 144.7 | 680 | 628 | 2,940 | 3.8 | 56,716 | 31,170 | 87,886 | 57 | 16 | 2,135 | -10 |
| Malaysia | 23.8 | 86.5 | 3,640 | 198 | 8,340 | 6.5 | 88,521 | 74,384 | 162,905 | 80 | 59 | 4,655 | 4,095 |
| Philippines | 77.0 | 80.8 | 1,050 | 336 | 4,360 | 3.3 | 33,589 | 31,373 | 64,962 | 92 | 59 | 1,028 | 1,355 |
| Singapore | 4.1 | 99.4 | 24,740 | 100 | 24,910 | 7.8 | 121,731 | 115,961 | 237,692 | 86 | 63 | 5,782 | 8,593 |
| Thailand | 61.2 | 120.9 | 1,970 | 401 | 6,550 | 3.8 | 64,223 | 60,190 | 124,413 | 76 | 32 | 1,990 | 3,529 |
| Cambodia | 12.3 | 3.3 | 270 | 19 | 1,520 | 4.8 | 1,531 | 1,476 | 3,007 | 80 | | 62 | 218 |
| Laos | 5.4 | 1.6 | 310 | 9 | 1,610 | 6.4 | 320 | 437 | 757 | | | | 33 |
| Myanmar | 48.3 | na | na | na | na | na | 1,760 | 2,461 | 4,221 | | | 180 | 274 |
| Vietnam | 79.5 | 32.6 | 410 | 169 | 2,130 | 7.6 | 15,100 | 16,000 | 31,100 | | | 947 | 1,691 |
| ASEAN-6 | 380.0 | 537.5 | 1,414 | | | | 364,780 | 313,078 | 677,858 | | | | |
| ASEAN-10 | 525.5 | 575.0 | 1,094 | | | | 383,491 | 333,452 | 716,943 | | | | |
| NEA-3 | 1,446.6 | 6,152.9 | 4,253 | | | | 821,494 | 734,778 | 1,556,272 | | | | |
| ASEAN+3 | 1,972.1 | 6,727.9 | 3412 | | | | 1,204,985 | 1,068,230 | 2,273,215 | | | | |

Source: World Bank (2003).

power parity (PPP), the Chinese economy was 1.5 times larger, making China the largest economy in East Asia.

— China's current per capita GNP is still below US$1,000, while Japan's is about US$40,000 in nominal terms. When adjusted for PPP, the differential shrinks markedly, although Japanese per capita GNP is still 6.5 times higher than that of China. Using per capita GNP as a proxy for the level of economic development, China is more developed than the CLMV countries (Cambodia, Laos, Myanmar, and Vietnam) and Indonesia. Using this same measure, it is less developed than the rest of ASEAN, Asia's NIEs (Hong Kong, Singapore, South Korea, and Taiwan), and Japan. However, China's average per capita GNP masks vast differences among its economic regions and provinces, particularly between the rich coastal provinces and the impoverished western interior region. This growing economic divide could threaten continued economic dynamism and social stability in the country.

— China has been enjoying sustained high economic growth since the early 1980s, led by booming FDI and exports. In the 1990–2001 period, China's economy grew an annual average of 10 percent. In contrast, the Japanese economy has been stagnant for a decade, while the other East Asian economies have been severely buffeted by the Asian financial crisis of 1997–1998. Official projections are that China's economy will continue to grow at an annual rate of around 7 percent for the next 10–15 years.

— Although manufactures form the bulk of China's fast-expanding export of goods, its competitiveness still lies in low value-added and labor-intensive products. China now enjoys comparative advantages mainly in labor-intensive industries such as textiles, garments, and some agricultural products.

China's economic rise and its WTO accession have given rise to a vibrant debate on its role in the region. Whether China's increasing regional weight is perceived as a threat or an opportunity depends on several factors.

First, China's sheer size and its economic dynamism create a sense of threat among its smaller Asian neighbors, notwithstanding the general acceptance that a globally integrated and prosperous China is good for the region. Hence many countries wish to see the rising power of China counterbalanced by the presence of Japan and the United States. China has to assure its neighbors that it will be a responsible and benign power. So far it has sought to do so by acceding to the WTO and conforming to its rules and regulations, and by participating in the ASEAN Regional Forum (ARF) and the ASEAN + 3 process. Recognizing East Asians' concerns over the "China threat," Chinese officials and scholars have stressed the beneficial role China is playing in the region. In particular, they note that China has proposed a free trade area (FTA) with ASEAN. Other cited benefits include China's large and rapidly increasing domestic market, the growing number of Chinese tourists and expanded Chinese investment in the region, and the stability of the Chinese currency.

Second, the sense of economic threat or opportunity depends on whether China's economy is complementary or competitive vis-à-vis the other East Asian economies, and whether these economies are able to exploit the complementary opportunities and overcome the competitive threats. Differences in resource and factor endowments, production structures, and productiveness lead to being complementary, while having similarities leads to a competitive relationship. For a large economy such as China, it is difficult to determine whether it is complementary or competitive, as its various regions have dissimilar levels of economic competence and comparative advantage. For example, the industrial and financial sophistication of the Shanghai region contrasts sharply with the very low level of development of the western interior region. For every East Asian economy, there is a region or province in China that is its competitor.

Table 2 shows China's complementary-competitive relationship with the other East Asian economies vis-à-vis exports to the U.S. market. The export structures of China and Japan are complementary, reflecting the wide development gap between the two economies. In terms of value, China and Japan competed in about only 16.3 percent of their exports to the United States in 2000, mainly in relatively low value-added products in which Japan has lost comparative advantage. Japan's comparative advantages are in products of capital and technology-intensive industries such as automobiles, electrical and mechanical equipment, chemical fibers, and semiconductor devices. In these high value-added categories, China's export competitiveness still lags far behind Japan (and some other more advanced East Asian exporters). However, Japan cannot be complacent, as China's export structure is becoming more competitive. The percentage of product competition between China and Japan in the U.S. market increased very rapidly in just one decade, from the low base of only 3 percent in 1990 to 16.3 percent in 2000. As Japanese and other multinational corporations increasingly invest in China and transfer advanced state-of-the art technology, the pace of catch-up could accelerate.

Table 2 also shows that ASEAN countries have more reason to be concerned about the "threat" that China poses. Using per capita income as a

Table 2. Competition between China and the rest of
East Asia in the U.S. Market

| | % of Product Competition in the U.S. Market | | |
|---|---|---|---|
| | 1990 | 1995 | 2000 |
| Hong Kong | 42.5 | 50.5 | 55.9 |
| Japan | 3.0 | 8.3 | 16.3 |
| South Korea | 24.0 | 27.1 | 37.5 |
| Taiwan | 26.7 | 38.7 | 48.5 |
| ASEAN: | | | |
| Indonesia | 85.3 | 85.5 | 82.8 |
| Malaysia | 37.1 | 38.9 | 48.7 |
| Philippines | 46.3 | 47.8 | 46.1 |
| Singapore | 14.8 | 19.2 | 35.8 |
| Thailand | 42.2 | 56.3 | 65.4 |

Source: Kwan (2002).

proxy, the major ASEAN economies are at a similar level of economic development and competitiveness to China, while the Asian NIEs are at a more advanced stage of economic development. In particular, the export structures of China and Indonesia, as reflected in their exports to the U.S. market, show an 82.8 percent overlap in 2000, while those of China and Thailand show a 65.4 percent overlap. The "China threat" has impelled ASEAN to commission the McKinsey consulting firm to undertake a study on ASEAN competitiveness, and to explore new directions for ASEAN integration. ASEAN has also readily accepted China's FTA proposal.

## GROWING ECONOMIC INTERDEPENDENCE IN EAST ASIA

Economic interdependence among East Asian economies has grown in tandem with the region's dynamic economic growth, spurred by increasing demand as well as rising supply capabilities. This can be observed from the growth in intra-regional trade and investment, as well as in the flow of financial capital and the movement of tourists, businessmen, and professionals.

The share of intra-regional trade has been rising. Table 3 shows that it reached 47.6 percent in 2001 for the 11 East Asian economies comprising the Northeast Asian Five (China, Hong Kong, Japan, South Korea, and Taiwan) and the ASEAN-6 (Indonesia, Malaysia, the Philippines, Singapore, Thailand, and Vietnam). For Hong Kong, Singapore, and Taiwan respectively, intra-regional trade accounted for over 50 percent of all their trade. For Japan, the figure was lower, at 39.1 percent. For all 11 East Asian economies, the percentages for intra-regional trade are higher than the percentages for trade with either the European Union or the United States. However, a note of caution is necessary in drawing conclusions regarding the relative importance of intra-regional trade versus trade with the EU and U.S. markets. A large share of intra–East Asian trade comprises intermediate products such as information technology (IT) parts and components, synthetic fibers and products, and chemical products. The European Union and the United States remain crucial markets for East Asian exports of final products.

The rapid growth in intra-regional trade in the 1980s and 1990s is due to several developments:

— The transition from command economies to market economies, and the ensuing trade and investment liberalization of China and the CLMV countries, as well as further trade and investment liberalization in the market-oriented economies of the Asian NIEs, Indonesia, Malaysia, the Philippines, and Thailand.

— Rapid industrialization in the region, particularly in industries with highly segmented production that facilitated outsourcing of parts and components. The IT industry is a very good example, with trade rapidly expanding between firms and industries, and within the region. The automobile and garment industries are other examples. East Asian manufacturers are increasingly involved in webs of production and specialization in various parts of the supply value chain.

— Involvement in production networks and specialization along the value chain reflects the growing role of FDI in the region. In particular, Japanese FDI has played an important integrating role through its production and distribution networks. A significant part of intra-regional trade is between Japan and other East Asian economies.

## EMERGENT EAST ASIAN ECONOMIC REGIONALISM

### Driving Forces of Regionalism

In 1967, Indonesia, Malaysia, the Philippines, Singapore, and Thailand formed ASEAN to promote regional peace, security, and prosperity. Membership was extended to Brunei in the 1980s, and to Cambodia, Laos, Myanmar, and Vietnam in the 1990s. In 1992, ASEAN agreed to form the

## Table 3. East Asia—Intra-regional Trade and Trade with the World, 2001

| Exporter/Importer | Japan | China | Hong Kong | Korea | Taiwan | NEA-5 | Indonesia | Malaysia | Philippines | Singapore | Thailand | Vietnam | ASEAN-6 | EA-11 | U.S. | EU | World |
|---|---|---|---|---|---|---|---|---|---|---|---|---|---|---|---|---|---|
| Japan | – | 30,941 | 23,249 | 25,288 | 24,214 | 103,692 | 6,403 | 11,013 | 8,190 | 14,714 | 11,873 | 1,776 | 53,969 | 157,661 | 121,153 | 64,351 | 403,247 |
| % | | 7.7 | 5.8 | 6.3 | 6.0 | 25.7 | 1.6 | 2.7 | 2.0 | 3.6 | 2.9 | 0.4 | 13.4 | 39.1 | 30.0 | 16.0 | 100.0 |
| China | 45,078 | – | 46,503 | 12,544 | 5,006 | 109,131 | 2,847 | 3,223 | 1,622 | 5,795 | 2,504 | 1,805 | 17,796 | 126,927 | 54,319 | 40,965 | 266,661 |
| % | 16.9 | | 17.4 | 4.7 | 1.9 | 40.9 | 1.1 | 1.2 | 0.6 | 2.2 | 0.9 | 0.7 | 6.7 | 47.6 | 20.4 | 15.4 | 100.0 |
| Hong Kong | 11,261 | 70,407 | – | 3,430 | 4,642 | 89,740 | 843 | 1,635 | 1,925 | 3,852 | 1,899 | 543 | 10,697 | 100,437 | 42,327 | 27,547 | 191,244 |
| % | 5.9 | 36.8 | | 1.8 | 2.4 | 46.9 | 0.4 | 0.9 | 1.0 | 2.0 | 1.0 | 0.3 | 5.6 | 52.5 | 22.1 | 14.4 | 100.0 |
| Korea | 16,506 | 18,190 | 9,452 | – | 5,835 | 49,983 | 3,280 | 2,628 | 2,535 | 4,080 | 1,848 | 1,732 | 16,103 | 66,086 | 31,211 | 19,627 | 150,439 |
| % | 11.0 | 12.1 | 6.3 | | 3.9 | 33.2 | 2.2 | 1.7 | 1.7 | 2.7 | 1.2 | 1.2 | 10.7 | 43.9 | 20.7 | 13.0 | 100.0 |
| Taiwan | 12,714 | 4,727 | 26,858 | 3,264 | – | 47,563 | 1,469 | 3,050 | 2,141 | 4,037 | 2,118 | 1,720 | 14,535 | 62,098 | 27,552 | 18,302 | 122,410 |
| % | 10.4 | 3.9 | 21.9 | 2.7 | | 38.9 | 1.2 | 2.5 | 1.7 | 3.3 | 1.7 | 1.4 | 11.9 | 50.7 | 22.5 | 15.0 | 100.0 |
| NE Asia-5 | 85,593 | 124,322 | 106,091 | 44,539 | 39,711 | 400,256 | 14,847 | 21,556 | 16,418 | 32,489 | 20,248 | 7,579 | 113,136 | 513,392 | 276,655 | 170,851 | 1,134,401 |
| % | 7.5 | 11.0 | 9.4 | 3.9 | 3.5 | 35.3 | 1.3 | 1.9 | 1.4 | 2.9 | 1.8 | 0.7 | 10.0 | 45.2 | 24.4 | 15.1 | 100.0 |
| Indonesia | 13,010 | 2,201 | 1,290 | 3,772 | 2,188 | 22,461 | – | 1,779 | 815 | 5,364 | 1,064 | 322 | 9,344 | 31,805 | 7,745 | 7,745 | 56,321 |
| % | 23.1 | 3.9 | 2.3 | 6.7 | 3.9 | 39.9 | | 3.2 | 1.4 | 9.5 | 1.9 | 0.6 | 16.6 | 56.5 | 13.8 | 13.8 | 100.0 |
| Malaysia | 11,770 | 3,821 | 4,063 | 2,963 | 3,263 | 25,880 | 1,563 | – | 1,287 | 14,913 | 3,360 | 474 | 21,597 | 47,477 | 17,808 | 11,964 | 88,202 |
| % | 13.3 | 4.3 | 4.6 | 3.4 | 3.7 | 29.3 | 1.8 | | 1.5 | 16.9 | 3.8 | 0.5 | 24.5 | 53.8 | 20.2 | 13.6 | 100.0 |
| Philippines | 5,057 | 793 | 1,580 | 1,044 | 2,127 | 10,601 | 133 | 1,112 | – | 2,308 | 1,358 | 62 | 4,973 | 15,574 | 8,843 | 6,195 | 32,151 |
| % | 15.7 | 2.5 | 4.9 | 3.2 | 6.6 | 33.0 | 0.4 | 3.5 | | 7.2 | 4.2 | 0.2 | 15.5 | 48.4 | 27.5 | 19.3 | 100.0 |
| Singapore | 9,335 | 5,332 | 10,822 | 4,687 | 6,262 | 36,438 | 2,832 | 21,126 | 3,081 | – | 5,299 | 2,105 | 34,443 | 70,881 | 18,746 | 16,280 | 121,786 |
| % | 7.7 | 4.4 | 8.9 | 3.8 | 5.1 | 29.9 | 2.3 | 17.3 | 2.5 | | 4.4 | 1.7 | 28.3 | 58.2 | 15.4 | 13.4 | 100.0 |
| Thailand | 9,942 | 2,850 | 3,284 | 1,226 | 1,908 | 19,210 | 1,360 | 2,713 | 1,152 | 5,263 | – | 794 | 11,282 | 30,492 | 13,193 | 10,476 | 64,909 |
| % | 15.3 | 4.4 | 5.1 | 1.9 | 2.9 | 29.6 | 2.1 | 4.2 | 1.8 | 8.1 | | 1.2 | 17.4 | 47.0 | 20.3 | 16.1 | 100.0 |
| Vietnam | 2,344 | 909 | 227 | 336 | 377 | 4,193 | 154 | 286 | 280 | 768 | 294 | – | 1,782 | 5,975 | 948 | 3,523 | 12,035 |
| % | 19.5 | 7.6 | 1.9 | 2.8 | 3.1 | 34.8 | 1.3 | 2.4 | 2.3 | 6.4 | 2.4 | | 14.8 | 49.6 | 7.9 | 29.3 | 100.0 |
| ASEAN-6 | 51,533 | 15,925 | 21,292 | 14,047 | 16,147 | 118,945 | 6,049 | 27,044 | 6,622 | 28,658 | 11,389 | 3,761 | 83,523 | 202,468 | 67,384 | 56,259 | 375,904 |
| % | 13.7 | 4.2 | 5.7 | 3.7 | 4.3 | 31.6 | 1.6 | 7.2 | 1.8 | 7.6 | 3.0 | 1.0 | 22.2 | 53.9 | 17.9 | 15.0 | 100.0 |
| East Asia-11 | 137,126 | 140,247 | 127,383 | 58,586 | 55,858 | 519,200 | 20,896 | 48,600 | 23,041 | 61,146 | 31,637 | 11,340 | 196,660 | 715,860 | 344,039 | 227,110 | 1,510,305 |
| % | 9.1 | 9.1 | 9.3 | 8.4 | 3.7 | 34.4 | 1.4 | 3.2 | 1.5 | 4.0 | 2.1 | 0.8 | 13.0 | 47.4 | 22.8 | 15.0 | 100.0 |
| U.S. | 57,452 | 19,182 | 14,028 | 22,181 | 18,122 | 130,965 | 2,521 | 9,358 | 7,660 | 17,652 | 5,989 | 460 | 43,640 | 174,605 | – | 158,767 | 729,100 |
| % | 7.9 | 2.6 | 1.9 | 3.0 | 2.5 | 18.0 | 0.3 | 1.3 | 1.1 | 2.4 | 0.8 | 0.1 | 6.0 | 23.9 | | 21.8 | 100.0 |
| EU | 39,190 | 26,378 | 19,965 | 13,765 | 11,354 | 110,652 | 3,908 | 8,212 | 3,883 | 12,889 | 6,327 | 1,564 | 36,783 | 147,435 | 210,706 | 1,403,800 | 2,312,553 |
| % | 1.7 | 1.1 | 0.9 | 0.6 | 0.5 | 4.8 | 0.4 | 0.2 | 0.2 | 0.6 | 0.3 | 0.1 | 1.6 | 6.4 | 9.1 | 60.7 | 100.0 |
| World | 316,139 | 220,987 | 173,796 | 131,019 | 94,362 | 936,303 | 34,470 | 72,276 | 39,728 | 109,480 | 55,496 | 14,162 | 325,612 | 1,261,915 | 1,092,607 | 2,230,962 | 5,980,846 |

Source: Adapted from Japan External Trade Organization (2003).

ASEAN Free Trade Area (AFTA). Southeast Asian countries thus became party to a formal RTA, while the Northeast Asian economies of China, Hong Kong, Japan, South Korea, and Taiwan did not yet participate in any RTA.

In 1990, Malaysian Prime Minister Mahathir Mohamad proposed the East Asia Economic Group (EAEG), later changed to East Asia Economic Caucus (EAEC), in reaction to the nascent North American Free Trade Agreement (NAFTA) and the emerging single market in Europe. The Malaysian proposal never took off, because of strong U.S. opposition and a lack of support from Japan and other East Asian countries. Non-supporters were reluctant to see a division in the Asia Pacific region, given their strong desire that the United States maintain geostrategic and economic interests in East Asia.

Instead, East Asian countries supported the Asia-Pacific Economic Cooperation (APEC) regional grouping, which included members on both sides of the Pacific, most particularly East Asian economies and the United States. APEC got off to a good start. In 1994 APEC reached a landmark decision, and adopted the Bogor goal of trade liberalization by 2010 for developed members and 2020 for developing members. Since then, however, APEC has not lived up to expectations. For members keen on trade and investment liberalization, APEC's open regionalism and voluntarism has failed to produce the desired pace of liberalization. Membership is also too large and diverse to forge an APEC-wide FTA. For members keen on economic and technical cooperation rather than liberalization, APEC's ecotech program appears too piecemeal.

Since then, various bilateral and regional FTAs have been signed, or are under consideration or negotiation. Table 4 lists negotiated and implemented RTAs in East Asia, and those under consideration or negotiation. The list continues to grow. RTAs are not confined to countries within the same geographical region or subregion. There are RTAs between Northeast Asia and Southeast Asia—such as ASEAN + 3, ASEAN-China, ASEAN-Japan, ASEAN-South Korea, and Japan-Singapore. There are RTAs between Southeast Asia and other regions—such as ASEAN-CER (with Australia and New Zealand), ASEAN-EU, and Chile-New Zealand-Singapore. Bilateral FTAs have proliferated—both between countries in the region, and with countries outside the region. For example, Singapore has FTAs with Australia, Canada, Chile, the European Union, India, Japan, South Korea, Mexico, New Zealand, and the United States; Japan with Mexico, Singapore, South Korea, and Thailand; and South Korea with Chile and Japan.

## Table 4. Free Trade Agreements in East Asia

| | Year | Participants | Notes |
|---|---|---|---|
| **Agreements in force** | | | |
| ASEAN Free Trade Area (AFTA) | 1992 | ASEAN-10: Brunei, Indonesia, Malaysia, Philippines, Singapore, Thailand, Cambodia, Laos, Myanmar, Vietnam | ASEAN formed in 1967, AFTA implemented in January 1992. AFTA supplemented by agreements on services, investment, and monetary co-operation involving swap arrangements and regional surveillance. |
| ASEAN+3 | 1999 | Asean-10, China, Japan, South Korea | Chiang Mai Initiative in monetary co-operation involves swap arrangements and regional surveillance. |
| Vietnam-U.S. trade and investment agreement | 2001 | Vietnam, U.S. | This falls short of an FTA. |
| Singapore-New Zealand FTA | 2001 | Singapore, New Zealand | Implemented in January. |
| Japan-Singapore Economic Partnership Agreement (JSEPA) | 2002 | Japan, Singapore | Signed in January, implemented in November. It is an FTA-plus. |
| Singapore-EFTA (European Free Trade Association) FTA | 2002 | Singapore, members of EFTA | Signed in June 2002, implemented in January 2003. |
| **Agreements under consideration/negotiation/study** | | | |
| ASEAN-China Comprehensive Economic Cooperation | 2002 | ASEAN-10, China | FTA to be realized within 10 years. Framework Agreement adopted at Nov. 2002 Summit. |
| ASEAN-Japan Comprehensive Economic Partnership | 2002 | ASEAN-10, Japan | FTA component to be realized within 10 years. Agreement to proceed reached at Nov. 2002 Summit. |
| ASEAN-CER | 2002 | ASEAN-10, Australia, New Zealand | Trade and investment agreement, falls short of FTA. |
| East Asia Free Trade Area (EAFTA) | ? | ASEAN-10, China, Japan, South Korea | Proposal made at ASEAN+3 Summit. East Asia Vision Group submitted its report in Nov. 2001, followed by a report from the East Asia Study Group in Nov. 2002. The FTA is now being studied by the economic ministers |
| ASEAN-India Regional Trade and Investment Agreement | ? | ASEAN-10, India | Proposal at Nov. 2002 Summit. |
| Chile-New Zealand-Singapore Trilateral FTA | ? | Chile, New Zealand, Singapore | |
| China-Japan-South Korea Trilateral FTA | ? | China, Japan, South Korea | |
| Pacific-5 FTA | ? | Australia, Chile, New Zealand, Singapore, U.S. | |
| **Bilateral FTAs under consideration/negotiation/study** | | | |
| China with: | | Hong Kong, Macau, Thailand | |
| Hong Kong with: | | China, Macau | |
| Japan with: | | Malaysia, Mexico, Philippines, South Korea, Taiwan, Thailand | |
| Malaysia with: | | Japan | |
| Philippines with: | | Japan, U.S. | |
| Singapore with: | | Australia, Canada, Chile, India, Mexico, South Korea, Taiwan, U.S. | |
| South Korea with: | | Japan, U.S., Singapore, Chile | |
| Taiwan with: | | Japan, New Zealand, Panama, Singapore, U.S. | |
| Thailand with: | | Australia, China, India, Japan | |

Malaysia and Thailand are now also jumping onto the bilateral FTA band-wagon. Many countries are members of two or more RTAs, with the re-sult that there are overlapping RTAs.

Global, regional, and domestic economic and political pressures have driven this growth in economic regionalism in the past decade.

## Responding to Regionalism in the Americas and Europe

East Asia is the only sizeable economic region in the world without any formal RTA. NAFTA and the European Union are seen to offer numerous benefits to their members and to discriminate against nonmember coun-tries. As outsiders, East Asian economies and exporters are subject to dis-criminatory practices and trade diversion due to these two blocs. Concern has grown with the continual expansion of the European Union to cover central and eastern Europe, the surge in RTAs in Latin America, and the emergence of the Free Trade Area of the Americas (FTAA) by 2005. East Asians are hence pressuring their governments to form similar RTAs.

## Meeting the Globalization Challenge

East Asia is pursuing regionalism to better manage the risks of globaliza-tion as well as to ensure international competitiveness. A larger regional market and greater security of market access would enable individual economies and firms to achieve economies of scale and scope; reduce trans-action costs, with the falling of trade and investment barriers; pool in-vestment, technological, and management resources; and enhance productivity.

## Disappointment with the WTO and APEC

Trade liberalization under the GATT/WTO has become increasingly dif-ficult with its large and diverse membership. The Uruguay Round took over seven years to negotiate. Failure to launch a new trade round in Se-attle in 1999 highlighted the increasing difficulties of securing multilat-eral trade liberalization. Although the Doha Round was launched in December 2001, it remains to be seen whether its objectives can be achieved within the given timeframe of 2005. In contrast, RTAs among "like-minded" countries are speedier to negotiate and they produce more fo-cused results. There is also concern about APEC's ineffectiveness in liberalizing trade and investment among its members. Open regionalism and nonbinding principles are supposed to achieve APEC's Bogor trade and investment liberalization targets of 2010 for developed economies and 2020 for developing economies, but there are questions about whether these targets can be achieved in this fashion. APEC's effectiveness suffered a severe blow with the failure of the Early Voluntary Sectoral Liberalization (EVSL) initiative. In general, APEC has failed to check the momentum of regionalism in North and Latin America.

## Responding to the Regional Financial Crisis

The 1997–1998 Asian financial crisis gave strong new impetus to East Asian regionalism as it highlighted the reality of regional contagion. It also illustrated the desirability of regional cooperation, to prevent another crisis emerging and to help improve regional economic stability and resilience. Another impetus to regional cooperation was acute disappointment over the nature of assistance that the European Union, the International Monetary Fund, and the United States provided to the region in crisis. Leaders and officials of Southeast and Northeast Asia met subsequently under the ASEAN + 3 initiative to discuss financial and monetary cooperation. In the search for economic recovery, RTAs look increasingly attractive as they could help secure market access and additional investment resources, and they could facilitate better resource allocation and economic efficiency.

## The Rise of China

China's increasing economic weight contributes to the growing regional realization that East Asia could form a large and dynamic economic bloc able to harness regional resources for solving regional problems. East Asia could also be a more effective voice in the global arena hitherto dominated by Western interests. With the inclusion of China, East Asia incorporates a third of the world's population, a quarter of the world's GDP, and two-fifths of the world's foreign exchange reserves. Having secured its entry into the WTO, China has now become interested in RTAs. Apart from promoting its political interests, China is looking at regional economic integration to help it develop new markets and promote outward investment for Chinese enterprises. In November 2001, China proposed a RTA with ASEAN. This initiative is aimed at overcoming Southeast Asian anxiety over the "China threat," as well as ensuring that it is not kept out of Southeast Asia by Japan and the United States.

## The Changed Position of Japan

Until recently, Japan had pursued a multilateralist trade strategy. Yet it too is now looking at RTAs. A decade of stagnation, the loss of economic dynamism, and the challenge to remain internationally competitive have resulted in Japan wanting dependable access to overseas markets. China's rise has also added to Japanese concerns about its international and regional competitiveness. Japan's first RTA initiative was with South Korea. After three years of study and consideration, agreement was finally reached in March 2002 to start official discussion about forming a bilateral FTA. Negotiations with Singapore started later, but were speedily concluded by January 2002. The Japan-Singapore Economic Partnership Agreement (JSEPA) was implemented that November. In the wake of China's proposal for an FTA with ASEAN, Japan also proposed an ASEAN-Japan economic partnership agreement in January 2002. It is currently negotiating an ASEAN-wide framework agreement as well as various bilateral agreements.

## The Changed Position of the United States

When Malaysian Prime Minister Mahathir first proposed the EAEG in 1990, it met with strong U.S. objection and a negative response from Japan. So the initiative failed. The Japanese proposal for an Asian Monetary Fund to help countries battered by the Asian financial crisis was similarly stillborn due to U.S. and IMF objections. Since then, the United States no longer seems to be opposing regional cooperative initiatives in East Asia. It has raised no objections to the initiatives between ASEAN-China, ASEAN-Japan, ASEAN + 3, and even the East Asia FTA. It is even negotiating FTAs of its own. It has signed a trade and investment agreement with Vietnam, completed negotiations on an FTA with Singapore, and proposed an U.S.-ASEAN FTA. It is also negotiating a trade and investment agreement with Thailand.

Chia Siow Yue

## ASEAN Economic Integration Agreements

The ASEAN-10 members are diverse in size and resource endowments, levels of development, and industrial and technological competence. Economic, financial, and development cooperation and integration in ASEAN has taken various forms, but it has not been inward looking. Even now, intra-ASEAN trade accounts for only about 25 percent of the region's total trade, while 60 percent of tourists and 90 percent of foreign investments are from outside the region.

The centerpiece of ASEAN economic cooperation and integration is AFTA, which entails progressively reducing tariffs to the 0 percent–5 percent level by 2008 for intra-ASEAN trade in goods. By January 2002 and six years ahead of schedule, AFTA realized the tariff level target of 0 percent–5 percent on 95.7 percent of tariffs and 90 percent of intra-ASEAN trade in goods among the ASEAN-6 (Brunei, Indonesia, Malaysia, the Philippines, Singapore, and Thailand). The CLMV countries have until 2010 to achieve the 0 percent–5 percent tariff level target. In 1999, ASEAN agreed to bring all intra-ASEAN tariffs down to zero for the ASEAN-6 by 2010, and for the CLMV countries by 2015. The intention is for all intra-ASEAN tariffs to be completely eliminated by 2015. This end-date is still far away, but accelerating the pace of tariff elimination on intra-regional trade and dismantling nontariff barriers would create a seamless regional market which would facilitate trade, and improve efficiency and competitiveness.

The 1995 ASEAN Framework Agreement on Services (AFAS) and the 1998 Framework Agreement on the ASEAN Investment Area (AIA) supplement AFTA. AFAS recognizes that tradeable services have dynamic growth potential, and that efficiency and productivity in the production of goods is closely linked to efficiency and productivity in the provision of services. ASEAN has identified business services, transportation, telecommunications, and finance to be priority services. However, apart from cooperation in tourism and some opening of the financial services market with the entry of foreign banks in the wake of the Asian financial crisis, not much progress has been made. AIA addresses the fact that trade liberalization has to be accompanied by liberalized investment and facilitation measures to be effective. ASEAN has expanded the sectors to be opened up—beyond manufacturing—to include agriculture, forestry, fisheries, and mining. It has also brought forward the end-date for national treatment to 2010 for ASEAN-6, and 2015 for the CLMV countries. As with the AFTA schedule, the AIA liberalization schedule is too slow to enable AFTA and AIA to reinforce each other, or to counter strong FDI interest in China.

There are increasing calls for ASEAN to be more integrated and competitive in order to meet the economic challenges ahead, particularly those challenges stemming from China. As noted, ASEAN has commissioned the consulting firm McKinsey to study ASEAN's competitiveness issues, and to chart a road ahead. ASEAN governments are also exploring progression from AFTA, AFAS, and AIA toward an integrated ASEAN Economic Community (AEC). An AEC would consolidate existing efforts in trade and investment liberalization and facilitation, and would widen and deepen ASEAN economic integration. Making ASEAN a borderless trade and investment zone would improve the region's productivity and competitiveness, and help sustain economic growth.

## ASEAN + 3 Initiative

The ASEAN + 3 initiative involves the ASEAN-10 countries, and China, Japan, and South Korea. Started by ASEAN, ASEAN + 3 was, at the outset, an informal gathering of the 13 countries' foreign ministers on the sidelines of the main ASEAN Ministerial Meetings. It provided a vital first forum for Southeast and Northeast Asian political leaders and policy makers.

The initial ASEAN + 3 Heads of State Summit was convened in December 1997, during the Asian financial crisis, to discuss modalities for financial cooperation. A proposal for an Asian Monetary Fund, first mooted by Japan in Seattle, never developed further due to concerns that it might undermine the role of the IMF. The subsequently agreed upon Chiang Mai Initiative (CMI) has two features. First, it is a network of bilateral swap agreements (BSAs) between ASEAN countries, China, Japan, and South Korea to provide liquidity to central banks in need. Several BSAs have been signed, typically between a Northeast Asian country and a Southeast Asian country. Second, it is the regional surveillance mechanism to monitor exchange rates, macroeconomic aggregates, and sectoral and social policies. By surveying these policies, it hopes to catch early warning signals to prevent another financial crisis from occurring. ASEAN + 3 finance ministers meet regularly to discuss monitoring, surveillance, and further financial cooperation.

The ASEAN + 3 process started with financial cooperation, and seems now to be moving toward broader economic cooperation and integration.

There have been several ASEAN + 3 Heads of State Summits, as well as Ministerial Meetings on finance, economics and trade, labor, agriculture and forestry, tourism, energy, and the environment. There have also been discussions on moving beyond swaps and surveillance to deeper monetary and financial integration. Optimists portray the CMI as the forerunner of an Asian Monetary Fund and an eventual common currency for East Asia. Critics question whether the present 13 members satisfy the criteria for an optimum currency area, and they note the political and economic obstacles to such deep integration. There is also the issue of sequencing—should financial and monetary integration move ahead of trade integration? Without trade integration and macroeconomic policy coordination, deepening monetary and financial cooperation would be difficult.

## ASEAN-China Comprehensive Economic Cooperation

A proposal from Chinese Premier Zhu Rongji for ASEAN-China cooperation at the November 2000 Summit led to the formation of an ASEAN-China expert group and the issuing of a report, *Forging Closer ASEAN-China Economic Relations in the Twenty-First Century*. The report made the following recommendations:

— Establishment of an ASEAN-China FTA within 10 years. It should provide for differential treatment and flexibility for the CLMV countries and also for an "early harvest" of mutually agreed goods to be liberalized without having final agreement on a full FTA.

— A wide range of trade and investment facilitation measures.

— Technical assistance and capacity building to ASEAN members, particularly Cambodia, Laos, and Myanmar.

— Expanded cooperation in areas such as finance, tourism, agriculture, human resource development, small and medium-sized enterprises, industrial cooperation, intellectual property rights, the environment, forestry and forestry products, energy, and subregional development.

A Framework Agreement on ASEAN-China Comprehensive Economic Cooperation (AC-CEC) was signed in November 2002. It commits ASEAN and China to start negotiations on an FTA that will cover trade in goods and services, investment liberalization and facilitation, as well as other areas of cooperation. The target is to establish the FTA by 2010 for ASEAN-6, and by 2015 for the CLMV countries, with flexibility on sensitive commodities and preferential tariff treatment for the CLMV countries. Given the differences in development levels and competitiveness between the ASEAN-10 economies, it will be difficult for ASEAN countries to maintain a common position in negotiations on trade liberalization with China. There is a strong possibility of some ASEAN countries entering into bilateral arrangements with China. Thailand is reportedly already in bilateral negotiations with China.

Regardless of the ten-year time frame for completing the ASEAN-China FTA, China has agreed to open up certain agricultural product sectors early so that participating countries can benefit from increased trade before the FTA actually comes into force. Not all ASEAN countries have agreed to participate, however.

In recognition of the wide economic disparities between ASEAN countries, China has offered the CLMV countries preferential treatment. It has, for example, agreed to implement accelerated subregional development cooperation arrangements, such as for the Greater Mekong subregion. It has also agreed to reduce the debt obligations of the less-developed ASEAN members, and to launch an IT training program for ASEAN. China is also cofinancing completion of the railway linking Singapore and Kunming.

China's motivations for the initiative toward ASEAN have raised a great deal of interest, not only in ASEAN, but also in Japan and the United States. China's motivations are both political and economic. Politically, China wishes to remain on friendly terms with its southern neighbors, and to allay ASEAN concerns about China's increasing economic muscle. Closer economic relations with ASEAN would help China build geopolitical clout in Southeast Asia, and contain the influences of Japan, Taiwan, and the United States. China is also eyeing the ASEAN region for both markets and natural resources, especially oil.

ASEAN governments readily welcomed China's initiative for a number of reasons. China is the largest new market for ASEAN products and services, and it could serve as an engine of growth. Closer ASEAN-China economic ties would enable ASEAN to benefit from China's growing economy, reduce economic dependence on the European Union and the United States, and help offset the knock-on effects for ASEAN of Japan's sluggish economy. China's entry into the WTO also means its trading relationships have to be based on international rules and practices. Chinese tourists are already a key factor in the growth of tourism in ASEAN, and China is a rapidly expanding market for Thai agricultural produce. With the CEC, ASEAN could attract more Chinese tourists and Chinese FDI.

The CLMV group has lower wage costs than China, and should be more successful in attracting FDI. China's offer of special treatment and development assistance for the CLMV countries should help them accept the Chinese initiative.

Nonetheless, ASEAN countries remain deeply concerned about China's competitive strengths and advantages—its ability to flood global, regional, and national markets with cheaply produced goods—and its huge capacity to attract FDI. Intensified competition will give rise to further dislocation costs in ASEAN. Some ASEAN leaders, such as Singapore's Goh Chok Tong, have been exhorting ASEAN to integrate faster and more deeply, and to become more competitive to meet the challenges from China and those from globalization.

## ASEAN-Japan Comprehensive Economic Partnership

The Japan-Singapore Economic Partnership Agreement (JSEPA), signed in January 2002 and implemented that November, marked Japan's first departure from the multilateral trade track. Negotiations were completed within a record 14 months, and reflected strong political and economic ties, as well as the economic complementarity of the two countries, particularly Singapore's lack of an agricultural sector that could compete with Japanese agriculture. Singapore and Japan are the two most developed economies in Asia. They share many economic and strategic interests, and work closely in many regional and international forums. Although the JSEPA includes the liberalization of trade in goods, services, and investment found in many traditional FTAs, it also includes cooperation in key growth areas such as IT, science and technology, financial services, tourism, and human resource development.

Japan proposed a formal economic partnership agreement with ASEAN in January 2002, soon after ASEAN accepted China's proposal for an ASEAN-China FTA and immediately after the signing of the JSEPA. In November 2002, ASEAN and Japan signed a joint declaration to develop a framework for an ASEAN-Japan Comprehensive Economic Partnership (AJ-CEP), and to provide for separate bilateral partnership agreements. Bilateral discussions have started with Malaysia, the Philippines, Thailand, and Vietnam. A committee of senior officials will draft the framework, monitor progress in bilateral agreements, and report back to the next summit scheduled for November 2003.

Japan's preference for a network of bilateral agreements under a general AJ-CEP agreement recognizes the difficulty of negotiating one comprehensive package. Japan regards bilateral pacts as more "realistic" as they allow each ASEAN member a different liberalization schedule. Also, given the sensitivity of agriculture in Japanese politics and economics, and that several ASEAN countries are major exporters of agricultural products, bilateral agreements make it easier to recognize and resolve these issues. However, some in ASEAN are concerned that bilateral agreements enable Japan to "cherry pick," and that they undermine ASEAN solidarity and negotiating leverage, particularly as Japan may not have a bilateral arrangement with every ASEAN country.

What motivates the Japanese overture and ASEAN's ready acceptance? Japan too is concerned about China's economic ascendancy, and how it could undermine Japan's position as the premier economic power in East Asia and its influence in Southeast Asia. A formalized relationship between Japan and ASEAN would help consolidate Japan's trade and investment relations with Southeast Asia, while a rejuvenated ASEAN would also help Japan avoid putting all its investment eggs in the China basket. The timing of Japan's initiative toward ASEAN is, obviously, in reaction to the ASEAN-China FTA proposal.

For ASEAN, the Japanese initiative—following the Chinese overture— helped affirm ASEAN's role in East Asian politics and economics. ASEAN recognizes Japan as the world's second largest economy and as the regional growth engine, yet it is also concerned about Japan's long economic slump, the sharp decline in Japanese FDI to ASEAN, and the drop in ASEAN-Japan trade in recent years. Overall, the AJ-CEP helps anchor Japanese interests in Southeast Asia, while also counterbalancing China's overwhelming influence and muscle.

## Conceptual Issues

The proliferation of overlapping regional and bilateral FTAs has given rise to debate among economists on a number of issues.

### The Systemic Effects on the WTO and the Global Trading System

A perennial debate is whether regional and bilateral RTAs are stumbling or building blocs for the GATT/WTO multilateral trading system. Indeed, do they assist or impede the WTO Doha Round of multilateral trade negotiations currently underway?

By their very nature, RTAs are discriminatory, favoring members and penalizing nonmembers through trade and investment diversion, so they do infringe on the basic WTO principle of nondiscrimination. Yet Article XXIV of the GATT allows RTAs, provided that they cover substantially all trade, and do not raise barriers against nonmember countries. RTAs among developing countries are also covered by an "enabling clause" which allows for special and differential treatment under the GATT/WTO. Critics argue that Article XXIV is too weak and has never been enforced, and that RTAs set bad precedents, with the exclusion of sensitive sectors and products, or inclusion of non-WTO compliant environmental and labor standards. The "spaghetti bowl" effect of overlapping RTAs with different rules of origin and different trade and investment rules and standards is a further complication.

Critics overemphasize the stumbling bloc effects of RTAs and overlook the building bloc effects. These have generally been WTO-consistent in covering substantially all trade and not raising barriers against nonmembers. Participation in a RTA forces a country to liberalize its trade and integrate more deeply, thereby opening the political and psychological door to broader liberalization in the WTO. The evidence so far is that East Asian countries have not turned away from multilateralism, as countries continue to maintain a global orientation in trade and investment, and a strategic interest in the Doha Round. For countries with limited financial and human negotiating resources, negotiating several RTAs could divert resources from the Doha Round process. For better-endowed countries, there are, in fact, advantages, in that the negotiating experience gained with RTAs can be usefully deployed to the Doha Round negotiations. Overall, participation in RTAs seems to help countries accept global liberalization under the WTO.

The term "FTA" is, in many ways, a misnomer, as new regional and bilateral initiatives are no longer traditional GATT/WTO-sanctioned FTAs focusing on tariff removal. "New age" or "WTO plus" FTAs today include trade facilitation such as harmonization, mutual recognition of technical standards, and investment liberalization and facilitation. They also incorporate technical and development cooperation in areas such as human resource development, infrastructure development, IT, research and development, small and medium-sized enterprise development, and environmental protection. ASEAN + 3 has also been initiating monetary cooperation and integration ahead of efforts in trade integration. Furthermore, apart from the economic impact, FTAs also have positive political and diplomatic effects among member countries.

East Asian economies are pursuing a multi-tier track of entering into regional, subregional, and even bilateral RTAs while continuing unilateral reforms and liberalization, and supporting the multilateralism of the WTO. The objectives of the multi-track approach are to foster national economic competitiveness, improve market access, attract investments, acquire financial stability, and secure specific development objectives pertaining to services, human resources, research and development, IT, and small and medium-sized enterprises.

## Measurement and Distribution of Gains and Costs

FTAs can help expand trade opportunities, attract investment, and speed up domestic structural reforms, among other economic effects.

A simulation study on an ASEAN-China FTA, cited in the report of the ASEAN-China study group, shows that if both sides reduced their tariffs to zero, exports would expand by US$13 billion a year (48 percent) from the ASEAN-6 to China and US$10.6 billion (55.1 percent) from China to ASEAN-6. The FTA would grow Chinese GDP by 0.27 percent and that of the ASEAN-6 by 0.86 percent. A similar simulation study on an ASEAN-Japan FTA shows that the FTA would raise exports from Japan to ASEAN by 27.5 percent, and from ASEAN to Japan by 44.2 percent, while it would boost GDP by 0.07 percent in Japan and 1.99 percent in ASEAN. Such simulation studies, it should be cautioned, focus largely on standard trade creation and trade diversion effects from removing tariff barriers, and they fail to capture many of the dynamic effects of FTAs.

The proliferation of overlapping RTAs has also given rise to a "hub-and-spoke" effect. In trade literature, hubs are criticized for reaping more benefits than spokes, since each hub has free market access to all the spokes, while each spoke only has free market access to the hub. But the issue of unequal gains for hubs and spokes may be overblown, as spokes can also become hubs. For example, the United States is the hub with its FTA arrangements with Canada and Mexico in NAFTA, and also in its various bilateral FTAs with Chile, Israel, Jordan, Singapore, and many more countries. However, Canada and Mexico have also been negotiating FTAs with other partners, in which they themselves become hubs. Hence, the American first-mover advantage as a hub is rapidly eroded by the emergent

Canadian and Mexican hubs. In East Asia, Singapore is the forerunner in forming bilateral FTAs. As ASEAN countries individually and collectively sign on to various FTAs, Singapore's initial hub advantage will disappear as other ASEAN countries themselves become hubs.

## Transaction Costs

The proliferation of regional and bilateral RTAs in East Asia has given rise to serious overlapping and a "spaghetti bowl" effect, with rules of origin forming a complex matrix. The trade-deflection impact of diverse rules of origin, and the transaction costs of cross-border business deserve closer study. How do businesses in each country cope with multiple rules of origin, and multiple product and technical standards for exports to different destinations? How can a consolidated East Asian FTA emerge from subregional and bilateral FTAs with different rules of origin and standards? To enable RTAs to become building blocks with ever-widening memberships, having common rules of origin and standards—perhaps incorporated as part of the WTO under a revised Article XXIV—would be desirable.

## Emergent East Asian FTA or Community?

The ASEAN + 3 process has spawned ideas for an eventual East Asian FTA or East Asian Community. At the November 1998 Heads of State Summit, Korea proposed an East Asia Vision Group (EAVG) to present a vision for East Asian cooperation. The EAVG submitted its report, *Towards an East Asian Community*, in October 2001, with the following main recommendations:
— Evolve the ASEAN + 3 Summit into an East Asian Summit.
— Establish an East Asian FTA, starting with the interim step of linking existing FTAs in East Asia.
— In the long term, create an East Asian Community with cooperation encompassing all aspects of society, namely, economic, political, security, environmental, social, cultural, and educational elements.
A follow-up study group of senior officials appointed to evaluate the EAVG recommendations submitted the *Final Report of the East Asia Study Group* in November 2002. The report recommends, in the short term, forming an East Asia Forum, an East Asia Business Council, and a network

of East Asian intellectuals, as well as promoting East Asian studies. It suggests that forming the East Asian Summit and the East Asian FTA should be medium- to long-term goals. An East Asian Summit should evolve from the ASEAN + 3 process in a manner comfortable to all member countries—to alleviate ASEAN concerns that it may become marginalized if the pace is too fast, and to nurture a greater sense of ownership among the Northeast Asian countries. An East Asian FTA would encompass existing subregional and bilateral FTAs, and create the world's largest market of almost two billion people. ASEAN + 3 leaders agreed to explore the phased evolution of the ASEAN + 3 Summit into an East Asian Summit, and they also tasked economic ministers to study and formulate options on the gradual formation of an East Asia FTA and report the results to the 2003 Summit.

There are many reasons to work toward an East Asian FTA or East Asian Community.

— A region-wide framework seems a logical development in view of the already high degree of de facto market integration in East Asia, the ongoing ASEAN + 3 process, the emerging ASEAN-China and ASEAN-Japan cooperation agreements, and the proliferating bilateral FTAs.

— The formation of the FTAA and the expansion of the European Union to incorporate a growing number of central and eastern European countries in coming years will pressure East Asia into forming a counter bloc, as East Asian businesses and exporters see themselves increasingly discriminated against in those markets.

— East Asian economic integration would improve the region's competitiveness in both home and global markets through improved market access, better economies of scale, better use of comparative advantages and complementarities, lower business transaction costs, learning from best practices, and strategic alliances in innovation and research. These would lead to increased domestic and foreign investments, higher economic and income growth, and increased employment opportunities.

— Forming an East Asian FTA or East Asian Community is also about more than economics. Just as the European Community has played a pivotal role in maintaining peace and stability among western European member countries, and ASEAN has helped keep the peace between Southeast Asian member countries, an East Asian FTA or Community could play a similar role in East Asia. When the economies of East Asia become more interdependent and intertwined, awareness of a shared future and common destiny will emerge, and this will help deter intra-East Asian conflict. The discipline of regional timeframes and schedules would also act as pressure points for domestic reforms. Such a large regional grouping would also enable East Asia to have a stronger global voice and greater bargaining leverage vis-à-vis Europe and the Americas.

An East Asian FTA or Community could only be realized over the long term as there are severe challenges to its actualization. At the political level, there is no common vision for East Asia, as was the case with the founding members of the European Union. An East Asian identity is also slow in emerging. ASEAN, for example, has already been in existence for 35 years, yet a strong ASEAN identity has not emerged. Countries have to be convinced that they have a common destiny, and that the political and economic gains of "being together" outweigh the costs and pull of national sovereignty. A further problem is the degree of historical mistrust among East Asian nations, particularly between China and Japan. Confidence building and community building are long processes, and they must begin now. The existing ASEAN + 3 process is a confidence-building exercise, but more needs to be done. There should be political, social, and cultural exchanges among East Asian communities at various levels, including between political leaders, policymakers, intellectuals, professionals, students, youth, and artistic groups.

At the economic level, the disparate development levels and economic competencies pose obstacles to intra-regional trade and investment liberalization, and the free movement of capital and people. Countries will want to open up at varying paces, and exclude different nationally sensitive sectors. Many countries will not want to surrender the degree of national sovereignty necessary for creating common institutions, rules, disciplines, and policies. However, economic disparity should not be an insurmountable obstacle, as such diversity also makes for economic complementarity. And as the region's economies develop and restructure according to comparative advantage, there will be less protectionist sentiment and fewer sensitive sectors—so long as there are built-in mechanisms to ensure that all member countries benefit. Indeed, notwithstanding growing intra-regional economic ties, not all perceive an East Asian FTA as absolutely necessary for national growth and prosperity. There are strong links with North America and Europe for trade, investment, finance, and technology, as well as strong dependence on the U.S. security umbrella. Some wish that regional economic integration would also mean stronger ties with Australia-New Zealand, Europe, and North America.

The hierarchy of economic integration ranges from sectoral integration to free trade areas, customs unions, and finally common markets and economic communities. Given the region's diversity and sensitivity on national sovereignty, an economic community along the model of the European Union—with its harmonized policies, rules, and standards; supranational institutions; and surrendered national sovereignty—would be difficult to achieve in the near term. Moving toward something similar in East Asia has to be a long-term process. ASEAN has been in existence since 1967, and it is far from becoming an economic community. As spelled out in the EAVG report, the East Asian Community would involve deep economic and political integration, which would require a common political vision and similar interests.

There are also issues regarding membership. Namely, who would be members of the East Asian FTA or Community, and what would be the criteria for membership. Official proposals have so far focused on the ASEAN-10, China, Japan, and South Korea. This core group is divided though on whether or not to include Australia, Hong Kong, Mongolia, New Zealand, North Korea, and Taiwan. Membership and the modalities of cooperation and integration are closely intertwined.

Given its growing weight in regional economics and politics, China would have to play a pivotal role in the emergence of an East Asian FTA or East Asian Community. A Chinese hegemon could be feared by its smaller neighbors, so a strong China-Japan partnership would be crucial—as the French-German partnership has been to the creation and evolution of the European Union. Another option would be to have the East Asian FTA or Community built on three pillars—China, Japan, and ASEAN—so that Southeast Asia would not feel marginalized and that ASEAN could play a balancing role between China and Japan. However, for ASEAN to be a successful third pillar, its members would have to be more deeply integrated and cohesive than they are at present.

## CONCLUSION

The recent past has been a relatively peaceful period for East Asia, with no ideological wars or major border conflicts among member states. Although the East Asian economic miracle ended in 1997 with the advent of the Asian financial crisis, the region is showing resilience and remains, economically, the world's most dynamic.

East Asian regionalism is on the march, with a proliferation of subregional and bilateral agreements in place or under negotiation and study. A complex matrix of overlapping FTAs with uncoordinated rules and standards is emerging, leading to a "spaghetti bowl" effect and to the appearance of "hubs and spokes." Harmonizing all rules and standards would be necessary for East Asia to evolve into a free trade area or economic community.

Economic integration in East Asia has to be perceived as a win-win situation for individual member states, the East Asian region, and the world. For this perception to emerge, the more advanced member states in East Asia need to help less-developed member states with financial and technical assistance to enable them to catch up economically, and to exploit the opportunities offered by the huge integrated market.

An economically integrated East Asia would also contribute to regional peace and stability, as closer economic interaction promotes political and security dialogue and cooperation. A peaceful, stable, and prospering East Asia would be good for the world.

East Asian economic integration should not, however, splinter the world into three antagonistic economic blocs, and so undermine the multilateral trading system embedded in the WTO. East Asian economies must maintain their high commitment to the multilateral WTO process, and be active in the ongoing Doha Round to help ensure its successful conclusion. The lowering of trade and investment barriers among East Asian members should be accompanied by lowered trade and investment barriers with other countries in the world.

ASEAN also needs to be more cohesive and integrated. Enlarging its membership to include the CLMV countries, the Asian financial crisis, and a growth in bilateral spats have all damaged ASEAN's image of cohesiveness recently. Broadening ASEAN's membership has resulted in a two-tier ASEAN and has complicated its traditional consensus-oriented approach. The financial crisis severely damaged several ASEAN economies, with some countries since experiencing political and social unrest, and a breakdown in law and order. Preoccupation with domestic economic, political, and social problems has diverted the attention of ASEAN leaders and policymakers from moving ASEAN forward. Bilateral spats between ASEAN member states over border issues, migrants, and national sovereignty have also added to the international image of ASEAN as a "house divided." If ASEAN wants to push ahead with economic integration and further political and security cooperation, it needs to close ranks. A strong ASEAN could then contribute to creating a strong East Asia.

## BIBLIOGRAPHY

ASEAN-China Expert Group on Economic Cooperation. 2001. *Forging Closer ASEAN-China Economic Relations in the Twenty-First Century.* Jakarta: ASEAN Secretariat.

Chia Siow Yue. 2002a. "ASEAN and Emerging East Asian Regionalism." Paper presented at a seminar on "Towards Asian Integration: The Role of Regional Cooperation" at the Asian Development Bank's 35th Annual Meeting. Shanghai, May.

———. 2002b. "Regional Economic Cooperation in East Asia: Approaches and Processes." Paper presented at the "International Conference on East Asian Cooperation," organized by the Institute of Asia Pacific Studies, Chinese Academy of Social Sciences. Beijing, August.

———. 2003. "Emergent Regionalism and Bilateralism in East Asia." Paper presented at the Festschrift for Peter Lloyd, organized by the University of Melbourne. Melbourne, January.

East Asia Vision Group. 2001. *Towards an East Asian Community: Region of Peace, Prosperity and Progress.* Jakarta: ASEAN Secretariat.

Japan External Trade Organization. 2003. *Prospects for Free Trade Agreements in East Asia.* Tokyo: Japan External Trade Organization.

Kwan, C. H. 2002. *The Rise of China and Asia's Flying Geese Pattern of Economic Development: An Empirical Analysis Based on U.S. Import Statistics.* Tokyo: RIETI Discussion Paper, Series 02-E-009, July. Tokyo: RIETI.

Tay, Simon, Jesus Estanislao, and Hadi Soesastro, eds. 2001. *Reinventing ASEAN.* Singapore: Institute of Southeast Asian Studies.

World Bank. 2003. *World Development Report.* Washington, D.C.: World Bank.

# 5

## The Cultural Implications of the Rise of China on the Region

### WANG GUNGWU

This chapter focuses on the cultural changes occurring in China today, in the context of the challenge and threat that a strong and prosperous China might pose to the region. Culture is addressed in its conventional context, as values seen through people's creative arts, education, religion, and social cohesion, but also as political culture and as the culture of trade, industry, and economic development.

Clearly the theme, the "rise of China," governs the significance or otherwise of China's culture on its neighbors and beyond. If China were not rising, China's cultural problems would be of interest only to the Chinese themselves. When one considers historical examples where the cultural developments of a country actually become significant, there is always an assumption that the country's wealth and power determined that culture's impact on the cultures of others. If wealth and power did not accompany that culture, the culture is likely to have remained a set of local phenomena that might be intellectually or aesthetically interesting, and might be worthy too of belonging to museums if it is appreciated beyond the country's borders.

Chinese culture has made universalist claims as a civilization in the past. Whether or not those claims were justified and whether much of the culture was essentially a local expression of people's genius that influenced other peoples in China's neighborhood is not the point here. One could ask though if the culture of modernity that predominates today (that is, the modernity that the West has globalized, in fact, that largely originates from Western culture) can make the universalist claims that it does. This culture of modernity has been successfully proactive in the region for more than a hundred years, and it is now one that most countries, including China, have accepted as the major guiding culture of the future. Is this modern culture universal? If so, then once that culture is widely accepted, all the countries that embrace it could be expected to share the same cultural values eventually. If that were the scenario, what would be the significance of China espousing that culture? It is possible that a China that has truly risen would transform that culture of modernity in its own way so that a new manifestation might emerge. If that were to happen, what would be the implications, not only for the region, but also for what could be described as modern culture?

What then does "the rise of China" really mean this time round, compared with the times in the past when China may be said to have risen? There are three main eras in history when China rose to become the most powerful and prosperous country in the region. The first rise was the Qin-Han unification of the first bureaucratic empire that lasted from the third century B.C. to the third century A.D. The second rise was the Sui-Tang reunification that followed a series of tribal invasions and the ascendancy of Buddhism within China. The third was the most powerful rise before modern times, namely that of the Ming and Qing dynasties when the Confucian tradition was reconstructed and reinforced as a new orthodoxy. Seen in this longer perspective, the present rise of China, after 100 years of decline since the late nineteenth century and 40 years of division between 1911 and 1949, may be quite different. It is certainly necessary to consider whether the past has left indelible marks on today's leaders, and what this might mean for China's future position in the region. Indeed, China's current division is an active component of its rise today, and its reunification could be considered incomplete until Taiwan returns to the fold.

The title of the chapter also suggests that, for there to be cultural implications beyond its own territories, China's rise this time needs to be seen in a longer perspective. In addition, the experience of China's neighbors during the previous times when China was wealthy and prosperous needs to be considered.

## HISTORICAL CONTEXT

The Qin-Han centuries left a strong impression on the cultures of the various Yue peoples in what is now southern China. The influence of their culture has been argued to be so extensive that the commonly adopted name of China came from the name Qin because of their success in unifying the large empire. Also, the people who created the core of that culture have been called the Han people, thus bearing forward the name of the Han dynasty for two thousand years. These are examples of the impact of the Qin-Han empires' political culture. The cultural implications of Chinese power can be divided into direct and diffuse consequences. The direct impact was felt in the agricultural lands of its immediate neighbours, notably Korea and Vietnam, countries that have long absorbed major elements of Chinese culture. While the impact was long lasting, it was confined mainly to the elites of those two countries. The diffuse implications were, however, more extensive. They include the impact of China's export goods and technology, the best known of which are silks, paper and printing, ceramic ware, and features of military and maritime technology. These are examples of China's economic culture impressing itself upon China's neighbors.

In terms of the culture of values, Qin-Han China seems to have been far less successful. Indigenous religions and their rituals and practices did not spread much beyond its borders. The educational ideals offered were elitist if not esoteric, even for the Chinese populace itself. The written language was unique and complex and, from the start, hard for anyone to master. The ubiquitous family system was so intensely linked to an almost sacred place for male ancestors that many neighboring societies that did not share that emphasis on lineage simply rejected the culture that stressed its importance. As for the creative arts, except for the techniques and designs associated with trade in manufactured goods and thus associated with economic culture, not much seems to have been appreciated outside China's borders during this first period of prominence.

By the time of China's second rise, the powerful culture of the Tang empire was consolidated all over southern China and had spread overland toward the "Western Region" and to what is now known as Manchuria and Mongolia. Key elements of that culture also crossed the sea to Japan, and that cultural contact still resonates in Japan today. But, with the exception of Japan and the parts of Manchuria closest to the Tang border, much of that culture did not take root, and most of the western and northern areas of penetration shook off that culture when the Tang dynasty fell. Nevertheless, Tang political culture was quite different to that of the Qin-Han. It was the product of a mixture of Buddhist spiritual and tribal military conquest, some popular and localized religious responses, and an elitist Confucian restoration. Within China, this political culture was indeed a powerful amalgam and together it shaped the cosmopolitan culture that is often identified with the Tang capital Changan. But its appeal as political culture outside China was limited. More important was the culture of trade, industry, and development that was based on the openness with which the Tang empire has always been associated. As a result of that openness, foreign merchants and travellers came from afar and did much to enrich the lives and tastes of all Chinese. The new cultural ingredients that were brought to China during the period of division between the fourth and sixth centuries strengthened Chinese culture, and led to one of the truly efflorescent periods of Chinese history.

The question of how much the culture of values that emerged impacted the region is harder to determine. The advance of Buddhism to Korea and Japan may be included because certain key features of Mahayana Buddhism had undergone Sinicization before transmission. In Vietnam and parts of southwestern China like the Nan Zhao kingdom in Yunnan, other sources also influenced the Buddhism that took root. In any case, apart from religion, the impact from Tang Chinese classical and literary education and the creative arts (including music and dance, painting and calligraphy, architecture, and the plastic arts) was greatest among the aristocracy and the official classes. This was even truer of the Confucianism that had diminished for over 200 years but was restored to importance in the seventh century. This influence was packaged with the more popular features of Buddhism and Taoism before being exported. Indeed, despite its overwhelming wealth and power, Tang China probably imported as many cultural artefacts from great distances as it exported to its immediate vicinity. What might have been seen as universal was China's Buddhist manifestations which had already begun to permeate many parts of Chinese philosophy and the creative arts. The rise of China did have cultural implications in what it exported. Equally important was how that which it imported enhanced its own cultural richness.

In comparison with the Qin-Han and the Sui-Tang images of power and wealth, the third rise, of the Ming and Qing dynasties, with the peak of development occurring between the fifteenth and eighteenth centuries, was less spectacular but no less powerful. China's cultural impact during this period was of a different quality. The Mongol invasion and subjugation had virtually destroyed the brilliant culture of the Song dynasty (the Mongol Yuan dynasty lasted over 90 years), so Chinese political culture had become far more conservative and inward-looking. The

Ming founders concentrated on the physical defense of its borders and on restoring the great institutions of the Han and the Tang. Indeed, apart from the networks of officially approved trade and the aberrant maritime expeditions of Zheng He to the Indian Ocean, the Chinese were not much interested in projecting their culture. Chinese scholars themselves have recognized that the closed-door policy of the Ming became a source of weakness. Manchu conquerors largely retained this policy toward China's maritime frontiers after 1644, and Chinese culture became increasingly protective, so it is no wonder that there was little capacity to resist the incoming new cultures that enterprising and aggressive Europeans then brought to the region. While the Manchus and their northern frontier allies, the Mongols, expanded overland into Central Asia when necessary for security, most significantly, they retained much of the political culture of the Ming Chinese. By then, this had become highly integrated and very complex, and somewhat daunting to people not familiar with its main features. In short, it was not a culture that the Manchu Qing could or wanted to export much beyond the neighborhood. In the yet-to-be Sinicized parts of southwestern China (Yunnan and Guizhou, in particular), the neighboring states of Korea and Vietnam, and even in Japan, it was largely a question of what the rulers and elites of these countries were prepared to accept.

Underlying this were relatively closed and tightly controlled trading relations with foreign states and an official ban on private Chinese trade abroad, both of which inhibited the growth of a more extensive entrepreneurial culture. Nevertheless, it may be argued that, despite such discouragement, Chinese economic or trading culture greatly affected the development of the port cities and kingdoms of Southeast Asia. But, since this coincided with the advent of far bolder merchants from Europe who were backed by their ruling classes, the cultural implications were relatively subdued and indirect.

Between a defensive political culture and a constrained economic culture, it would have been surprising if a culture of values were more prominent. There were exceptions, in the form of Chinese sojourners who managed to leave China and make their homes in the region. At one level were members of the literati who escaped to Japan, Korea, and Vietnam at the fall of the Ming in the seventeenth century, and at another level, the anti-Manchu Chinese and their supporters who also left after several failed rebellions during the nineteenth and twentieth centuries. So pockets of exported Chinese values survived throughout the region, wherever small communities were able to form. Some of these migrants replicated cultural institutions, as manifest in art and architecture; temples, shrines, and cemeteries; drama and classic stories; and even some educational centers. But, apart from Japan, Korea, and Vietnam, there are few signs to show that their culture of values reached out among the peoples in whose midst these Chinese settled.

This fact, and other indications that China's culture during this period did not travel far, allow two complementary interpretations that may appear contradictory. The first interpretation is that this third time that China rose, under the Ming and Qing, cannot be compared with the first two so far as regional impact is concerned. This is because the world, and also the region, had changed. There were considerable developments, including those arising from ideas and institutions outside the region, and those from earlier Chinese influences. Also, simultaneously, was the presence of peoples from the West who were more technologically advanced and who had their own dynamic cultural values to offer against the relatively stagnant if not decadent Chinese values that severely limited Chinese influence. The second interpretation questions the link between cultural implications and China's rise. The fact that China is rising may not necessarily have cultural implications. Much depends on the total environment in which China may be said to have risen. For example, the rise of China relative to what, and what kinds of rise would be meaningful? One needs to look closely at the guiding ideas and institutions that lie behind the rise.

## THE RISE OF CHINA TODAY

Bearing these two interpretations in mind, a legitimate question is whether the current rise of China is not a lesser phenomenon than many people suppose. One may also question whether China's rise would necessarily have cultural implications of great significance.

It could be assumed that China's rise to regional power for the fourth time will have cultural implications for the region. The significance of these implications could be determined either by comparing the present rise with the three earlier times, or by using new sets of criteria to reflect the dramatic changes in the world since the nineteenth century. Should the present be compared with the first flush of power of the Qin-Han, or the second burst of revivalist strength during the Tang, or the third complacent and defensive phase of the Ming-Qing? Which is the most relevant to today?

It would be quite easy to argue that the revolutionary force of modern China is comparable with the explosive power of the Qin-Han unification. To a similar degree, that force totally transformed existing polities and established new kinds of relationships with China's neighbors. It is also possible to show that China today is more like the Sui-Tang recovery. It is an example of a country whose power has been renewed after fighting off invaders, absorbing new foreign ideas, and opening the country to external trade and new technology. And there is the view that focuses on the borders of the Qing empire as the foundations of a new, modern nation-state. These borders are new and encompass dozens of recognized minority nationalities, and the impact of the idea of such a nation is still to be fully felt. There is a credible appeal to continuity with the Ming-Qing heritage that is central to the newly forceful Chinese nationalism.

What is most striking is that all three of the earlier eras contribute to the shape and direction of China's rise today. Mao Zedong as Qin Shihuang the great unifier, and the People's Republic of China as a redefined Han empire, recalls the first rise. A China opened to an outside world of new ideas and technology and new markets remind us of the second, a cosmopolitan Tang China. And the challenge of ethnicity and nation molding after being introduced to new concepts of sovereign borders ties the present to the third, the immediate past of the Manchu Qing dynasty. Analogous features of the past three eras do not make the task of examining future cultural implications any easier, but these similarities help one recognize the many unpredictable elements in China's long history. All these elements should be placed in a global, twenty-first century perspective.

The world has clearly changed beyond recognition after European colonialism and imperialism. The West's dominance of the region for 200 years and the present superiority of American wealth and power provide a totally different backdrop for this fourth time that China is rising. It is tempting to say that China's past is not relevant as long as the new power equations remain. But there are some given factors that will not go away. The size of China in the region and the political weight that this carries cannot be wished away. Also, both within China and among its neighbors, the memory of China's historical power, albeit dormant for the time being, is not far from the surface of regional consciousness. If proof is needed, the project that resulted in this book itself reflects the theme's potential to engender concern and uncertainty. Not least, there are the implications of the cultural vestiges transmitted to some neighbors, via language and value systems, that need to be taken into account. In addition, how do the Chinese feel about the cultural challenges ahead? What resources do they have to deal with the culture of modernity and what do they expect to contribute to that culture? Trying to answer both these questions may be the most useful way to tackle the cultural implications of the rise of China this time round.

In terms of political culture, China's decision in the twentieth century to jettison the Confucian state in favor of a revolutionary creed was obviously a major shift in political culture. The new creed derived from the historical experiences of western Europe, and it vainly projected the Utopian ideal of liberation from the cycles of endless tension and the Darwinian culture of war that nation-states needed in order to survive. It has left a legacy of aggressive nationhood that China as a new nation-state has to learn to cope with. The failure of revolutionary socialism has now opened China to the rival secular and materialist faith in capitalism. Under the conditions China faces today, attempting to return to a traditional political culture is likely to fail. The continuing struggle to forge a new cultural amalgam without accepting the full force of liberal ideology that accompanies capitalism will engage China's leaders for a long time to come. The implications for the region are that China needs to be left alone to digest and internalize these changes, and that it will be keenly sensitive to any kind of threat to itself while it is readjusting, with difficulty, to the new stage of global politics. Given its size, China only needs to be internally stable and united for it not to fear its immediate neighbors. But it knows enough history to fear that a power further away, like the United States, could invoke a "China threat" scenario to instigate a hostile alliance in the region against China. Under the circumstances, it would be sheer stupidity for China to provide any power with that excuse to disrupt China's own developmental and survival agenda.

A new economic culture is needed to help China survive the challenge of a globalized market economy. Here the commitment to development is absolute, and the cultural implications of an increasingly competitive environment for the Chinese people are grim. But China has passed the point of no return on two vital points: it has to meet the expectations of its 1.3 billion people, and it has to generate adequate resources to prevent the country from ever being successfully invaded again. The demanding task of keeping up the rapid economic growth it has so far achieved, and of organizing an equitable, socially just distribution of the newly created wealth, makes it likely that China will have to stay on this treadmill at all costs. It therefore seems misleading to talk of China catching up and threatening other great powers. What is at stake are the following: the survival of the Communist Party in the face of massive discontent; the stability of existing social institutions; and, ultimately, the fate of a China trying to stay united within its present borders. The implications of this economic culture are that it needs peace and goodwill in general and within the region particularly, not just for now, but for the long haul. The unenviable task is attaining a relatively fair, equitable, and all-round, well-off society for its enormous workforce.

What about China's culture of values? Does it provide a counterweight to the apparent leaning toward modern political and economic culture, or does it inevitably follow where politics and economics lead? Like Japan, India, and the Islamic world, China has a deep-rooted ancient culture of values and, in its own way, it has tried to resist having this culture replaced altogether by values from the West. It recognizes that there is much that is appealing in the new values—because they are modern and progressive. The Chinese people, inheriting a humanist and rational tradition, are prone to opt for secular alternatives to their outworn ideas and institutions. In rejecting Confucianism and all manifestations of religion, the generation of revolutionary leaders has made it easier for Chinese to embrace scientific and philosophical premises from the West. The result of this acceptance of fresh assumptions for the building of the new state and society has been profound. It has rendered it far more difficult for the next generation of Chinese to contemplate any return to an earlier set of cultural values. This is not to deny that traditional values have survived in the countryside among the millions of rural families and lineages. But the rate at which urban and industrial society is growing, and the necessity for rural workers to seek their livelihood in that society, is challenging those values these workers are either happy to abandon or are forced to leave behind.

The last 100 years have been most trying for the majority of Chinese attempting to keep faith with their culture of values. The transition has been long and bitter. The battle for a convergence of old values with which people are comfortable and the values that promise to free them from drudgery and poverty is likely to go on indefinitely. For the moment, if one observes the young in the major towns and cities of China, it might appear that the result is foregone. The culture of modern values, whether coming directly from the West, or indirectly from Japan, Korea, or Chinese communities in Taiwan, Hong Kong, and Singapore, are winning hands down. Only a handful of older urban elites and their counterparts in the countryside care enough for the traditional values, and they are in no position to reverse the tide, certainly not by the old methods of moral exhortation and upbraiding.

## Conclusion

Does this mean the end of the inherited culture of values for China? Developments in history rarely follow logic and straight lines. The roots of that heritage are deep and manifest themselves in many different ways. The gains and losses registered so far have been in political and economic culture, but the impact of that transformation can be both a threat to, and an inspiration for, the culture of values. And precisely because cultural values are diffusely found at all levels of society and can permeate people's consciousness deeply, and because they are notoriously slow to change in every society, what happens to them is unpredictable. In aesthetics and philosophy; through literature, drama, film, music, dance, and the fine arts; in every classroom and lecture hall; and through every kind of design and fashion, creative convergences can occur readily to give fresh life to older values. Even the challenge of new religions, whether indigenous or foreign in origin, can produce unexpected consequences. As more and more Chinese seek spiritual expression in their lives, they have the collective power to transmute inherited values into new manifestations that could serve new and yet unforeseen needs.

As China's recent rise exposes its people to radical changes in the culture of values, what are the implications for the region? The mental and emotional turmoil the Chinese people have experienced during the twentieth century is still little known today among China's neighbours. And, as long as the Chinese themselves are engaged in the travails of reinventing themselves, their culture of values is unlikely to be exemplary for others. Most of China's recent experiences seem to have been particular rather than common to the region, and the task of identifying some of its universal features to warn others who are striving for similar changes has yet to begin. There are, of course, lessons in China for others to learn from if they so choose. But the more immediate lessons are those pertaining to China's political and economic culture, rather than its culture of values. Until such time as the Chinese can demonstrate how they have retrieved and revived key parts of that culture of values through innovative use of the modern culture they have full-heartedly accepted, the cultural implications of China's rise are likely to be peripheral and unconvincing. But the region would do well to study the history of China's multiple struggles. However painful and devastating these have been, they have jolted most Chinese to a fresh energy and dynamism that China has not seen since the first unification of China over 2,000 years ago.

# CHINESE PERSPECTIVES

# 6

## Political Developments in the Rise of China

### Yang Guangbin

Along with wide-ranging economic reform, China's politics has changed in the past 20 years too. Chinese politics has transformed from the totalism[1] of Mao Zedong (1949–1978) to today's authoritarianism. China's domestic political scene now could be compared to the situations in South Korea and Taiwan before those societies democratized, although there are also substantial differences between China and the other two cases. To clarify the analogy, it is necessary, first, to classify the major features of Chinese politics; then to analyze the strengths and weaknesses of the Chinese system; and, finally, to outline prospects for political change.

### The Current Pattern of Chinese Politics

To understand the analogy between China and Korea, it is helpful to understand the general situation in South Korea before democratization. Before it democratized, Korean society typified a society with an authoritarian regime. Its politics was characterized by the following: The state limited social activities and interest groups, while it encouraged a market-oriented economy. Due to its weak authority, the regime used coercive means to control the situation. The elite who controlled power usually came from the army, and the army played a crucial role in politics. When its ideology collapsed, the regime ruled by enforcing its power.

These characteristics definitely describe some features of the present Chinese system.

YANG GUANGBIN

## China as a Binary System

China has followed a binary path since the early 1990s. On one hand, the Chinese Communist Party (CCP) has strengthened political control over society, especially after the 1989 Tiananmen incident. On the other, it has encouraged market-oriented reforms.

China has amended its constitution three times since 1988. The 1988 amendment recognized the legitimacy of private enterprise, the 1993 amendment established a socialist market economy, while the 1999 amendment acknowledged that non-state-owned enterprises were as important as state-owned economic entities. These constitutional amendments underscore the extent to which the Chinese state has encouraged economic freedom and the development of private enterprise.

The Chinese government has ordered state-owned enterprises to reform their governance structures to conform to international standards, and many local authorities have been encouraging foreign and domestic investors to purchase state-owned entities. The central and local governments are pushing market-oriented reform.

At the same time, there have been no amendments of a political nature to the constitution. Indeed, the constitution notes that China upholds the leadership of the CCP. As economic reform deepened, Deng Xiaoping suggested that political reform too should proceed. In 1987, the Thirteenth National Congress of the CCP decided on political reforms. These included canceling the CCP's core leadership groups[2] in government agencies; abandoning the CCP's Commission of Politics and Law[3] at all levels of government; abrogating government counterparts[4] in all CCP committees; and disallowing the CCP's Inspecting Discipline Commission to hear criminal cases.[5] The purpose of these reforms was to separate the CCP and the government. But the reforms failed due to the Tiananmen incident.

The CCP has centralized power over politics in the following ways:

— In terms of personnel arrangements, the CCP's Politburo Standing Committee selects all members of the CCP's Central Committee, who number over 500. Similarly, the Politburo Standing Committee nominates all major provincial and ministerial officials.

— In terms of relations between the central government and local regions, the CCP and the central government tightly control local governments through a system of *nomenklatura*. All governors and CCP provincial and municipal heads directly under the central government are not native to those areas. For example, because of its advanced development, in the early 1990s, Guangdong Province was at odds with the central government. Provincial leaders, including Ye Xuanping and Xie Fei, who were natives, were then promoted to positions in the central government, and replaced with nonnatives. The central government has subsequently successfully controlled Guangdong Province. To ensure tight relations between the central government and wealthy provinces—such as Guangdong, Zejiang, and Shandong—or prosperous municipalities— such as Beijing and Shanghai—the CCP head is usually a Politburo member.

— In terms of provincial politics, an increasing number of CCP heads— about 20—are directors-general of provincial people's congresses. In the 1980s, only three CCP heads were in the position of director-general. Having CCP heads in this position guarantees CCP control over the local government and the congress, as well as over local cadres.

— In terms of propaganda and ideology, alien voices are generally prohibited in official media. The voices of some media outlets, such as *Strategy and Management* and *Southern Weekend,* are allowed to differ from official ones to a very limited extent. Since 1989, the first principle for all propaganda departments has been not to make mistakes. Under these circumstances, applying for a license to publish a new magazine about humanities and social sciences is difficult.

In short, strengthened CCP leadership and consolidated central government authority, together with enhanced economic freedom, are the major characteristics of China's current political and economic relations.

## The CCP and the State Tighten Control over Society

In the 1980s, relations between the state and society were highly strained, especially for intellectuals and young students. Since the 1990s, relations between the CCP, government, and society have changed enormously. The reasons for this are as follows.

First, the collapse of the former Soviet Union allowed people from all walks of life in China to recognize that there could be chaos in China too without the CCP's leadership.

Second, the CCP itself became less theoretical and more practical, which in turn gained it societal support. In the 1980s, any measure encouraging markets was criticized as capitalism. Yet now the CCP encourages the socialist market economy.

Third, the intellectual elite and those engaged in enterprise have benefited from practical policies, which have resulted in more comfortable relations between the state and the elite. In the 1980s, income distribution was so unfair that intellectuals' income was lower than that of those who had little education. At the same time, there was only limited tolerance of thoughts different to the official line. So intellectuals were highly dissatisfied with both their spiritual and material lives. Since the 1990s, the market economy has provided opportunities for intellectuals to improve their living standards, and the CCP has given up romantic theories.

Fourth, different kinds of associations or civil organizations have appeared in the past 20 years, but various CCP organizations and governmental agencies tightly control them. Under laws governing social groups, the relevant CCP department and administrative agency must first approve the registering of a social group.

Although dependent on approving agencies, civil organizations do try to influence the CCP and the government to revise current policies or formulate new ones in order to maximize their own interests. This is manifest in the activities of many local and professional organizations (Yu 2002).

## The "End of Ideology"

The "end of ideology" suggests that there are no longer ideological arguments about China's chosen economic direction. Many of the political fluctuations in the 1980s were caused by ideological conflict. Earlier, if one suggested market-oriented policies, one would be denounced for promoting a capitalist direction. Deng suggested in 1992 that it was meaningless to argue about the differences between socialism and capitalism, adding that if something were good for China's economic development, then that way was the correct path. This pronouncement effectively ended ideology in China, and it marked the turning point in Chinese economic reform. China's economic reform has since proceeded virtually unhindered.

The "Three Represents," new CCP guidelines that Jiang Zemin expounded, suggests that the CCP must represent the fundamental interests of all ethnic groups, the most advanced productive forces, and advanced culture. The "Three Represents" was written into the CCP's new constitution at the Sixteenth National Party Congress in November 2002, and it is hoped that it will encourage the elite from all groups—

entrepreneurs especially—to become CCP members. The "Three Represents" is felt to be a watershed in CCP history as it symbolizes how the CCP has turned into a cultivator of private property, not its destroyer.

In terms of these three points—China's dualistic path of economic reform and political control, the CCP and government tightening control over society, and the "end of ideology"—China appears to have fallen into the authoritarian pattern. Like South Korea depended on its army to control society, the CCP network attempts to control every corner of Chinese society, making China a very good example of authoritarian political practices.

## THE ADVANTAGES AND PROBLEMS OF AUTHORITARIAN POLITICS

### Advantage One: Strong Ability to Mobilize[6]

As examples of authoritarian politics, an important difference though between China now and Korea before it democratized lies in their party systems. Over the course of its long revolutionary history, the CCP has developed grass-roots organizing skills, enabling it to establish itself in every nook of society. From its roots deep in society to the upper reaches of power, the CCP has established a system of committees to control government and society.

In the Chinese system of *nomenklatura*, all major lower-level officials are nominated and approved by higher-level CCP departments. Naturally, nominating officials are responsible for nominated officials and vice versa, so government officials must be in line with the CCP.

In the past 20 years, the CCP has chosen a strategy of economic reform as first priority, with political reform lagging behind. This choice compares well with the opposite strategy that the former Soviet Union followed. China's economic success can be attributed partly to its party system that guarantees a strategy will be implemented.

### Advantage Two: Power in Technocratic Hands

Since the early 1990s, political power has been transferred to technocrats from the revolutionary generation. The advantage of the technocratic approach is that ideological differences are ignored and that the focus is on getting a job completed. Today's technocrats may have different opinions on whether development should be fast or slow, but they appear to agree on the issue that caused serious political differences in the 1980s— namely, the direction in which development should proceed.

Since 1992, technocrats have headed China's leadership. In the third generation of leaders headed by Jiang, all members of the Politburo Standing Committee majored in engineering and technology. This also holds true for the fourth generation of leaders under Hu Jintao, who took over from Jiang on November 15, 2002. All nine members of the Politburo Standing Committee have engineering backgrounds. Four of the nine are graduates of Qinghua University, China's cradle of engineering. According to Chinese practice and regulations, Hu will be in power for ten years.

China's recent history, and that of other countries, suggests that technocratic governance without ideological conflict is a helpful contributor to stable economic growth.

## Problem One: Low Political Participation and High Political Corruption

A negative consequence of the strategy of economic development as priority and slowed political reform is a low degree of political participation. Ordinary people are not felt to have a chance, much less a right, to influence the process of policymaking. The *nomenklatura* system means that nominated officials are responsible to each other, not to the people or voters. In this system, common wisdom in China is that lower-level officials follow many illegal measures. Serious corruption has hurt the legitimacy of the CCP.

## Problem Two: Tense Relations between Grass Roots and Local Authorities

Low political participation reflects corruption and strained relations between grass-roots society, local governments, and local CCP authorities. These can be attributed to new relations between the central government and local governments. Under the traditional centralized system, the major purpose of local authorities was to mobilize people to finish the plans of the central government. With economic reform, however, centralized center-local relations have been transformed into a decentralized "pressurized system." Under this system, the central government distributes specific economic tasks to provincial authorities, who turn over some of the economic tasks to city authorities, who likewise assign some tasks to township authorities. As noted, the futures of lower officials are in the hands of higher authorities, so lower-level authorities have incentives to complete the assigned tasks. Higher authorities are able to give political and economic awards and penalties to those lower-level authorities according to how they accomplish their tasks. To finish their assigned tasks, lower authorities, especially at the township level, collect money or materials directly from society's grass-roots.

This system definitely drives local authorities to find ways to develop local economies. But it has created problems between local authorities and the grass roots, as authorities have abused their power.

## *Problem Three: The State's Administrative Monopoly Weakens the Political System*

Compared to other authoritarian regimes, China's economic system, with its heavy dominance of state-owned enterprises, generates problems. In China, although the non-state-owned economy has grown significantly, state-owned enterprises still monopolize many sectors of the economy. Historically, state-owned enterprises in China have been attached to a ministry or an administrative component. For example, China Telecom was attached to the Ministry of Information Industry. Thus, in the early stages of building a market economy, administrative monopolies played a dominant role in economic life. High transaction or institutional costs definitely limit competition.

## PROSPECTS FOR POLITICAL REFORM IN CHINA

It is widely suggested that China is facing serious problems due to its choice of political system. The question keeps arising whether China is adopting political reform, and, if it does not adopt adequate reforms, what its prospects might be in the short and medium term.

## Is Political Reform Underway?

China has adopted political reform, although not necessarily by the standards of Western political science.[7] It is also unlikely that China will undertake political reform in the sense of Western political scientists in the next five years, namely, during Hu's first term. In China, many political problems are closely related to the political party system, specifically the principle of the CCP's *nomenklatura*. Maybe public elections could reduce corruption and check officials' behavior, but the likely result would be loss of control. It is very hard to get the party in power to reform itself.

Also, Hu's team is comprised of typical technocrats who are not motivated to promote the type of political reforms that Western political scientists urge. It is very likely that Hu's team will introduce administrative reform in order to reduce inefficiency and promote administrative competence. Administrative reform does have political meaning though, as such reform enhances the market economy and political democracy cannot exist without a market economy.

The CCP's Sixteenth National Party Congress declared that the first 20 years of this century would be crucial for China for building a "well-off society in an all-round way," to use Jiang's words. This means that economic projects—rather than political reform—will still be the CCP's top priority. With respect to political reform, the CCP Congress referred mainly to administrative reform and how to improve the CCP's control over officials.

## PROSPECTS FOR CHINESE POLITICS

If China does not introduce political reform as recommended by Western political pundits, will political instability and societal collapse then necessarily follow? The simple answer is no.

First, in history, political instability and collapse have derived mainly from tense relations between the state and society. In the past ten years in China, relations between the social elite, including enterpreneurs and intellectuals, and the state have been more comfortable. Partial political disturbances due to tense relations between local authorities and society's grass roots, however, should not be excluded.

Second, it seems unlikely that Hu's team would split over economic policy priorities. China's special political and economic relations—where the state monopolizes political and economic power—typically mean that any economic problem results in political controversy. The disaster of the Great Leap Forward in 1958–1959 resulted in the Cultural Revolution, which brought political, economic, and social catastrophe to China. The economic failures of CCP Chairman Hua Guofeng made him step down from office. The 1989 incident resulted mainly from currency inflation that went along with the economic shortages of 1987–1988. Many of the power struggles were not caused, as some Western observers suggest,[8] by factionalism and elite politics. Rather, they derived mainly from China's special political-economic relations. Although China has adopted economic reform in the last 20 years, political-economic relations remain basically unchanged. Under these circumstances, any economic disaster will have immediate political implications.

Third, the CCP's organs embody every part of society and the government. The CCP's ability to control circumstances exceeds expectations, but it doesn't mean that it will play a magic role under conditions of economic deterioration. As noted, the material difference between China and other authoritarian entities lies in the party system. The underlying principle of the People's Liberation Army is that the CCP commands the gun, and the gun is never allowed to command the CCP. Also, the political commissar system guarantees traditional relations between the army and the CCP. The CCP controls administration through its core leadership groups and committees, all CCP members and officials identifying with the party belong to a CCP branch, and higher-placed CCP committees have direct power over lower-level committees. Since 1998, the CCP has also begun to set up branches in social associations.[9] The CCP therefore leads and controls society and the state.

However, if political reform were at a standstill in five years' time, it may be very difficult for the CCP to find a way to keep corruption within limits, and relations at the grass roots would become extremely strained. If China's economic development bogged down and unemployment rose rapidly over a certain period, it would be very hard to mobilize people, considering the low rate of political participation. In modern politics, people are happy to share benefits, not hardships.

Therefore, China seems to be in a dilemma. And it cannot be classified as a first-class power until it resolves its political problems through political reform.

# NOTES

1. Totalism means that state power controls all fields of society without legal or moral bounds.
2. There is a core leadership group of five, all nominated by the CCP Central Committee, in every government ministry. The group, which is responsible for major personnel arrangements in the government agency, reports to the Secretariat of the CCP Central Committee.
3. The CCP's Commission of Politics and Law handles the judicial departments at all levels of government.
4. At all levels, departments of the CCP Central Committee control corresponding government agencies. For example, the education department of the CCP Committee directly controls the government education agency.
5. Regulations of the CCP's Inspecting Discipline Commission say that, in the case of a government official suspected of an offense, if he or she is a CCP member, the Commission can first investigate before passing the case to the judiciary.
6. In political science, "mobilization" refers negatively to organization and, to some extent, to manipulation. The reality of Chinese politics is that the CCP has highly organized and mobilized society. Many Chinese believe that, considering China's honeycomb-like society, it is very necessary for Chinese to be organized to accomplish tasks.
7. For Western China watchers, political reform mainly suggests democratization, including public elections and separating the CCP and the government. They usually deny that administrative reform belongs in the category of political reform.
8. Factionalism or elite politics is a very popular approach for Western China watchers when studying Chinese politics. Typical of this genre is the *Cambridge History of China* (MacFarquhar and Fairbank 1990 and 1992).
9. In February 1998, the CCP's Central Department and Ministry of Social Affairs jointly issued a *Circular of Establishing the Party's Branch Within Social Groups*. It requires all social groups comprising more than three CCP members to establish a CCP branch of the basic sort.

BIBLIOGRAPHY

Lieberthal, Kenneth. 1995. *Governing China.* New York: W.W. North & Company, Inc.

MacFarquhar, Roderick, ed. 2002. *Zhongguo zhengzhi: Mao Deng shidai* (The politics of China: The eras of Mao and Deng). Chinese Edition. Hainan: Hainan Chubanshe (Hainan Publishing House).

MacFarquhar, Roderick, and John K. Fairbank, eds. 1990. *Jianqiao zhonghua renmin gongheguo shi* (The Cambridge history of China: The people's republic, part I: the emergence of revolutionary China, 1949–1965). Shanghai: Shanghai Renmin Chubanshe (Shanghai People's Publishing House).

———. 1992. *Jianqiao zhonghua renmin gongheguo shi* (The Cambridge history of China: the people's republic, part II: revolution within the Chinese revolution, 1966–1982). Chinese edition, Hainan: Hainan Renmin Chubanshe (Hainan Publishing House).

North, Douglass C. 1981. *Structure and Change in Economic History.* New York: W.W. North & Company, Inc.

Rong Jingben, ed. 1998. *Cong Yalixing tizhi xiang minzhu hezuoxing tizhi zhuanxing* (Transformation from the pressurized system to a democratic system of cooperation: Reform of the political system at the county and township levels). Beijing: Zhongyang Bianyi Chubanshe (Central Compilation and Translation Press).

Yang Guangbin. 2003a. *Zhongguo jingji zhuanxing zhongde guojia quanli* (State power in Chinese economic transition). Beijing: Dangdai Shijie Chubanshe (Press of the Contemporary World).

———. 2003b. *Zhongguo zhengzhi daolun* (Introduction to Chinese politics and government). Beijing: Zhongguo Renmin Daoxue Chubanshe (Press of Renmin University of China).

Yu Keping, ed. 2002. *Zhongguo gongmin shehui de xingqi yu zhili de bianqian* (The emerging of China's civil society and its significance to governance in reform China). Beijing: Shehui Kexue Wenxian Chubanshe (Press of Social Science and Documents).

*Zhonggong shiliuda zhengzhi baogao* (Political report of the Sixteenth National Congress of the Chinese Communist Party). 2002. Beijing: Renmin Chubanshe.

*Zhonggong shisanda zhengzhi baogao* (Political report of the Thirteenth National Congress of the Chinese Communist Party). 1987. Beijing: Renmin Chubanshe.

# 7

# A Sustainable Chinese Economy?

## MEN HONGHUA

Economic reform and opening to the outside world since the late 1970s have made China the fastest-growing economy in the world. Since 1978, China has succeeded in achieving an average annual growth rate of over 9.4 percent, with the average annual growth rate of its exports also exceeding 13 percent. Its modernization program has made remarkable headway. Even during the 1997–1998 Asian financial crisis and in its wake, China has maintained its growth momentum and consolidated its financial stability. According to the World Bank's estimates of purchasing power parity (PPP), China has become the second largest economy in the world, after the United States. As Nicholas R. Lardy said, "For all these countries in Asia, China is such a large force, the only rational response is to figure out how to work with it" (*New York Times* 28 June 2002).

Though China's economic performance so far has been a true miracle, its continued success remains far from assured (Kim 2003). In fact, there have been disputes regarding the accuracy of growth rates cited by the Chinese government and the sustainability of the high levels of growth. In 2001, Thomas Rawski published a paper expressing his doubts that China's gross domestic product (GDP) statistics reflect actual economic performance, which touched off a great debate among economists in China and abroad. Impressive levels of GDP growth have also not resulted in an equitable society. In 2002, the Political Report of the Sixteenth Party Congress of the Chinese Communist Party (CCP) proposed the goal of establishing an "all-round, well-off" society in the next 20 years, but the challenges to achieving this target are enormous.

The key questions concerning the future of China's economy are whether China's fast economic growth is a reality, a myth, or just a bubble, and whether China can continue to sustain high growth rates for the foreseeable future. In the view of this author, provided China can overcome certain challenges, its high-speed economic development could be maintained in the foreseeable future. At the same time, Deng Xiaoping's (1993) observation from 11 years ago should be remembered, "For a big developing nation like China, it is impossible to attain fast economic growth steadily and smoothly at all times. Attention must be paid to stable and proportionate development, but stable and proportionate are relative terms, not absolute."

## CATCHING UP: CHINA'S PATH TO MODERNIZATION

In the terms of both population and GDP, China was the largest economy on the planet until the early nineteenth century. It lost its lead with the Industrial Revolution, and its economy experienced a long period of decay from 1820 to 1949. After the founding of the People's Republic in 1949, China's process of industrialization and modernization began. However, due to domestic political instability, China's economic takeoff did not begin until 1978.

As a latecomer to modernization, China has had no choice but to chart a new path in catching up with the rest of the world and achieving a modern economy. Three great powers, namely, the United States, Japan, and China, have modernized in a short period of time, and, as a result, have given huge impetus to the world economy.

Since China's economy was so small compared to other modern economies shortly after its founding, its efforts in catching up have so far been impressive. In 1952 China was one of the poorest countries in the world. The per capita GDP of western Europe was 7.15 times higher than that of China, and the GDP per capita of the United States was 18.8 times higher (fig. 1). According to Augus Maddison (1998), China's average annual growth rate from 1952 to 1978 was 4.4 percent, which was lower than the world's growth rate of 4.52 percent. From 1978 to 1995, however, China's growth rate was 7.49 percent, which was much higher than the world's growth rate of 2.7 percent. China's per capita GDP growth rate in 1952–1978 was 2.34 percent, which was lower than the 2.56 percent figure for the world. But China's per capita GDP growth rate for 1978–1995 was 6.04 percent, which was again much higher than the 1.01 percent for the world. After more than 20 years of modernization, China now ranks as the sixth largest economy in the world (Liu, Wang, and Li 2002, 1; Zeng

2002, A6). China has become the world's preeminent low-cost manufacturer, not only of traditional labor-intensive goods like footwear, toys, apparel, and sporting goods, but increasingly of information technology products, hardware, and electronics (Lardy 2002a). Since late 2000, the outlook for the U.S. economy has been gloomy, economic recovery in Europe has faltered, and Japan's economy remains afflicted by recession and deflation, so economists are now talking about China being the new engine of the world economy.

### Figure 1. China in the World Economy

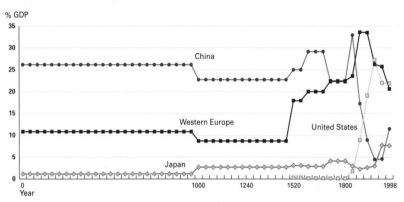

Source: Maddison (2001).

China's economic development and modernization reflect the "advantages of the latecomer" and some unique characteristics. By introducing technology and equipment from advanced countries, studying the know-how and lessons from precedents, and exploiting its own comparative advantages, China has speeded up its modernization drive. And maintaining this rapid economic development, in a way, now determines the legitimacy and prestige of China's political leaders. Other impetuses to its development have been its own history of humiliation in the nineteenth and early twentieth centuries, and the examples set by the advanced countries.

In the era of the globalized, knowledge-based society, China is undergoing profound and, indeed, accelerated transformation. This is so much so that China might leap over several stages of development to transform itself simultaneously from a traditional society to a modern society, from a predominantly agrarian economy to a knowledge-based economy, and from a planned economy to a modern market economy.

# A NEW STAGE OF ECONOMIC DEVELOPMENT

Since 1978, China's successful economic transformation focused mainly on GDP growth. Yet, as Harvard economist Dwight Perkins points out, "much of the early success of market reforms resulted from the basic simplicity of the task" (Nye 2002, 20). Economic achievements correlated with other issues and sustained economic development was the inevitable result. With further economic development, various social conflicts stand out, and now China must make some fundamental readjustments to guarantee economic sustainability.

First, in its guiding ideology, China must pay more attention to the value of institutional innovation. From the viewpoint of institutional theory, China's economy has achieved its goals by institutional negation. For example, the transformation from a totally planned economy to a modern market economy has involved the negation of the planned economy. Likewise, the negation of total public ownership has resulted in the present ownership system in which various economic ownership forms coexist. Institutional factors will play key roles in China's further economic development.

Second, in economic strategy, China should stress the quality of growth. Successful modernization should achieve the goals of economic growth and social development simultaneously. In general, China's fast economic growth has been inefficient, relying mainly on capital inflows, inputs of natural resources, and cheap human resources. The negative effects of this—income inequality, environmental degradation, and social injustice—will hinder further economic development.

Third, China should pursue a strategy of "leaping over" economic developmental stages. Harvard economist Michael E. Porter regards there to be four stages in economic development. They are factors-driven, investment-driven, technology-driven, and innovation-driven development. Currently, China is between the investment-driven and technology-driven stages, and has an eye on innovation-driven development.

In sum, in the new stage of economic development that China is now entering, it will need to focus on institutional innovation, the quality of growth, and structural adjustments. The key will be to abandon the expansive growth style and turn to market-oriented sustainable growth.

Since 1978, the goals of China's reforms have been to transform the ownership system and set up a market economy, improve foreign trade, and integrate into the world economy. These aims have nearly been achieved. In the last 20 years, almost all areas and sectors that could open to the outside world have been opened up, and almost all preferential policies have been put in place. The first stage of reform and opening up has now been completed; the issuing of the Political Report of the CCP's Sixteenth Party Congress marks the beginning of a new stage. This new era has certain characteristics. First, reform and preferential policies have become second nature, and market mechanisms will be the major drivers of the economy. Second, the main bodies of economic development are no longer government and state-owned sectors, but are now the market and nonstate sectors. The nonstate sector will play increasingly important roles in China's economy.

Third, with China's entry into the World Trade Organization (WTO), the effects of international factors—such as globalization—on China's economy will be greater than ever. Fourth, China's central government will pay more attention to the quality of economic growth, environment protection, employment, and social stability.

The main goals of the new stage are to promote domestic economic integration, guarantee the effective utilization of various resources, and set up a comprehensive and effective framework for the market economy. Specifically, this will involve breaking down protective barriers, promoting corporate governance, and guaranteeing the independence of judicial powers. Setting up an "all-round, well-off society," the primary mission of the new stage, means stressing the quality of economic growth, but also democratic rights and improving the ecological environment. Accomplishing this mission will depend on whether China can maximize the effects of positive factors while curbing the effects of negative ones.

## SOURCES OF SUSTAINABLE ECONOMIC GROWTH

In China, any important reform measure stems from decisions of the Central Committee of the CCP and the central government, reflecting a "top down" pattern of decision making. With the processes of economic development and social diversification, forces emerge from below and outside that increase and give impetus to new "growth points," resulting in the emergence of autonomous economic development.

Since the CCP Central Committee and the central government make decisions about reform, CCP Party Congresses mark the cycle of China's economic development. In 2002, a new generation of leadership took office, and its authority depends on achieving fast and sustainable economic growth to fuel further economic development. It released the Political Report of the CCP's Sixteenth Party Congress that set out the key tasks for the next 20 years. Some experts regard economic growth as the only policy that helps meet all of Beijing's broader strategic goals (Gershman 2003).

China's reform is, to a great extent, related to the learning process and ability of its leaders. Until now, they have followed the realistic practice of learning by "trial and error," enshrined in the slogan "to cross the river by feeling the stones." They have learned from experiences abroad, introduced advanced management methods, and adapted institutional innovations to suit national conditions. The success of reform over the last 20 or so years has proved that Chinese leaders possess adequate policy-making ability. Indeed, China has now begun to enjoy comparatively mature economic decision-making.

A country's human resources, capital, natural resources, and level of science and technology can determine the durability of economic growth. One of China's tasks is to determine how to develop its population of 1.3 billion people so that it changes from a country with a large population to one with huge human resources. China's large labor supply has already resulted in it being the production center for global consumables. Its huge population also means that it is an enormously attractive market. Its thrifty people have furthermore allowed China to enjoy a high savings rate since the 1980s. Foreign direct investment (FDI) is another vital engine of

Figure 2. FDI in China (1990–2002)

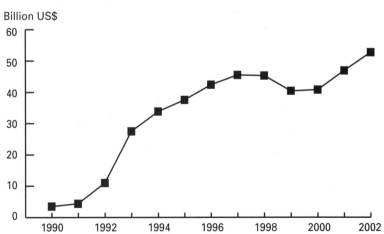

domestic economic growth, and China became the largest recipient country of FDI in 2002, with sums that reached US$52.7 billion (fig. 2). China is short of some natural resources, yet its high foreign exchange reserves of around US$286.4 billion ensure its ability to import necessary resources and raw materials. In the last few years, educational levels and use of science and technology have improved greatly. High-tech industries have become the engine of economic development in China's coastal areas.

In accordance with its "gradient theory," China has followed varied policies toward different domestic regions, bringing about gradient differences and dissimilar comparative advantages between East China, Central China, and West China. A better integrated domestic market would give great impetus to economic development. In the last few years, China has begun to set up regional economic belts with its neighbors. Since the 1997–1998 Asian financial crisis, it has also made great effort to enhance regional integration. China's proposal for a free trade area between China and the Association of Southeast Asian Nations is a good example.

The institutional obstacles to nonstate capital have almost been eliminated. Even so, the contribution of nonstate capital to GDP reached 50 percent in 2000, and the private sector has become the main source of new jobs (Lardy 2002b). The Political Report of the CCP's Sixteenth Party Congress confirms the equal political status of nonstate sectors and promised legal protections as a key to helping grow the nonstate economy.

China's entry into the WTO marked a new stage in its reform and opening up (Hai 2001). Its foreign trade has increased rapidly, and its economic structure is adjusting accordingly. Entering the WTO has also enabled China to remain a reliable and favorite market for foreign investors. China's accession to the WTO was definitely a boon for both China and the international trading regime. No country has increased its role in the international trading system as fast as China has in the last 20 years.

In addition, its successful bids for the 2008 Olympic Games and the World Expo will bring long-term economic benefits. Goldman Sachs estimates that the Olympic Games will increase China's annual GDP by 0.3 percent from 2002 to 2008 (Pang 2002, A7).

## SEVERE CHALLENGES AHEAD

The described political, economic, social, and international factors suggest that China has laid the foundation for sustainable development. Yet it is also facing many interconnected challenges to successful economic development. Problem areas include institutional, social, and issue-related factors, potential-for-conflict areas, and international issues. The challenges they present should not be underestimated; China's economic growth depends, to a great extent, on its ability to overcome these challenges.

First, in terms of institutional factors, China is undergoing unprecedented structural adjustments. After almost two decades of fast economic growth when demand exceeded supply, the tables have turned, and supply now exceeds demand in many sectors. Yet the economic structure is slow in adapting. Agriculture is experiencing a most difficult period, with prices having plummeted. Traditional industrial sectors like timber, textiles, iron and steel, coal, and machinery have ceased to expand, and are being forced to restructure. Nontraditional sectors like electronics, telecommunications, computers, biotechnology, and insurance are all growing rapidly, but do not yet form pillars in the economy.

The gap in development levels between different domestic regions is enlarging, and no integrated nationwide market has been established. Structural differences between rural and urban China have existed for centuries, but China's modernization drive has exacerbated these.

Trying to establish an economic market system has negatively impacted social justice. By adopting the market-oriented strategy, the price system has become distorted, income differentials have expanded, and the creation of privileged social strata has accelerated. The strategy seems to emphasize economic growth for the present, while it ignores a sustainable future.

Another scourge is rampant corruption. While no country has been able to stamp out corruption completely, the extent of this ill varies widely. In China, corruption is mainly institutional. "Bureaucratic privatization" occurs, with powerholders employing various means to steal, annex, and divide public assets. Annual losses due to corruption are suggested to be about 14.5 percent–14.9 percent of GDP (Hu 2000b).

Second, growing inequality and unemployment are creating enormous social costs. Rising inequality is a prominent feature of China's economy; in fact, there has never been a society that experienced such a rapid deterioration in income distribution in a 20-year period. The ever-growing disparities among regions—between the hinterland and coastal areas, between the urban and rural areas, and within urban and rural areas respectively—are severe. Because of China's preferential policies toward different regions, the growing disparities between the coast and inland regions draw a great deal of attention. West and Central China have born the cost of East China's development, with West China lagging particularly far behind. Most of the more than one quarter of all Chinese who subsist on less than US$1 a day are concentrated in the peripheral but strategically important areas of Tibet, Xinjiang, and Inner Mongolia. This is the main reason China launched the Western Development Program in September 1999.

Great disparities also exist between urban and rural dwellers. According to the National Bureau of Statistics of China, the Gini coefficient of the wealth of Chinese urban dwellers rose from 0.35 of 1988 to 0.43 in 2002 (fig. 3). If tax evasion, corruption, and other rent-seeking activities were included, the figure rose to 0.51.

**Figure 3. Per Capita Income in Rural and Urban China**

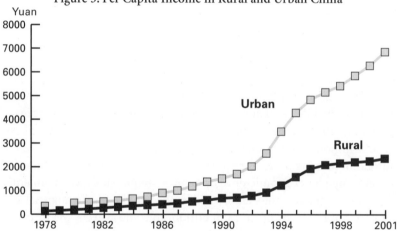

Income inequality is increasing between urban dwellers and peasants. In the urban areas in 2002, the top tenth of society earned 45 percent of total income, and the bottom tenth earned 1.4 percent, with many people falling below the poverty line (table 1). In rural China, agricultural prices have plummeted in the past six years, and 870 million peasants have born this brunt and so been the losers from reform. The growing mismatch between population and resources could lead to severe social unrest and threaten the very foundations of economic development. If extreme inequality is not lessened, the masses will no longer support reform.

Meanwhile, China is experiencing unprecedented high unemployment. The National Bureau of Statistics of China estimates that about 45 million

Table 1. Growing Inequality in Urban China (1990-2002)

| Year | Gap between Top 20 and Bottom 20 | Share of Bottom 20 in Total Income | Share of Top 20 in Total Income | Share of Top 10 in Total Income |
|---|---|---|---|---|
| 1990 | 4.2 times | 9.0 percent | 38.1 percent | 23.6 percent |
| 1993 | 6.9 times | 6.3 percent | 43.5 percent | 29.3 percent |
| 1998 | 9.6 times | 5.5 percent | 52.3 percent | 38.4 percent |
| 2002 | 13.3 times | 4.9 percent | 64.3 percent | 45.0 percent |

workers were laid off in 1995–2001. By the end of 2001, the real rate of unemployment was running at 8 percent–9 percent, which is much higher than the official figure of 3.6 percent, and the total number of unemployed was 18 million–19 million. Such large-scale unemployment could lead to severe social consequences.

And discontentment is growing. High unemployment and income inequality are together making the masses feel insecure, with workers, peasants, urban dwellers, and even cadres feeling dissatisfied.

Third are the negative effects of such issue-area factors as banking risks and environmental degradation. The delay of banking and financial reform challenges the credibility of China's economic reforms, with confidence in the banking system being especially low. By now, the total amount of bad debt in China's state-owned banks is about 40 percent of GDP. Since the state-owned banks have born certain responsibility or costs of reform, some part of their bad debt is quasi-national debt. Devoid of autonomous motivations for reform, the backward banking and financial system impedes economic development. Foreign banks will soon enter the Chinese market, but state-owned banks and the fragile financial system are not ready for fierce competition. In some aspects, the future of China's economy depends on banking and financial reform.

China also has a widely damaged natural environment, with some ecologists regarding China's present ecological environment as a nightmare. China's drinking water resources are less than 25 percent of the world average; its forest resources are less than 12.5 percent; and its grassland resources are less than 50 percent. Pollution has grown along with GDP, as the catching-up strategy has paid little attention to environmental protection. Over 80 percent of China's sewage flows untreated into its streams and rivers, and more than 60 percent of Chinese cities have severe water shortage problems. The World Bank estimates that air and water pollution cost China about 3 percent–8 percent of GDP, while the *People's Daily* reckons that environmental pollution causes annual losses of US$34.3

billion, which cancels out a large part of economic achievements.* In recent years, due to the sandstorms it experiences from environmental degradation, Beijing began to pay close attention to its ecological environment. Investment in environmental protection in 1998–2002 reached US$70.21 billion, and flagrant environmental pollution is being curbed. Environmental degradation has not yet been alleviated, however.

Fourth, in terms of factors that could lead to conflict, one of the most severe challenges is Taiwan's search for "independence." Intermittent escalations in cross-Strait tensions since 1996 have reminded all that any severe conflict across the Taiwan Strait would have a grave economic impact, and would certainly disturb China's economic development drive. Increasing "splittist" tendencies in Tibet and Xinjiang, and territorial disputes on the Diaoyu Islands and in the South China Sea also have the potential to create huge economic disruption.

Fifth, international factors do play an important role in China's economy. As it integrates further with the world, China gains more opportunities for development, while at the same time it is affected more directly by any global uncertainties. As a new member of the WTO, China must also bear some adjustment costs. Neighboring instabilities such as the nuclear crisis with North Korea also have negative effects on its economy. Nontraditional security issues, such as organized transnational crime, terrorism, and narcotics trafficking, may also influence China's economy in the foreseeable future.

Some of the noted negative factors are latent, while others—banking problems, income inequality, corruption, and environmental degradation—constitute immediate severe threats to China's economy. To meet these challenges, China must undertake further reforms.

## FURTHER REFORM NEEDED

Severe challenges and good opportunities coexist in China's economy. It is widely believed that China's new leaders under Hu will push forward with further necessary reform. In the last 20-odd years, negative factors (see table 2) have gained strength, and various interest groups have formed, so any reforms will be contested. So the new leaders will have to be resolute

---

*<http://www.worldbank.org/home/htm/extpb/annrep97/overview.html, and http://www.renminbao.com/rmb/articles/2002/10/12/4363.html> (5 March 2003).

## Table 2. Main Factors Affecting China's Economic Development

| Types of Factor | Posititive Factors | Negative Factors |
| --- | --- | --- |
| Institutional | New leaders took office. Learning ability of Chinese leaders. | Severe economic structural restrictions. The negative effects of the catching-up strategy. Corruption. |
| Social | The masses expect further reform. Positive effects of Olympic Games and World Expo. | Income inequality Unemployment. Dissatisfaction of the masses. |
| Issue-area | Advantages in some resources. Nonstate capital. | Banking risks. Environmental degradation. |
| Conflictual | Huge domestic market, with gradient regional development. | Tendencies in Taiwan for "independence" Ethnic splittists in Xinjiang and Tibet. Territorial disputes with neighbors. |
| International | Setup of regional economic belt. Boom effects of China's WTO membership. | Uncertainty in the world economy. Adjustment costs of China's entry into the WTO. |

to reform further and achieve necessary breakthroughs. Otherwise, the economic situations in China could worsen.

In terms of further reform, the following suggestions are offered. First of all, China should change its economic strategy guidelines. From 1978, China shifted its policy orientation from equity to efficiency. These two goals of equity and efficiency are often in conflict, but the optimal choice for sustainable economic development lies with a development strategy that stresses both evenly.

Second, more attention must be paid to economic security. Since the sources of economic risk are varied after China's accession to the WTO, China should perfect its crisis management mechanisms, and work out reserve schemes for possible economic risks and crises.

Third, government functions should be transformed in accordance with the requirements of a modern market economy. The government has dominated economic reform, and its functional transformation needs to play a key role in further development. In the last few years, the Chinese government's functions have changed greatly, yet its intervention in the economy has essentially not lessened. The "proactive fiscal policy" of recent years has provided it with new leverage. In the future, government functions should stress providing social foundations for sustainable development, such as making and implementing sound macroeconomic policies, and establishing a decent social safety net.

Fourth, great efforts should be made to set up a nationwide integrated market. China's fragmented market means the economy develops unevenly, and this hinders the achievement of many goals. Setting up an integrated nationwide market would help utilize and deploy resources rationally, give free rein to regional advantages, and help realize China's "economic unification."

Fifth, the adoption of "green GDP," in which close attention is paid to environmental protection, should be encouraged. GDP reflects economic growth, but not its effects on the environment; only green GDP, a new measure of international competitiveness, reflects this reality. As one of the great economic powers, China should adopt the idea of green GDP, to show awareness of its international responsibilities and benefit future generations in China.

Though China's economic progress is a reality, on the whole, it remains a poor country. Indeed, China has a long way to go before its achieves its new mission of having an "all-round, well-off" society in 20 years. In conclusion, China should pay close attention to the challenges posed by negative factors. If China continues to reform and open up, it will enjoy sustainable economic development, and will have a key role to play in the world economy.

## BIBLIOGRAPHY

Bach, Christian et al. 1996. "China and the WTO: Tariff Offers, Exemptions, and Welfare Implications." *Weltwirtschaftliches Archiv* 132(3): 45–66.

Carpenter, Ted Galen, and Dorn James, eds. 2000. *China's Future: Constructive Partner or Emerging Threat?* Washington, D.C.: CATO Institute.

Deng Xiaoping. 1993. "Zai Wuchang, Shenzhen, Zhuhai, Shanghai Deng di de tanhua yoadian" (Excerpts from talks given in Wuchang, Shenzhen,

Zhuhai, and Shanghai, 18 January–21 February). In *Deng Xiaoping wenxuan disanjuan* (The selected works of Deng Xiaoping, volume III).

Foy, Colm, and Angus Maddison. 1999. "China, A World Economic Leader?" *The OECD Observer*, no. 215 (January): 1–8.

Gershman, John. 2003. "China Not a Military Threat: China Puts Economic Growth Above Hegemony." (20 February). <http://www.resistinc.org/newsletter/issues/2002/01/gershman.html>.

Hai Wen. 2001. "Jiaru shijie maoyi zuzhi shi zhongguo xiandaihua jiIncheng de yige xin lichengbei)" (Entry into the WTO: A new milestone in China's modernization process). *Guoji Jingji Pinglun* (International Economic Review), no. 3–4: 37–42.

Hu Angang. 1999. *Zhongguo fazhan qianjing* (China's development prospective ). Hangzhou: Zhejiang Renmin Chubanshe Zhejiang (People's Publishing House).

———. 2000a. *Zhongguo tiaozhan fubai* (China challenges corruption). Hangzhou: Zhejiang Renmin Chubanshe Zhejiang (People's Publishing House).

———. 2000b. "Public Exposure of Economic Losses Resulting from Corruption." *World Economy & China*, no. 10: 44–49.

International Center for the Study of East Asian Development (Kitakyushu). 2001. "Recent Trends and Prospects for Major Asian Economies." Special Issue, *East Asian Economic Perspectives* 12(2).

International Monetary Fund. 2002. *World Economic Outlook: Recessions and Recoveries*. Washington, D.C.: International Monetary Fund.

Kim, Samuel S. 2003. "China as a Great Power." 21 February. <http://www.currenthistory.com/archivessep97/kim.html>.

Lardy, Nicholas. 1994. *China in the World Economy*. Washington, D.C.: Institute of International Economics.

———. 2002a. "The Economic Future of China." Speech at the Texas Asia Society, Houston, 29 April. <http://www.ciaonet.org/conf/aoc_spch02/Lan01.html>.

———. 2002b. "China Will Keep on Growing." *Asian Wall Street Journal* (14 June). <http://www.brook.edu/views/op-ed/lardy/20020614.htm>.

Liu Guoguang, Wang Luolin, and Li Jingwen, eds. 2002. *Zhongguo jingji xingshi fenxi yu yuce* (The analysis and forecast of China's economy). Beijing: Shehui Kexue Wenxian Chubanshe (Social Sciences Documentation Publishing House).

Maddison, Augus. 1995. *Monitoring the World Economy 1820–1992*. Paris: Organization for Economic Cooperation and Development.

———. 1998. *China's Economic Performance in the Long Run*. Paris: Organization for Economic Cooperation and Development.

———. 2001. *The World Economy: A Millennial Perspective*. Paris: Organization for Economic Cooperation and Development.

National Bureau of Statistics of China (Zhongguo Guojia Tongjiju). 1999, 2000, 2001, 2002. *China Statistical Abstract 1999, 2000, 2001, 2002*. Beijing: Zhongguo Tongji Chubanshe (China Statistics Press).

Nye, Joseph S. Jr. 2002. *The Paradox of American Power: Why the World's Only Superpower Can't Go It Alone*. New York: Oxford University Press. Quoted from Dwight Perkins. 2000. "Institutional Challenges for the Economic Transition in Asia." Paper presented at the Australian National University, September.

Organization for Economic Cooperation and Development. 2002. *China in the World Economy: Challenges of Domestic Policies*. Paris: Organization for Economic Cooperation and Development.

Pang Jinju. 2002. "Zhongguo jingji duaisu chixu fazhan de denengxing" (Possibilities of China's fast and sustainable economic growth). *Zhongguo Jingji Shibao* (China Economic Times) (14 January).

Rawski, Thomas. 2001. "What's Happening to China's GDP Statistics." *China Economic Review* 12: 347–354.

World Bank. 1993. *The East Asian Miracle: Economic Growth and Public Policy*. New York: Oxford University Press.

World Trade Organization. 2000, 2001, 2002. *Annual Report*. Geneva: World Trade Organization.

Wang Shouchun. 2000. "Guanyu zhongguo jingji xin zengzhangyuan de tantao" (A discussion on the new source of economic growth in China). *Shuiwu yu Jingji* (Taxation & Economy) 15(6): 44–46.

Yu Yongding. 2001. "Macroeconomic Management of the Chinese Economy since the 1990s." Working paper of the Institute of World Economics and Politics, Chinese Academy for Social Sciences, Beijing. <http://www.iwep.org.cn/pdf/07wp_rcif.pdf>.

Zeng Peiyan. 2002. "Guomin jingji he shehui fazhan de lishixing bianhua" (Historic changes in the national economy and social development). *Renmin Ribao* (People's Daily) (17 September).

# 8

# China's Foreign Trade Policy after WTO Accession

## Wang Rongjun

Since China formally joined the World Trade Organization (WTO) in December 2001, its economy has continued growing strongly and attracting much foreign investment, while the world's major economies have struggled with sluggish growth or recession. Exactly how WTO entry has contributed to China's ongoing strong economic performance is greatly debated, but WTO accession has definitely meant that China's "reform and opening" have entered a new stage—they are now institutionalized.

The clearest signs of institutionalized reform and opening are the changes that have been made in Chinese foreign trade policy. The first-year WTO commitments that China's government has fulfilled include cutting tariffs, opening most industries to foreign competition, amending or repealing old foreign trade laws and regulations, and issuing new ones that comply with WTO rules and principles. The changes that have been made to fulfill these WTO obligations are not just perfunctory policy adjustments; the changes are permanent, reform-deepening transformations of China's trade regime. As interaction with the outside world increases in both scope and scale, trade policy has attracted attention from an increasing range of interest groups. New players and forces are now trying to participate in shaping China's trade policy. Perceptions of trade policy have shifted too.

This chapter focuses on the recent changes in China's foreign trade policy in the context of WTO accession. First, it analyzes changes in trade policy thinking in the light of WTO accession by examining policy debates. It then discusses trade policy practices and adjustments, especially the Chinese government's efforts to fulfill its WTO commitments. Finally, it explores the significance of the post–WTO changes in China's trade policy.

Perceptions of trade policy issues are emphasized throughout, as present thinking and policy practices will significantly influence the future path of China's foreign economic policy.

## TRADE POLICY DEBATES AFTER WTO ACCESSION

### The Role of Foreign Trade in China's Economy

China's imports and exports have expanded continuously since the 1990s. China's trade has grown at a much faster rate than its gross domestic product, and its trade dependency ratio in 2001 was 44 percent, or 1.47 times higher than in 1990. China exports much more than it imports, and, with the exception of 1993, it enjoyed fast-growing trade surpluses in the 1990s. Foreign trade became China's main engine of economic growth in the 1990s, contributing 7.5 percent on average to GDP growth (Zhang 2002). A 10 percent increase in Chinese exports was, for example, found to have resulted in a 1 percent increase in GDP in the 1990s, if both direct and indirect contributions were considered (Lin and Li 2002).

In a debate that mirrors an earlier one about the advantages and disadvantages of China joining the WTO, most Chinese scholars concur on the contribution of foreign trade to China's economic performance, although some minimize its importance. Interestingly, in the first year since China joined the world trading body, more scholars and policy analysts have joined the school that disavows the impact of foreign trade on the national economy. Many are suspicious about the current importance of the foreign trade sector, and are pessimistic about its future role. A study concerning the composition of GDP found that the contribution of international trade to China's economic growth over the past 20 years was very small (Zhu 1998). Some analysts have even contended that the relationship between GDP growth and trade surpluses is negative (Zhang and Hu 1999). Many scholars in this school are also concerned about the present growth trajectory of China's foreign trade, noting that an economy as large as China's that depends on foreign demand needs increasingly large international markets to maintain growth. They argue that the current environment is different to when Japan and the newly industrializing economies of Hong Kong, Singapore, South Korea, and Taiwan successfully used this model to grow in the 1950s through the 1970s, and that China will be unable to repeat these experiences. China's disproportionate dependence on the U.S. market also makes them question the sustainability of present trade growth rates.

But more scholars defend the contributions of foreign trade than query it. Apart from the larger numbers who subscribe to it, this school of thought is also the more comfortable position because it parallels the government's public position. Official statements and public media have expended significant resources since WTO accession emphasizing the importance of foreign trade.

## Comparative Advantage and Export Processing

China accepted the principle of comparative advantage only after adopting reform and opening in 1978, the initiation of which completely transformed China's trading system and its relations with the rest of the world. Domestic considerations have been the primary motivation in reforming China's trade policy, particularly improving the performance of its trade regime as it is so central to economic growth and development. Pre–WTO policy reforms included dismantling central planning, decentralizing and liberalizing trade, reducing a wide range of tariffs, relaxing exchange controls, and maintaining a realistic exchange rate. The principle on which to base socialist China's trade was greatly debated in the early and mid-1980s until policymakers recognized that China's trade could be based on comparative advantage.[1] Policies that favored utilizing its advantage in abundant and relatively low-cost labor would most help China's exports. In terms of this principle, China experienced extraordinary growth in the export of labor-intensive commodities, and export processing has prospered. The share of labor-intensive products in China's total exports increased to 74 percent in 1990 from 40 percent in 1980 (World Bank 1993).

However, faced with rising worldwide protectionism, especially newly created or upgraded barriers seemingly designed to target Chinese exports, some scholars and analysts have now started to wonder whether the principle of comparative advantage should still underpin China's exports.

This questioning is partly motivated by the fact that international markets have changed since China acceded to the WTO. Increased global protectionism since the end of the cold war and developed economies' growing concern about import surges from China since it joined the WTO have changed the international market for Chinese goods permanently. In order to sustain its outstanding export performance, some Chinese analysts are wondering whether the Chinese government might have to abandon or adjust the principle of comparative advantage, such as supplementing it with more active government participation.

Also, the labor-intensive industries upon which China has relied are beginning to meet with greater competition in international markets. Many labor-intensive products are over-supplied, while the demand elasticity of most of these products, especially goods used for daily life, is very small, with no hope of significant market enlargement soon.

Then there is the matter of China's formidable size. Most trade theories assume a small economy in which the object does not have the power to influence the international price of a commodity. As a big economy, China can influence or even set the price in some industries. Even so, low long-term prices for exports are causing deteriorating terms of trade. As China's exports have expanded, the difficulties of getting ahead have been increasing, as evidenced by the rising number of anti-dumping investigations against Chinese imports.

Suspicions about comparative advantage have led to questions about export processing. First, export processing is mostly comprised of trade in labor-intensive and low-end technological products. The design, technological component, and management of the goods that China's enterprises process are typically done outside of China, so China reaps a tiny part only of the profit coming from this kind of trade.

Second, export processing conflicts with the goal of establishing a more sound economic structure. A long-existing problem in the Chinese economy is excessive investment in industrial capacity and relative underinvestment in the service industry. This has resulted from agriculture and manufacturing being perceived as comprising the real economy, while tertiary or service industry was considered as subsidiary and as not creating real value. China has an enormous stake in promoting the development of tertiary industry, especially knowledge-intensive industry. If policy remains tilted toward export processing and related manufacturing, the industrial structure will remain weak, and serious unemployment will not be alleviated.

Third, China's interior and western regions are not suited for export processing. These areas are quite different geographically from the coastal areas, with no nearby ocean routes for easy expansion of export processing and small, poor markets in neighboring countries. Export processing is unlikely to prosper in these areas.

Supporters argue that the processing ability of domestic enterprises has increased tremendously over the last 20 years. Export processing is firmly rooted in China's industrial structure, and comprises quite a significant share of total industrial output and employment. Export processing is furthermore a solid launch pad for upgrading domestic industries and for starting China's industrialization.

Comparative advantage and export processing are still the basis of official policy, with the Communist Party's Sixteenth Party Congress, for example, recently re-endorsing comparative advantage, despite its noted disadvantages. The thinking is that the vital contribution of labor-intensive exports to China's economic growth is not easily replaced, and that China's almost unlimited labor supply means that labor-intensive industries have the potential to continue growing. Labor-intensive industries are also allowing the accumulation of national wealth and human capital to provide the basis for a later structural shift to capital-intensive industries. The development of industry, including labor-intensive industries, is a process of accumulating production know-how, management knowledge, and market experiences. And upgrading labor-intensive industries is a process of learning, absorbing, and digesting advanced technologies, with relatively low costs and within a short time, to provide the foundation to be internationally competitive in capital-intensive industries (Fan 1998). Labor-intensive products have relatively small demand elasticity, and their future growth prospects are not large compared with other products. Yet, as they are mostly daily necessities, demand will be stable, and absolute volumes will still be great. In addition to textiles, toys, and other traditional exports, labor-intensive industries include consumer electronics and general machinery, areas with great potential for further expansion.

## Industrial/Enterprise Competitiveness

There are two opposite opinions on the international competitiveness of Chinese industries and enterprises—one that considers Chinese enterprises not to be internationally competitive, and the other that regards China's industrial and enterprise competitiveness to be sufficient for China to shortly become the world's factory.

The Chinese Society for Enterprise Evaluation belongs to the former school and, using indicators developed in Switzerland by the IMD and

WANG RONGJUN

the World Economic Forum, it has evaluated the competitiveness of major Chinese enterprises.

According to this evaluation system, the international competitiveness of Chinese enterprises is rather weak. They compare unfavorably with the companies of the United States and other major developed economies, as well as with those of some relatively small economies like Ireland and Denmark (see table 1). The most competitive advantage of Chinese enterprises—indeed, almost the only advantage that Chinese enterprises enjoy—is the cost of labor (see table 2). It should, however, also be noted that the sample of this analysis is 1,000 large state-owned enterprises that are not necessarily China's most competitive companies.

Table 1. Transnational Comparison of Competitiveness, 1999

| Country | Score | Rank |
|---|---|---|
| United States | 100 | 1 |
| The Netherlands | 91.94 | 2 |
| Canada | 91.04 | 3 |
| Switzerland | 90.52 | 4 |
| Singapore | 89.97 | 5 |
| Finland | 89.42 | 6 |
| Hong Kong, SAR | 88.06 | 7 |
| Sweden | 87.04 | 8 |
| Ireland | 83.68 | 9 |
| Denmark | 82.89 | 10 |
| China | 25.72 | 38 |

Source: Zhang (2003).

Table 2. International Competitiveness of Chinese Enterprises
in Terms of Management, 1999

|  | 1995 | 1996 | 1997 | 1998 | 1999 | Average |
|---|---|---|---|---|---|---|
| Management competitiveness | 30 | 34 | 30 | 36 | 37 | 33.4 |
| Labor productivity | 36 | 38 | 42 | 46 | 38 | 40 |
| Labor cost | 12 | 2 | 1 | 3 | 11 | 5.8 |
| Enterprise performance | 28 | 37 | 31 | 35 | 39 | 34 |
| Management effectiveness | 36 | 32 | 29 | 34 | 33 | 32.8 |

Source: Zhang (2003).

For those who belong to the China-as-global-production-center school, China's remarkable foreign trade performance and the rapid increase of foreign direct investment into China in the year after WTO accession validates their viewpoint. That many world-renown multinationals have set up branches and manufacturing bases in China, and that world retail giants like Wal-Mart and Carrefour have established their global procurement centers in China are also considered hard evidence of China's competitive strength.

When endorsing the idea of China as the world's factory, Chinese scholars typically mention China's ample supply of low-cost labor, its vast domestic market, the presence of political will, and reform-oriented policies. Also, China's manufacturing capacity is very strong. From 1978 to 2001, China's total industrial output increased 24-fold for an annual average increase of 17.4 percent. Manufacturing is the main component of Chinese industry, providing 88 percent of total output value over three years recently. In 2001, 91 percent of China's total exports were manufactured goods, while its share of total world manufactured exports increased to 7 percent. China has become the world's largest exporter of many manufactured goods, including motorcycles, watches, bicycles, computer monitors, color television sets, washing machines, refrigerators, air conditioners, microwave ovens, tape players and recorders, and print circuit boards (*China Economic Times* 8 April 2003).

The main counterarguments are that China's share of total output, total manufactured value, and total volume of global imports and exports are still quite small. Most manufactured goods are low value-added, and China is actually running a still-expanding deficit in the trade of high-technology goods. In 2001, machinery and transportation equipment was China's largest single import item, comprising 44 percent of total imports. Chinese enterprises are also still dependent on foreign suppliers for most core technologies and essential parts that they need, including product design and processing equipment. For example, Galanz Corporation of Guangdong Province, the world's largest microwave oven manufacturer, still imports magnetron, the oven's core component. And China desperately needs highly skilled labor (*Economic Daily* 22 July 2002). Most Chinese enterprises that are regarded as strong international competitors in their fields are actually low-end assemblers and processors in the transnational value chain. Take the electronics industry as an example. In 2002, the total sales income of China's electronics industry was almost 1,400 billion renminbi, or 11 percent of the world total, next only to the United States and Japan. But about half of the industry's output went abroad. China has become the manufacturing base for information technology (IT) products, with 90 percent of the world's 100 biggest IT enterprises having branches in China. China has also become the largest global manufacturer for Motorola, Nokia, and Acer. But the fact remains that Chinese IT manufacturing enterprises are just assemblers. About 60 percent of the industry's profit comes from chip and software design and production, and this normally goes to U.S. or other foreign-owned businesses, and 20 percent comes from other essential parts, usually supplied by Japanese or Korean enterprises. Chinese enterprises get less than 10 percent (Ma and Yang 2002).

## Globalization and Regionalism

The above debates have a huge bearing on China's attitude toward globalization and regionalism. Government documents considered globalization to be an unstoppable trend long before China's WTO accession. Since joining the WTO, the government has been stressing the benefits of participating in globalization more than the negative consequences. China's position in globalization is considered to be advantageous due to China's massive domestic market, its wide range of industries, and its capacity to provide a huge supply of low-cost labor for FDI. Its market-size advantage, its industrial production capabilities, and its low labor costs, combined with foreign capital, technologies, and management, suggest that a highly competitive open economy could be created. For post-WTO China, the major purpose of introducing foreign investment into domestic industries has changed from utilizing capital to introducing advanced technology, upgrading its industrial structure, and increasing international competitiveness. All of these help China build its own ability to develop core technologies.

Traditional development theory contends that developing countries becoming too reliant on foreign technologies could be held back permanently. This perception changed, particularly in the mid-1990s. With faster technological advances, investment in research and development tends to depreciate more quickly, so enterprises must apply high-cost technologies as widely as possible to recoup their investment. Also, industrial organization has changed from being vertically integrated to a horizontal division of labor in some industries, necessitating a global market to distribute development costs and create economies of scale. For companies with similar technology, those who get to market fastest are the ultimate winners. So owners of new technology tend to apply that technology simultaneously across the globe. A recent survey found that the proportion of Fortune 500 Chinese affiliates that use the parent companies' technologies has increased to 80 percent in 2002 from 43 percent in 2001 and 14 percent in the mid-1990s (Jiang 2002).

The Chinese government's position toward regional cooperation is more complicated. With the collapse of the "flying geese" model of East Asian economic development, East Asian countries have been thinking about how to integrate regional resources for a new division of labor. But, if the world factory argument is to be sustained, China's greater interest would be in fully immersing itself in globalization. So pursuing a strategy of globalization rather than regionalism might be a better inclination for China, as regional economic cooperation is less likely to benefit it as much. China is also yet to open its capital account, so the real benefits of regional currency cooperation would be difficult to realize. Finally, regional cooperation could play a limited role only in promoting economic growth and safeguarding China against outside risks.

From a political-economic perspective, however, active participation in regional economic cooperation is greatly in China's national interest. Neighboring East and Southeast Asian countries are concerned about what China's rise means to their economic and security interests. A positive Chinese posture toward regional economic cooperation would have at least three immediate potential benefits. First, constructive Chinese participation in regional economic initiatives would definitely help reduce conflicts and obstruct their emergence. Second, globalization is not necessarily fair and beneficial to developing countries. By cooperating with other East and Southeast Asian countries, China would better be able to secure its own interests in the globalization process. Third, being an initiator and coordinator of regional economic cooperation now would develop regional trust in China, and would enable it to play more important roles in the future. So participating actively in regionalism would be helpful for China's global strategy.

## TRADE PERFORMANCE AND TRADE POLICY PRACTICES AFTER WTO ACCESSION

### Trade Performance in 2002

On joining the WTO, as pledged, the Chinese government promptly reduced tariffs and abolished a number of nontariff barriers for 2002. From

January 1, 2002, tariffs were reduced, on average, to 12 percent from 15.3 percent on 5,300 items, covering 73 percent of the tariff schedule. For manufactured goods, the average tariff reduction was to 11.3 percent from 14.7 percent; for agricultural products, the average tariff reduction was to 15.8 percent from 18.8 percent. At the same time, nontariff barriers were lifted on grain, wool, polyester fiber, fertilizers, and some types of tires. Many expected China's trade surplus to decrease, as China's imports would likely rise quickly while exports would fall. In fact, the opposite occurred. The 2002 trade surplus actually increased significantly, to be about 50 percent higher than that for 2001. Machinery and electronic products comprised the fastest-growing export category, with a 32.3 percent increase over the previous year that was valued at US$157.1 billion. Increases for traditional labor-intensive exports such as garments, footware, and toys were 12.7 percent, 9.9 percent, and 7.9 percent, respectively (Zhong 2003). Exports to most major trade partners increased significantly, with the North American market growing the fastest. Exports to the members of the Association of Southeast Asian Nations (ASEAN) also increased rapidly. On the import side, China imported most from Japan, ASEAN, and Taiwan in 2002.

For various reasons, China's trade performance in the first year since joining the WTO was better than expected. China's domestic demand was relatively weak that year, which forced domestic enterprises to look for opportunities abroad, and the renminbi and the U.S. dollar both depreciated, so Chinese exports were particularly price competitive. The central government, along with local governments, adopted export-promotion policies, such as giving tax rebates and export credits, and providing credit insurance. That local governments adapted policies to suit specific regional situations was also important to maintaining export strength. FDI inflows increased significantly, and trade opportunities grew concomitantly (Jin Pei 2002).

But the most noteworthy development in the foreign trade sector was the rise of private businesses (table 3). The loosening of restrictions on foreign trade operations had started in 1999 and was then accelerated, as China promised in WTO accession protocols that foreign trade business would be completely open to private and foreign operators in three years. New rules issued by the then Ministry of Foreign Trade and Economic Cooperation (MOFTEC), now known as the Ministry of Commerce (MOFCOM), allowed provincial and even local trade officials to grant foreign trade rights. For example, Zhejiang Province is one of China's most developed areas for private enterprise. Collective or private enterprises accounted for 80 percent of the 1,700 enterprises that obtained foreign trading rights in Zhejiang in 2002, and they were responsible for a third of total exports. Zhejiang and Guangdong are the two Chinese provinces that export the most, with exports from private enterprises increasing 250 percent and 114.6 percent, respectively, in 2002. In 2002, Chinese exports by private enterprises totaled US$32.8 billion, which was 66.5 percent more than for 2001. As more and more Chinese private enterprises obtain permits for conducting foreign trade, their share of total imports and exports is expected to increase further (Xinhua News Agency 2002).

The satisfactory performance of the foreign trade sector alleviated con-

**Table 3. Imports and Exports of Enterprises in 2002 (US$100m)**

|  | Exports | Year-on-Year Change (%) | Imports | Year-on-Year Change (%) |
|---|---|---|---|---|
| State-owned enterprises | 1,228.6 | 8.5 | 1,144.9 | 10.6 |
| Foreign-invested enterprises | 1,699.4 | 27.6 | 1,602.7 | 27.4 |
| Collective enterprises | 188.6 | 32.6 | 94.8 | 18.5 |
| Private enterprises | 137.8 | 159.5 | 95.6 | 180.9 |
| Others | -1.3 | 12.5 | 14.1 | -49.7 |

Source: Ministry of Commerce (2003).

cern about foreign competition, while the rapid development of private enterprises in China's foreign trade has added a new element to the formulating of China's foreign economic policy.[2]

## Building Legal Frameworks and Expanding Market Access Efforts

There are two central focuses in China's trade policy after WTO accession—amending and adjusting laws and regulations that are inconsistent with WTO principles, and designing and establishing a WTO-compatible trade policy regime. These two processes are complementary rather than mutually exclusive, and their interaction directs Chinese trade policy. China's central government has been firm in pushing through the required policy reforms and adjustments, with the outstanding performance of the foreign trade sector reinforcing its efforts.

So China's trade policy in 2002 was oriented to amending or adjusting non-WTO compliant laws, and creating new ones that are WTO compatible. The National People's Congress made or amended laws, while the government did the same with ordinances. The State Council has processed 2,300 documents, of which 830 were repealed and 325 are being amended (Jin Liqun 2002). These laws and regulations encompass three main areas: general laws and regulations that define the overall rules for conducting foreign trade in China; laws and regulations regarding market access to sectors that were previously very protected; and laws and regulations dealing with trade remedies. This last category, the one that relates to trade remedies, is discussed separately, because of its special long-term significance, and because it is the most criticized part of China's policy adjustments.

Promulgated in 1994, *China's Foreign Trade Law* provides the fundamental legal basis and guiding principles for China's foreign trade policies. As the law itself is very general,[3] China issued the WTO-compatible Regulations on the Import and Export of Merchandise Goods and Regulations on the Import and Export of Technology in December 2001. They replaced previous laws and regulations regarding merchandise trade, such as Provisional Procedures on Operating and Managing Import and Export Commodities, which was promulgated on July 19, 1994, and Provisional Regulations on Managing the Import of Machinery and Electronic Products, which was promulgated on October 7, 1993. The two new regulations specifically define the general rules and principles established by the Foreign Trade Law, thereby fulfilling China's commitment to repeal or revise all laws, regulations, and other measures that were inconsistent with the principles of most favored nation, national treatment, or nondiscrimination.

Numerous other new laws and regulations covering nearly all aspects of trading with China have been issued or have come into force, all with the purpose of fulfilling China's accession commitments. For example, on January 1, 2002, new customs regulations took effect that aim to clarify how Chinese Customs calculates import and export duties. The regulations also allow trading companies to apply for a ruling on classification up to three months before goods are imported or exported, they waive tariffs, and they simplify the process for importing goods temporarily.

The amended laws and revised regulations will be promulgated or issued after proper legal procedures are followed. In the meantime, provincial and local authorities are still reviewing their laws and regulations to see if they are consistent with national laws. Provincial-level laws, regulations, and other regulatory measures that implement the central government's legal measures are submitted to the central government for review.

Some trade partners have criticized China's intellectual property rights (IPR) protections as inadequate. Upon accession to the WTO, the Chinese government committed itself to the WTO Agreement on Trade-Related Aspects of Intellectual Property Rights (TRIPs), so it is reviewing and amending China's intellectual property rights laws. China's amended patent law and its implementing rules, which took effect on July 1, 2001, streamline the patent application process, standardize patent infringement penalties, simplify enforcement procedures, and shift the burden of proof to defendants in patent infringement cases. Other IPR laws and regulations that address computer software, copyrights, trademarks, and criminal enforcement against counterfeiting were amended shortly thereafter. Some of the newly amended laws and regulations have protection levels that are even stricter than some developed economies. For example, the TRIPs agreement contains no specific requirements regarding software infringement by end users; it is up to WTO members themselves to determine the obligations of end users. While most developed members define infringement as unauthorized commercial use, China's newly amended software law extends infringement penalties to unauthorized noncommercial use.

In addition to amending previous trade rules and principles and creating new ones, the Chinese government has issued a series of regulations concerning foreign investment liberalization and market access improvement in banking, insurance, telecommunications, distribution, consulting, and some other service sectors. To conform to WTO commitments on foreign investment, China revised its Catalogue Guiding Foreign Investment in Industry and its Regulations Guiding Foreign Investment, both of which took effect on April 1, 2002. The industries in which wholly foreign-owned enterprises are now permitted have been expanded to 87.6 percent. New rules eliminate WTO-incompatible requirements on foreign exchange, advanced technology, export performance, and local content as conditions for investing by foreign-invested enterprises (Hu 2003). In July 2001, MOFTEC began loosening restrictions for domestic nonstate enterprises engaging in trade when it issued its *Circular Concerning the Rules Administering Trading Rights*. The objective of this circular was to shift MOFTEC out of managing trade to simply registering prospective domestic traders. These rules extend trading rights to private manufacturing firms as well as to private trading companies. To improve transparency, the rules set time limits for the approval process, so that the regulatory authorities can no longer hold up applications indefinitely. The rules also reduced the minimum capital requirement for wholly Chinese-invested enterprises to obtain trading rights. In July 2001, MOFTEC issued its *Circular Concerning the Extension of Trading Rights for Foreign-Funded Enterprises* which granted trading rights to some foreign-invested firms ahead of schedule (United States Trade Representative 2002).

The Chinese government has also worked to open the services market in accordance with WTO commitments. In the financial sector, some foreign banks have started to negotiate merger and acquisitions deals with the Chinese banks, and foreign financial institutions have been invited to form joint ventures to help dispose of nonperforming loans from the four major commercial banks. A number of foreign banks have received licenses to operate in areas newly liberalized by China's WTO commitments. Upon WTO entry, foreign investment in foreign currency services was allowed nationwide, and foreign or joint-venture banks such as the Bank of East Asia, Citibank, HSBC, and Standard Chartered have received licenses. The right to offer renminbi lending to foreign companies and individuals has been expanded to include Dalian and Tianjin, after successful pilot programs in Guangdong and Shanghai. Several Japanese and South Korean banks have applications pending or have been approved to provide renminbi services in Dalian and Tianjin. In the insurance sector, China's State Council has approved amendments to the 1995 Insurance Law. On December 13, 2001, the China Insurance Regulatory Commission (CIRC) approved New York Life Insurance, Metropolitan Life Insurance, Nippon Life Insurance, and another four foreign insurers to set up or to expand business operations in China.

In some areas, the opening of the services market is ahead of schedule for the first year of WTO membership. For example, foreign insurance companies are allowed to open businesses in Beijing and Tianjin. Some foreign retail branches are negotiating with their Chinese counterparts to take a majority share of their equity. From July 2002, foreign travel agents have started to form joint ventures or set up wholly owned subsidiaries in Shanghai. Well in advance of the phase-in dates for market access, CIRC issued four new insurance regulations that cover foreign insurance companies, insurance appraisal institutions, insurance brokerage companies, and insurance agency institutions.

## Building the Trade Remedy System

The most controversial part of China's trade policy adjustment efforts in the first year after WTO accession was in the area of trade remedies. Again, there are two sides to the efforts to build a trade-remedy system—one is reforming and adjusting current trade relief regulations and measures that are inconsistent with WTO requirements, and the other side is creating a WTO-compatible trade remedy system.

The most important first step was building China's own antidumping and countervailing system. China promised to repeal import quotas, import licenses, and most other traditional nontariff barriers at accession, or on January 1, 2004, or 2005, so other ways to protect domestic industries against unfair or improper trade practices will need to be found. In October 2001, three regulations that form the basis of China's new trade remedy system were introduced: Regulations on Antidumping Duties; Regulations on Countervailing Duties; and Regulations on Safeguard Measures. They replaced Regulations on Antidumping and Countervailing Duties that was issued in 1997.

Introducing WTO-compatible antidumping, countervailing, and safeguard measures is the only feasible way to move against unfair trade practices. Antidumping was the most-used tool in this regard in 2002, with cases in the steel and petrochemical industries. Countervailing and safeguard measures are still symbolic, but they could become important trade remedies in the future, especially safeguard measures that target so-called import surges.

But these three regulations are not enough to establish a comprehensive trade remedy system, at least for some policy analysts and scholars. They strongly favor adopting other measures to complement the three basic regulations, such as increasing financial subsidies to domestic agriculture. In its accession negotiations, China promised that agricultural support would not surpass 8.5 percent. However, current agricultural support is much lower than that. So there is room to increase financial support to domestic agriculture while staying compliant with WTO rules (Lv 2002).

WANG RONGJUN

## CONCLUSION

Since WTO accession, rule-based behavior has become one of the basic principles of government conduct. Even though rules themselves do not automatically lead to liberalization, ongoing efforts to impose a systemic set of rules will continue to boost economic performance.

However, Chinese authorities are still ready to intervene if necessary. The government is convinced of the importance of accelerating the development of high-technology industries to maintain international competitiveness in the face of globalization, so China will adopt policies that further this goal. Combined with increased foreign direct investment, the focus will be to expand technology-intensive manufacturing exports as rapidly as possible. Yet pushing high-tech exports will often need support in the form of policies such as tax rebates, as they are not necessarily in line with China's comparative advantage.

China displayed determination to fulfill its WTO commitments in the first year of accession to the world trading body. It adjusted its trade policy on two tracks: one was reforming and adjusting existing structures and practices to conform to its promises; the other one was building new rules-based trade policies. Outstanding performance of the foreign trade sector in 2002 reinforced China's confidence, and thus its determination. The success of these adjustments will be very significant for China's future. A U.S. scholar summed it up cogently: "If China's full incorporation into the world trading system is managed well, it seems likely that the reforms . . . will be seen as another watershed event contributing strongly to the modernization of China and its full integration into the world economy" (Pearson 1999).

## NOTES

1. Almost all influential Chinese economists and researchers in international economics were involved in the debate, the theme of which was whether or not the theory of comparative advantage could apply in China. See, for example, Xu (1999).
2. For a discussion of the role of government agencies and interest groups in formulating China's trade policy, see Pearson (1999) and Shen (2000).
3. The basic principles are: The country has a unified foreign trade system;

fair and free foreign trade is safeguarded; foreign trade dealers are en-
sured independent operational authority; the development of foreign
trade is encouraged; and trade relations with other countries and regions are promoted on the basis of equality and mutual benefit. See
Shi (2002).

## BIBLIOGRAPHY

Fan Gang. 1998. "Lun jingzheng li" (On competitiveness). *Guanli Shijie*
(Management World) 3.

Hu Jingyan. 2003. *Changes in China's FIE Policy after WTO Accession.* Forum
on Leadership and Policy Direction of China's New Administration. WTO
and China: Beijing International Forum, Beijing. Co-Sponsored by
MOFCOM and Beijing Municipal Government, November.

Jiang Xiaojuan. 2003. "Liyong jingji quanqiuhua de jiyu cujin jingji fazhan"
(Utilize the opportunity brought by globalization to promote economic
development). *People's Daily* (17 February).

Jiang Zemin. 2002. *Quanmian jianshe xiaokang shehui, kaichuang zhongguo
teseshehuizhuyi shiye xing jumian* (Build a well-off society in an all-
round way and create a new situation in building socialism with Chinese characteristics). Report to the Sixteenth National Congress of
the Chinese Communist Party. <http://english.peopledaily.com.cn/fea-
tures/16thpartyreport/home.html>.

Jin Liqun. 2002. *China: One Year into the WTO Process.* Address to the
World Bank. 22 October <http://www.worldbank.org/wbi/B-SPAN/
docs/IMF-WB–address–final.pdf>.

Jin Pei. 2002. "Zhongguo zhizao zou xiang shijie." ("Made in China" helps
energize the world economy). *Zhongguo Zhengquan Bao China* (China
Securities Journal) (18 July).

Li Heng. 2002. "A Year of Changes after WTO Accession: Review." *People's
Daily*, English version (12 December).

Lin Yifu and Li Yongjun. 2002. "Chukou yu zhongguo de jingji zengzhang"
(Foreign trade and China's economic growth: A demand-led analysis).
Beijing University. CCER Working Paper No. C2002008 (May).

Lv Bo. 2002. "Ruhe yindui maoyi bilei he jianli wuoguo de maoyi baohu
tixi" (How to deal with trade barriers and build China's trade safeguarding system). Beijing: Institute of Foreign Trade Studies, Ministry

of Foreign Trade and Economic Cooperation.

Ma Jiantang and Yang Zhengwei. 2002. "Shijie gongchang yu zhongguo jingji zhanwang" (The world's factory and the prospects of China's economy). SETC Economic Research and Consulting Center (July).

Ministry of Commerce. 2003. "Chukou qiye xingzhi" (Imports and exports of enterprises in 2002). <http://www.mofcom.gov.cn/article/200302/20030200070411-1.xml>.

Pearson, Margaret M. 1999. "China's Integration into the International Trade and Investment Regime." In Elizabeth Economy and Michel Oksenberg, eds. *China Joins the World: Progress and Prospects.* New York: Council on Foreign Relations Press.

Shen Bin. 2000. "The Political Economy of Trade Policy in China." Copenhagen: Copenhagen Business School WP10/2000 (August).

Shi Xiaoli. 2002. *WTO guizhe yu zhongguo waimai guanli zhidu* (WTO rules and China's foreign trade administrative system). Beijing: Zhongguo Zhengfa Daxue Chubanshe (Chinese University of Law and Politics Press).

"Siying qiye zheng zai dapo chuantong waimao geju" (Private enterprise is breaking the traditional pattern of China's foreign trade ). 2002. Xinhua News Agency (October 23).

United States Trade Representative. 2002. *2002 Report to the U.S. Congress on China's WTO Compliance.* Washington, D.C.: United States Trade Representative.

World Bank. 1993. *China's Foreign Trade Reform: Facing the Challenges of the1990s.* Washington, D.C.: World Bank.

Xu Qingjun. 1999. "Lun zhongguo maoyi fazhan zhanlue de yanjin" (On the evolution of China's trade stategy). Ph.D. dissertation.

Yu Yongding. 2002. "Cong zhongguo de jiaodu kan quanqiuhua" (Globalization from China's perspective). In *Globalization and the 21st Century—Collected Works of the First Sino-French Academic Forum.* Beijing: Shekou Wenxian Chubanshe (China Social Documentation Publishing House).

Zhang Shuguang. 2002. *Zhengce yu tizhi liandong—shichanghua jinchen zhong de hongguan jingji fenxi.* (Policy and system interaction: Macroeconomic analysis in the process of marketization).Shanghai: Shanghai Caijing Chubanshe (Shanghai Financial University Press).

Zhang Wenkui. 2003. "Zhongguo qiye jingzhengli zhuangkuang" (The state of competiveness of China's enterprises). *Review of Economic Research* 2.

Zhang Xiaoji and Hu Jiangyun. 1999. "Zai ziyou maoyi de beihou jingkou maoyi yu guoming jingji fazhan" (Behind free trade: Import trade and the Development of the national economy) *Guoji Maoyi* (InterTrade) 208(4).

Zhao Xiao. 2002. "Zhongguo juli 'shijie gongchang' yiran yaoyuan" (How far away is China from being the world's factory?). August. <http://www.china-review.com/zpym/execute.asp>.

Zhong Zhenyan. 2003. "Cong waimao fazhan kan jiaru WTO dui zhongguo chanye fazhan de yingxiang" (The impact of WTO accession on China's industry: From the perspective of foreign trade." *Zhongguo Jingmao* (China Trade) 3. Cited from <http://market.homeway.com.cn/lbi-html/news/special/cjzt/cjsj/pntr/12347417501.shtml>.

"Zhongyang jingji gongzuo huiyi zai Beijing juxing" (Central economic working conference held in Beijing). 2002. *People's Daily* (11 December).

Zhu Wenhui. 1998. "Zhongguo chukou daoxiang zhanlue de misi daguo de jinyan he zhongguo de xuanze" (The befuddlement of China's export-oriented strategy: Big country experiences and China's choice). *Zhanlue yu Guanl* (Strategy and Management) 5.

# 9

## The Shaping of China's Foreign Policy

### Ni Feng

Like other countries, China bases its foreign policy on an understanding of a number of fundamental issues. These issues include how China sees its own strength, its perception of the international stature it enjoys, its identity in the international community, and the kind of international environment in which it finds itself.

This chapter uses these issues to introduce China's foreign policy in five sections. The first section examines China's strength from the perspective of "comprehensive national strength." The second section discusses mainstream Chinese perceptions of China's international status as a rising regional power with some global influence. The third section describes the change in China's identity in the international community, from a revolutionary country that rejected existing international institutions to a responsible power with interests in the system. In the fourth section, East Asia provides the context for discussing those factors affecting the relative stability of China's international environment. The last section describes China's strategic choices for its foreign policy, including its desire to set up a win-win, cooperative framework; its interest in getting strategic backing from its neighbors; its wish to enhance solidarity and cooperation with other Third World countries; and its yearning to complete China's reunification.

### China's Strength

A country's strength is the basis and most important determinant of its foreign policy and international activities. Since the 1990s, China has used the concept of "comprehensive national strength" to measure its own strength (Huang 1992, Wang 1996). Chinese scholars define "comprehensive national strength" as the aggregate of a country's real and potential power in political, economic, military, scientific, technological, educational, and other areas at any given time. It is perceived as a strategic indicator of a country's stature (China Institute of Contemporary International Relations 2000a, 4). To date, the most influential studies in this area are a 2000 report from the China Institute of Contemporary International Relations (CICIR), *Assessing World Big Powers' Comprehensive National Strength*, and a study by the Chinese Academy of Sciences, *Evaluation of China's Comprehensive National Strength*.

The study from the CICIR* measures China's comprehensive national strength (CNS) in terms of economic, military, scientific and educational, resources, political, social, and international indicators. Researchers divided the seven indicators into two categories: CNS 1 or "hard" indicators, such as economic, military, and resources; and CNS 2 or "soft" indicators, including political, social, and international. The study measures China's CNS against that of Britain, France, Germany, Japan, Russia, and the United States, the six most powerful and influential nations in the world. Based on 1988–1998 data from the seven countries and statistical analyses, the conclusions that the researchers reached are noted in table 1.

Table 1. The Comparative National Strengths of Seven Countries

|      | U.S.A. | Japan | France | Britain | Germany | Russia | China |
|------|--------|-------|--------|---------|---------|--------|-------|
| CNS1 | 8371   | 5112  | 4270   | 4070    | 3918    | 3203   | 2175  |
| CNS2 | 6090   | 3096  | 3254   | 2830    | 2710    | 1604   | 1101  |

Source: CICIR (2000b).

In terms of ranking, China emerges seventh of the seven nations. The United States ranks first, far ahead of the other six, while Japan ranks second, with a CNS that is 60 percent that of the United States. France, Britain, and Germany appear at the same level, with their respective CNSs measuring half that of the United States. Russia's CNS is close to 40 percent of the United States' CNS. China's CNS accounts for a quarter of the United States' CNS; two-fifths of Japan's; half of France, Germany and Britain's; and two-thirds of Russia's.

---

* The CICIR report alone is introduced, as press reports suggest that the indicators used in the study from the Chinese Academy of Sciences and the conclusions reached there are very similar.

The study used a composite indicator for the three "soft" variables, with no specific breakdown. Table 2 reflects the results for the "hard" indicators.

Table 2. Rankings in Specific Areas

| | U.S. | Japan | China | Russia | Germany | France | Britain |
|---|---|---|---|---|---|---|---|
| Economy | 8924 | 6670 | 2511 | 2424 | 5143 | 4820 | 4850 |
| Science and Education | 9492 | 8641 | 1337 | 3124 | 6276 | 6904 | 6077 |
| Military | 9503 | 1338 | 1068 | 3172 | 1222 | 2085 | 2183 |
| Resources | 33 | 40 | 4621 | 5210 | 19 | 1918 | 1792 |

Source: CICIR (2000b).

As the table suggests, China ranks sixth in economic indicators. It measures slightly more than Russia, less than a third of the U.S. economy, and about half of Germany's.

In science and education, China's scoring is a seventh of that for the United States; one-fifth of France, Germany, and Britain's; and approximately half of Russia's. In relative terms, science and education is the weakest CNS indicator for China.

Militarily, China's score is about one-ninth of that for the United States, one-third of that for Russia, half of Britain and France's, and close to Japan and Germany's. This is also the area where the United States has the greatest advantage over the other countries. In fact, the U.S. scoring in the military area is close to the sum of the other six countries combined. This military preeminence is the most decisive factor in ensuring the United States the status of being the world's only superpower. Though ranked last, China's score in this realm is close to Germany and Japan's. Germany ranks slightly ahead of China in military capabilities, yet China's military spending is only 60 percent of Germany's; per capita military spending is only one-twelfth; export of conventional weapons is less than half; and military research and development spending is half.

In terms of resources, China trails behind first-ranking Russia. The United States comes in third, with Japan being sixth and Germany seventh. That Russia ranked first is no surprise, given its vast territory, rich fresh-water and energy resources, and per capita land ownership. China leads the United States largely because of its huge population base and its low percentage of aged relative to the total population. In 1998, the aged population in China—aged 65 and above—accounted for only 6.6 percent of the total population, compared with 12 percent–16 percent in the six other countries (CICIR 2000a, 24).

The seven countries could be divided into three categories: The United States would be in Category 1, while Britain, France, Germany, and Japan would be in Category 2 as they share the characteristics of limited resources and territory, with similar levels of economic, scientific, educational and military development. China and Russia would be in Category 3, because both are resource-rich great nations with underdeveloped economies, and similar scientific and educational levels.

The preceding analysis is Chinese scholars' basic assessment of China's CNS.

## China's International Status

China is undoubtedly a rising power, yet there are different opinions at home and abroad about what kind of power China is. The mainstream Chinese viewpoint is that China is a regional power with some global influence.

China's global influence stems from various sources. China's population is one-fifth or one-fourth of the world's total population. In terms of territory, China is the third largest country in the world. China is one of the five countries with permanent membership of the United Nations Security Council, and it is also one of five recognized nuclear powers. So China is an important player in issues involving international security, global strategic stability, arms control, and nuclear proliferation. At present, China's economy is the sixth largest in the world. Due to its fast-growing economy, China is the biggest new developing market, and it has become an important global manufacturing base. With China's accession to the World Trade Organization (WTO) and as the Chinese people continue working hard to attain a well-off society in an all-round way, China's impact on the global economy will only increase further.

In the meantime, China's influence and interests are focused mainly on the East Asian region. In geopolitical terms, China is located in the center of East Asia, and it is the strongest land power in the region. China plays an important role on the Korean peninsula. As it has good relations with both South and North Korea, China is able to exercise its unique and important influence for peace and stability in the area. Contacts between China and the countries of Southeast Asia are quite extensive, due to geographic proximity and the impact of overseas Chinese. In South Asia, China is Pakistan's ally, although it is making efforts to improve relations with India. In Central Asia, China's influence is increasing gradually. It is the initiator of the Shanghai Cooperation Organization, a grouping of China, Kazakhstan, Kyrgyzstan, Russia, Takijistan, and Uzbekistan that fosters regional cooperation and dialogue on issues of mutual concern. In North Asia, good relations between China and Russia have been a cornerstone of regional stability, yet relations between China, Japan, and the United States will, to some extent, dominate the region's future.

In geoeconomic terms, before 1979, China stayed out of the market system as a result of its closed-door policy. Since 1979, when China began economic reform and opening up, it began joining the global economic system, and became one of the "geese" in the "flying-geese" model of East Asian economic development. Due to its reforms, effective utilization of foreign direct investment, and excellent operation of its economy, China has now become a leading "goose" in the region, with its performance becoming more important as the economic growth engine in Asia Pacific. China has also been pushing economic integration in East Asia by initiating a free trade area between China and the Association of Southeast Asian Nations (ASEAN), and by suggesting a free trade treaty with Korea.

In short, in the international community, China's influence and status is rising. Yet, as its international stature grows, it is also facing restraints.

Although China's economic development is quite successful, its achievements are quite limited in many fields. For example, even though "China's rise" has become a hot subject, its per capita GDP approaches just US$1,000. As a developing country, it has to confront many challenges, such as limited resources, uneven development between the eastern coastal regions and the western interior, the gap between urban and rural areas, mismanagement of state-owned enterprises, bad loans, and so forth. In addition, as a society in transition, China is also dealing with dramatic shifts—from being an agriculture-based economy to an industry-based economy, from being a planned economy to becoming a market economy, from a traditional society to a modern society, and trying to establish efficient governing systems. All these challenges require China to concentrate most of its vigor on domestic issues, and to keep a low profile in the outside world.

China is also yet to complete its nation-building task. The challenge of realizing its reunification has depleted and consumed political, diplomatic, and economic resources that it could use elsewhere.

China is a land power, but its foreign trade and increasing oil imports rely on sea routes, so China has to keep good relations with maritime powers. Yet, at this point, these maritime powers are restraining its influence.

To a great extent, China's economic development and growth depend on external markets, capital, technology, and management. Dependence on these factors means that China is in a position where external influences easily have an impact on it.

China's rapid development is worrying some countries. In many countries, the fear of the "China threat" is rife, and China is regarded as a competitor or an adversary. Some countries assume their values and political system should be the world standard, and they disrespect global diversity.

All of these factors presently limit the role China can play in the international community.

## China's Identity in the International Community

A nation's understanding of the outside world is shaped in large measure by its identity in the international community. Different identities lead to different attitudes and policies toward the outside world. Changes within a country also lead to changes in its international identity. Since the late 1970s, when China adopted the policy of reform and opening up, China's international identity has undergone profound changes. China's participation in international conventions is a good indicator. Between 1949 and 1999, China acceded to 220 international conventions—34 during 1949–1979, but 185 during 1980–1999 (Ministry of Foreign Affairs of the People's Republic of China 2000). China is repositioning itself from a revolutionary country that rejected the existing international regime to a responsible power within the system. This change is evident in the following aspects.

First, China now sees itself as a beneficiary of the current international economic order, and it seeks to play an active role in it. Since the adoption of reform and opening, economic development has been the policy centerpiece of the Chinese government, so it has focused its foreign policy on creating a sound external environment for domestic economic development. After more than two decades of market-oriented reform and opening up to the West and the capitalist world, China has impressed the world with rapid economic growth, and with becoming increasingly integrated into the world economy. In 2002, China's foreign trade topped US$600 billion for the first time, making China the fifth largest trader in the world, while it received US$50 billion in foreign direct investment, the largest FDI inflow in the world. China has benefited from the existing international economic regime, yet it has also made its contribution to world economic stability. During the 1997 Asian financial crisis, China maintained the stability of its currency, effectively preventing the crisis from spreading to other parts of the region, and it provided financial support to Indonesia and Thailand. In short, the integration of the Chinese economy into the global economy has brought China closer to the international community.

Second, China is participating in international activities in an all-out manner. To use the popular Chinese catch phrases, China is seeking to *rongru shijie,* or integrate with the world, and to *yu guoji jiegui,* or become compatible with internationally accepted practices. In the arena of political security, China actively participated in the political settlement of the Cambodian issue. Indeed, it has participated in ten United Nations peacekeeping operations (Xiong 2002a, 3). It is fully involved in the quadripartite talks seeking a peaceful solution to the Korean nuclear issue. Beijing has also signed a declaration on conduct in the South China Sea with ASEAN, it is a keen participant in the ASEAN Regional Forum, and it is actively promoting the ASEAN + 3 model (ASEAN plus China, Japan, and South Korea). It has signed international arms control treaties such as the Nonproliferation Treaty, the Comprehensive Test Ban Treaty, and the Chemical Weapons Convention; it is complying with the Missile Technology Control Regime; and it has published three white papers on national defense to enhance transparency. China also created the Shanghai Cooperation Organization.

In the economic arena, China has participated keenly in APEC activities and agenda setting. During the sixth meeting of East Asian leaders in 2002, Chinese leaders proposed more than 20 initiatives, and signed or released more than 10 agreements or statements in support of regional cooperation (Wang 2003). After 13 years of effort, China finally joined the WTO in December 2001, and it has tried subsequently to fulfill its WTO obligations faithfully. For example, nearly 30 State Council departments have sorted out 2,300 pieces of legislation, repealed more than 830 of them, and revised 230 more. Local governments have also followed suit in compliance with State Council decrees (Zao 2002). The Supreme People's Court has abolished a number of judicial interpretations inconsistent with WTO rules and China's commitments, and it has promulgated new interpretations consistent with WTO rules (Li and Guo 2002).

These encounters with the outside world have benefited China practically, while they have also forged positive interactions for China with the international community. In the process, China has learned international rules, and it has agreed voluntarily to be bound by these rules. Hence it is projecting itself as a responsible power.

Third, China is adapting its strategic vision. Prior to 1978, China believed that war was inevitable, and that the United States and the Soviet Union, the two superpowers in the world, threatened its security. This perception informed a readiness for war. Such a conflict-oriented strategic vision meant that China was preoccupied with confrontation, rather than cooperation, in its dealings with the outside world.

From the late 1970s, however, this conflict-centered philosophy has undergone great change. Deng Xiaoping observed in the late 1970s that it was possible to delay the outbreak of war (Deng 1994, 77); in 1985, he noted that peace and development were the two themes for the world; and, in 1987, he asserted that war was avoidable (Deng 1993, 233). The third generation of Chinese leaders, headed by Jiang Zemin, characterized the current international situation as "peaceful, relaxed, and stable overall, with wars, tensions and turbulence occurring in parts of the world" (Jiang 2002a, 522). Based on this assessment, China now advances a strategy of "cooperation, interdependence, and respect for world diversity" (Xiong 2002b, 4–10). Most typical of this strategy is the new thinking on security. Jiang proposed that the "international community should embrace a new concept of security based on mutual trust, mutual benefit, equality and collaboration and endeavor to create a peaceful international environment of lasting stability, security, and reliability" (Jiang 2001, 48). In short, China has switched to a different strategic paradigm, one that sees the world in cooperative rather than confrontational terms.

China continues to use some older concepts such as "new international political and economic order." However, there are new interpretations to these concepts. In the past, for example, China would "encourage and promote the establishment of a new international order." The report of the Sixteenth Party Congress of the Chinese Communist Party in November 2002 noted that, "We stand for the establishment of a new international political and economic order that is fair and reasonable" (Jiang 2002b). This difference is more than semantic. Wang Yi explains that China proposes a new order "not to do away with or reject the existing order, but to amend and reform it by correcting what is irrational and unjust, so that this order reflects the common interests of the majority of nations and people, thereby contributing to the democratization of international relations. This new order that we advocate is not exclusive; rather, we hope it is open, inclusive, and win-win" (Wang 2003). This suggests that the main thrust of Chinese diplomacy today is not to create a new international order, but to join the existing order.

Of course, the change in China's identity is a step-by-step process. As China changes its orientation, it also needs other countries' understanding and cooperation.

## China's External Environment

For all nations, the international environment is a very fluid variable. The volatile nature of international relations means that the external environment facing all countries is constantly evolving. At the same time, there are structural factors that sustain the relative stability of the international environment for all countries. This section uses East Asia as the context for a discussion of those factors affecting the relative stability of China's international environment.

More than ten years after the end of the cold war, East Asia is exhibiting a compound structure of three competing postures in political and security matters. The three models are multipolarization, hegemonic stability, and multilateral security cooperation. The unique complexity of East Asia allows these competing models to coexist, but prevents any one of them from becoming the predominant model (Ni 2001, 7–16).

Multipolarization balances the various centers of power, and, compared with other regions, East Asia reflects the most intensive and sophisticated development of multipolarization. This is due to the fact that the region has such a concentration of great powers: four of the five recognized centers of power in the world are located in the region. East Asia is also home to a number of medium-sized powers and groups of nations with rising influence, such as ASEAN, North and South Korea, and Vietnam. One could say that the nature of international relations and the stage of development in the region resemble, to some extent, nineteenth-century Europe. Powers in the region, such as China and Russia, advocate multipolarization, while players such as ASEAN and Japan also endorse multipolarization in varying degrees.

Yet multipolarization is handicapped by the fact that it is more of a trend than a well-established fact, all the stakeholders do not agree on a clear objective, and U.S. dominance in the region's affairs remains hard to challenge for the foreseeable future.

The hegemonic stability model works because one power plays a key role, and it also drives the establishing of norms and rule. This model is alive and well in East Asia. The United States is the only superpower in the world, and its military presence in East Asia gives it control over the region's sea routes; most countries accept its role in the region, and they give it unparalleled ally support; and the United States is involved in nearly all important regional matters and plays a key role in those affairs, such as the Korean peninsula issue and the Taiwan issue.

At the same time, this model is hindered by the fact that other powers in the region moderate U.S. dominance; the U.S. role is hampered by its lack of geographic proximity to East Asia; and U.S. military dominance is only partial, as East Asia encompasses vast stretches of continental landmass.

The multilateral security model refers to an institutional arrangement between different countries to maintain order, manage conflicts, and sustain peace. While relatively underdeveloped in East Asia, increased multilateralism is an important hallmark of post–cold war international relations. And, for the following reasons, the region could be ready for creating a multilateral security mechanism. The multilateral security model and globalization are complementary; countries in the region are increasingly interdependent; the end of the cold war has resulted in less adversarial relations between countries, making it possible for them to cooperate on security matters; a number of East Asian countries actively advocate multilateralism; and positive progress has been made in fostering multilateral efforts, most notably in the ASEAN Regional Forum.

At the same time, there are constraints on the development of an East Asian multilateral security mechanism. The diversity and complexity of East Asia mean that multilateralism is not firmly grounded in the region, with regional multilateral security arrangements specifically remaining embryonic; and major regional powers have not taken multilateralism as the centerpiece of their foreign policies. Medium and small-sized countries were the primary catalysts behind the founding of the ASEAN Regional Forum, the principal multilateral security institution in the region, and its role in major security matters is limited.

Of the three outlined models, multipolarization and hegemonic stability are presently more important, while multilateralism has the most future potential. These three models contend with and check each other, but they also complement and embrace each other. Together, they constitute the political and security landscape of East Asia after the cold war. This is the regional setting in which China finds itself.

It is possible, of course, to view China's international environment from different perspectives. Other factors that could threaten China's security could, for example, be divided into four categories. In terms of economic security, issues that could negatively impact China include a downturn in world economic prospects, a possible financial meltdown, and a global energy crisis. Regarding political security, the main issues that could destabilize China include the West's political infiltration of China, ethnic and religious extremism, separatism, and terrorism. There are also concerns related to border security. Issues that could greatly impact China include turmoil in neighboring countries, border conflicts, and nontraditional security issues such as drug trafficking, epidemics, high-seas piracy, and refugee flows. Finally, there are matters related to China's reunification, with the main issue here being Taiwan (Wang 2002, 1).

## CHINA'S STRATEGIC CHOICES

China could be said to have made the following strategic choices:

First of all, China will make great efforts to set up an open, inclusive, win-win, and cooperative framework to realize peace and development. So China will continue developing and improving relations with other big powers, including the European Union, India, Japan, Russia, and the United States. Positive, cooperative, and stable relations with the other big powers are vital for improving China's international environment, and expanding its space in the international community; they would also contribute to creating a peaceful and flourishing world.

China will also continue to be active in multilateral diplomatic activities, and to play a role in the United Nations and other international or regional organizations. For example, China will participate more actively in UN peacekeeping operations than before. Multilateral diplomacy provides important forums in which China can show it is a responsible power and in which it can extend its influence.

In addition, China will try to promote dialogue and exchanges between different civilizations and cultures. Jiang noted in his report to the Sixteenth Party Congress of the Chinese Communist Party: "We stand for maintaining the diversity of the world and are in favor of promoting democracy in international relations ... countries that [have] different civilizations and social systems and [have taken] different roads to development should respect one another and draw upon one another's strong points through competition and comparison and should develop side by side by seeking common ground while shelving differences" (Jiang 2002b).

Second, China will look to neighboring countries for important strategic backing. In terms of politics, China will try to improve further relations with its neighbors. In the realm of security, China will initiate its new security concept, based on mutual trust, mutual benefit, equality, and collaboration. It will resolve border problems with its neighbors according to mutual understanding and accommodation, and deal with territorial disputes with its neighbors according to the principle of shelving controversy and enhancing joint development. It will also strengthen security cooperation with Russia and Central Asian countries within the framework of the Shanghai Cooperation Organization; it will actively participate in the ASEAN Regional Forum, and expand cooperation with ASEAN countries in nontraditional security issues; and it will try to set up dialogue mechanisms between China and both the U.S.-Japan and the U.S.-South Korea alliances. Overall, it will try to mediate crises and controversies around it, avoid intensifying existing contradictions, and strive to resolve these problems peacefully.

In the economic area, China will regard the China-ASEAN Free Trade Area as a turning point, and it will energetically promote economic integration in East Asia within the frameworks of ASEAN + 3 and ASEAN + 1 (its own dialogue with ASEAN). In energy issues, China will variously try to enhance cooperation with Russia and Central Asian countries, while coordinating positions with East Asian countries like Japan and Korea.

Third, China will continue to enhance solidarity and cooperation with other Third World countries, increase mutual understanding and trust, strengthen mutual help and support, broaden cooperation, and improve the efficiency of cooperation. As a developing country, China shares common ground with many other developing countries. Such commonalities include similar human rights situations, and interest in the role of the United Nations and in a new international political and economic order. China also looks to developing countries for important strategic backing.

Fourth, China will continue to push for its reunification. Originally, the Taiwan issue was a Chinese internal affair. Due to some countries becoming involved in it, the issue has now become a sensitive problem in relations between China and these countries. China will continue to implement the basic principles of "peaceful reunification" and "one country, two systems"; strive for direct mail, air, and shipping links at the earliest date; extend political, economic, cultural, and personnel exchanges across the Taiwan Strait; uphold the consensus of "one China" in the international community to block the activities of Taiwan separatist forces; and develop military capabilities indispensable to deterring risk-taking separatists.

## CONCLUSION

States conduct diplomacy based on their self-images and images of the outside world. In the past 20 years, China has undergone a profound transformation in how it views itself and the world. It no longer views itself as a country on the edge of the international community, but as a rising power, with limited but increasingly significant capacity to shape its environment. At the same time, while still considering the outside world as inherently anarchic with power remaining a yardstick in international politics, China today also believes that the world is moving toward a more civilized era, in which the probability of a global war is marginal.

China's growing confidence in its ability to shape its environment and its more positive outlook on the world are reflected in its diplomacy. While some of these changes may be subtle, they nonetheless represent fundamental shifts in the mindsets of its leaders, and are thus likely to influence the country's diplomatic conduct in the coming years.

By means of description and analysis of some fundamental elements of China's present day foreign policy, we can find that China is neither an expansionist state, nor one that wants to destroy the current international order. Like most states in the world, China's behavior focuses on the defense of its national interest. In the meantime, we can find more and more the color of liberalism in its diplomacy. China hopes that a moderate psychology will determine how the international community treats it and gets along with it. China does not seek privilege in the international community, just equal treatment. Equality will engender more mutual respect and trust between China and other countries in the world.

## BIBLIOGRAPHY

China Institute of Contemporary International Relations. 2000a. *Quanqiu zhanlue da geju—xin shiji zhongguo de guoji huanjing* (The global strategic structure—China's international environment in the new century). Beijing: Shishi Chubanshe (Current Affairs Press).

China Institute of Contemporary International Relations. 2000b. *Shijie zhuyao guojia zongheguoli pinggu* (Assessing world big powers' comprehensive national strength). Beijing: Shishi Chubanshe (Current Affairs Press).

Deng Xiaoping. 1993. *Deng Xiaoping wenxuan* (Selected works of Deng Xiaoping). Vol. 3. Beijing: Renmin Chubanshe (People's Press).

———. 1994. *Deng Xiaoping wenxuan* (Selected works of Deng Xiaoping). Vol. 2. Beijing: Renmin Chubanshe (People's Press).

Huang Shuofeng. 1992. *Da jiaoliang: Guoli qiuli lun* (Great game: National power, global power). Changsha: Hunan Chubanshe (Hunan Press).

Jiang Zemin. 2001. *Zai qingzhu zhongguo gongchandang chengli bashizhounian dahui shang de jianghua* (Statement to celebrate the eightieth anniversary of the Chinese Communist Party). Beijing: Renmin Chubanshe (People's Press).

———. 2002a. *Jiang Zemin lun you zhongguo tese de shehuizhuyi* (Jiang Zemin's viewpoints about socialism with Chinese characteristics). Beijing: Zhongyang Wenxian Chubanshe (Central Document Press).

———. 2002b. "Quanmian jianshe xiaokang shehui kaichuang zhongguo tese shehuizhuyi shiye xin jumian—Jiang Zeming zai zhongguo gongchandang shiliu ci daibiao dahui shang de baogao" (Building a well-off society in an all-round way, and creating a new situation of socialism with Chinese characteristics—Jiang Zemin's report to the Sixteenth National Congress of the Communist Party of China). *Renmin Ribao* (The People's Daily) (11 September).

Li Weiwei and Guo Chu. 2002. "Wo guo jiji luxing jiaoru shimao zuzhi youguan falu chengnuo" (Our country is actively carrying out its legal commitments to the WTO). <http://news.xinhuanet.com/newscenter/2002-12/02/conrent-647029.htm> (15 January 2003).

Ministry of Foreign Affairs of the People's Republic of China. 2000. *Zhongguo canjia duobian guoji gongyue yi lan biao* (China's work on multilateral treaties). <http://www.fmprc.gov.cn/chn/premade/24475/daiao.htm> 2 February 2003.

Ni Feng. 2001. "Lun dongya diqu de zhengzhi anquan jiegou" (Political and security structures of East Asia). *Meiguo Yanjiu* (American Studies Quarterly) 3: 7–16.

Wang Jisi. 2002. "Zhongguo guoji huanjing pinggu" (Strategic assessment of China's International Environment). *Xiandai Guoji Guanxi* (Contemporary international relations) 11: 1–25.

Wang Songfeng, ed. 1996. *Shijie zhuyao guojia zonghe guoli bijiao yanjiu* (A comparative study of the world big powers' comprehensive national strength). Changsha: Hunan Chubanshe (Hunan Press).

Wang Yi. 2003. "Zhongguo yu zhoubian guojia waijiao guanxi zongshu-yulinweishan yilinweiban" (Summarizing relations between China and its neighboring countries—good neighborship, good partnership). <http://www.news.sina.com.cn/c/2003-02-21/1129559135.shtml> (26 February 2003).

Xiong Guangkai. 2002a. "Zhongguo changdao de xin anquan guan" (China's new security concept). *Guoji Zhanlue Yanjiu* (International Strategic Studies) 3: 1–4.

——. 2002b. Jiang Zhuxi qiyi zhongyao jianghua dui guoji zhanlue sixiang de xin fazhan (New contributions to President Jiang Zemin's statement on 1 July about China's international strategic thoughts). *Guoji Zhengzhi Yanjiu* (Studies of International Politics) 3: 4–15.

Zao Xiuqin. 2002. "Zhongguo rushi yi zhounian dianping—luxing chengnuo xingshi quanli zouxiang gongying" (An anniversary of China joining the WTO—fulfill promises, exercise rights and advance toward win-win game). <http://news.xinhuanet.com/fortune/2002-12/06/content-651395.htm> (26 February 2003).

# Perspectives from Other Asia Pacific Nations

# 10

# Japan's Political Response to the Rise of China

## Takahara Akio

The rapid rise of China since the beginning of the 1990s has constituted a most dynamic development in East Asia, with far-reaching implications for the region and the world. It is significant not only because of China's formidable size, both in terms of territory and population, but also because its rise has coincided with the end of the cold war and the advent of globalization.[1] China in the early twenty-first century has emerged as a potential superpower and as a frontier of world capitalism.

The timing of China's emergence is also important when considering Japan's political response to China's impressive performance. In the 1990s, Japan seemed to be in flux on many fronts. Domestically, the domination of power by the Liberal Democratic Party (LDP) ended, and Japanese politics entered a period of continuous change. The Japanese economy floundered after the bursting of the "bubble" economy in the early 1990s. It appeared that many Japanese had lost their way and confidence in the face of globalization. In the realm of security, the raison d'être of Japan's alliance with the United States was questioned after the collapse of the Soviet Union, and the alliance seemed adrift in the first half of the 1990s (Funabashi 1997).

The Japanese business world responded positively to China's rise and expanded operations there, as Ohashi Hideo demonstrates and analyzes in this volume. However, the transfer of factories to China and the consequential hollowing out of industry in Japan stirred antipathy among some Japanese toward China. The Japanese emperor enjoyed a successful visit to China in 1992, but thereafter Japan-China relations gradually deteriorated in the mid-1990s. Factors that contributed to this decline included Taiwan's efforts to gain international recognition, such as the abortive attempt to send President Lee Teng-hui to the Hiroshima Asian Games in 1994; heightened emotions over the fiftieth anniversary of the end of the Second World War; Chinese nuclear testing in 1996; and, last but not least, reconfirmation of the Japan-U.S. security alliance in 1996. The basis of the problem, however, was a rise in nationalism in both countries—in China, because the Chinese were gaining self-confidence, and, in Japan, because the Japanese were losing their self-confidence.

Despite this downward spiral in sentiments, there were important developments in the latter half of the 1990s, particularly with regard to China's policy toward its neighbors, including Japan. China desired to become less isolated, with the risks of globalization having been brought home to all with the Asian financial crisis in 1997. China had earlier moved away from its revolutionary policy of "befriending distant states while attacking those nearby" (*yuanjiao jingong*), and, in the late 1990s, had started deepening ties with its neighbors, not only bilaterally, but also in multilateral regional forums. Chinese efforts bore fruit, for example, with the signing in November 2002 of a framework agreement for an economic cooperation pact with the Association for Southeast Asian Nations (ASEAN).

That China has taken up the challenge of free trade agreements and has embarked on promoting East Asian regionalism poses a serious challenge to Japan, which sees itself as the leading economy in East Asia. Japan has, in fact, been calling on China to engage in regional and world affairs since it first adopted reform and opening policies in the late 1970s and even after the June 4 incident in Tiananmen Square in 1989. This policy has remained basically unchanged to this day. Prime Minister Koizumi Jun'ichiro has made clear his appraisal that China's rise is not a threat, but an opportunity and a positive challenge, and he has praised highly Chinese initiatives promoting regional cooperation.

At the same time, China's rise and its deepening involvement in regional economic frameworks urge Japan and other neighboring countries to consider what security arrangements in East Asia should be. In seeking answers itself, China has presented a "new security concept," which includes fostering mutual trust, mutual benefit, equality and cooperation between nations, and peacefully solving conflict through dialogue. China's formation of the Shanghai Cooperation Organization with Russia and four other central Asian states, and its switch to a positive stance toward the ASEAN Regional Forum (ARF) are related to the new security concept.

This chapter analyzes the complex interaction between Japan's bilateral and regional policies and those of China. This task is assumed from the viewpoint of Japan's response to China's rise, while taking into account developments in China's policies toward Japan and the region.

## JAPAN'S POLICY TOWARD CHINA BEFORE CHINA'S RISE

Japan has strongly supported China's reform and opening policies since they were first adopted. Japan's idea has been to help China grow economically, and to assist its integration into the world economic system. The major means to achieving these goals has been providing official development assistance (ODA), technical assistance, and policy advice through the exchange of bureaucrats, technical personnel, academics, and students. Japan has also supported China's admission to international organizations such as the General Agreement on Tariffs and Trade (GATT) and, later, the World Trade Organization (WTO). Although the ODA charter prohibits the Japanese government from assisting countries that produce weapons of mass destruction and export arms, China was regarded as an exception. Japan was also the first country to cancel the economic sanctions it had adopted against China in 1989, in the wake of the Tiananmen incident.

At least four motivations underpinned Japan's desire to assist China's reform and opening. First, Deng Xiaoping's victory in the power struggles following Mao Zedong's death and his new policies constituted epochal change from the days of the Cultural Revolution when China was a source of instability in the region. With reform and opening, China found a vital interest in maintaining a peaceful international environment. Successful reform and opening in China were regarded as critically important to regional peace, stability, and prosperity.

Second, Japan considered that pragmatic forces within China's socialist government could be strengthened if the new economic policies—supported by Japan and other countries—brought tangible benefits to the Chinese people. In terms of aid policies, Japan is unique in its willingness to assist the development of socialist countries.[2] Socialism is not anathema to many Japanese; they understand that socialism in some parts of the Third World and in East Asia is largely a nationalist means.

Third, the Japanese understood the potential of China as a central player in the regional and global economy. Mainland China had, after all, been Japan's major trading partner before the Second World War. Semi-governmental trading arrangements were made even before relations were normalized in 1972. After normalization, Japan initially eyed China as an energy source, especially as an alternative supplier of oil and coal in the wake of the 1972 Organization of the Petroleum Exporting Countries (OPEC) oil crisis. China's economic progress was also considered an important element in the rapidly developing region. When Prime Minister Kaifu Toshiki visited China in 1991, the first leader of the Group of Seven industrialized countries to do so after Tiananmen, he said that, by supporting China's economy, Japan was contributing to regional stability and prosperity as a whole as the Chinese economy was linked to the economy of Asia Pacific (*Nicchu kankei kihon shiryoshu* 1998, 770).

Fourth, Japan realized that an effective way to change China's domestic system and behavior was to co-opt China into the global system. That was an important reason behind Japan's consistently positive position on admitting China into the GATT and the WTO, in contrast to the reluctance of some European and North American countries.

In terms of security issues, Japan and China did not perceive each other as a threat. Despite rhetoric about the imminent revival of militarism in Japan, China actually advised Japan to increase its military spending at times of need. This occurred, for instance, in the late 1970s and the early 1980s when Sino-Russian relations were tense.[3] For Japanese who faced the Soviet threat, China was hardly perceived as having the means or the intent to threaten Japan militarily. This was the case despite China's limited nuclear capabilities and bilateral disagreement over the Senkaku/Diaoyu Islands. The Chinese had started to claim these islands in 1970 after a regional commission of the United Nations, the Economic Commission for Asia and the Far East, announced there could be an oilfield in that area.

## China's Gradual Rise, and Frictions with Japan in the Mid-1990s

The Tiananmen incident changed the image of China in Japanese eyes. An annual Japanese government opinion poll recorded that the percentage of Japanese who felt an affinity for China fell to 51.6 percent in 1989 from 68.5 percent in 1988, while those who did not rose to 43.1 percent in 1989 from 26.4 percent in 1988.[4] The Japanese government joined the other Group of Seven industrialized countries in imposing sanctions on China, but it soon resumed its conciliatory policy. After the 1991 visit to

China by Kaifu, Japan responded positively to China's strong request for a visit in 1992 by the Emperor to commemorate the twentieth anniversary of normalized relations. Prime Minister Hosokawa Morihiro, who led the first coalition government after the LDP lost power in 1993, expressed deep remorse and apologies to those Chinese who suffered from Japan's invasion of China and its colonial rule there in a speech to the Japanese Diet (*Nicchu kankei kihon shiryoshu* 1998, 802). While these deeds and words expressed Japan's willingness to further consolidate Japanese-Chinese relations, the relationship actually deteriorated in the mid-1990s due to several factors.

The first issue was Taiwan. China strongly protested the reported idea of the Olympic Commission of Asia to invite Taiwan's President Lee to the Asian Olympic Games to be held in Hiroshima in October 1994. In the end, Xu Lide, Taiwan's vice premier, went to Hiroshima, in the capacity of chairman of the Committee for Inviting the 2002 Asian Olympic Games, but Beijing still protested vehemently.

Japan had no intention of changing its basic policy concerning Taiwan, as manifest in the 1972 Japan-China Joint Communiqué. Japan fully understood and respected Article 8 of the Potsdam Declaration. This article obliges Japan to implement clauses of the Cairo Declaration, which stated that one of the aims of China's war against Japan was to force Japan to return Taiwan, as well as Manchuria, to the Republic of China, which was the government of China at the time.[5]

However, Taiwan was now a democracy and a full-fledged economy. The Taiwanese desired more global recognition and the preservation of the status quo, while they wanted to avoid forceful reintegration with the mainland. A democratic leader had little choice but to endeavor to achieve the desires of his people. These factors, together with the historical and cultural affinity between Japan and Taiwan personified in Lee, contributed to rising sympathy among the Japanese public for Taiwan's situation.[6]

In China, power transferred from the so-called second generation of leaders to the third generation in September 1994. The Taiwan issue was the major policy area in which Jiang Zemin, who headed the third generation, asserted his leadership by announcing a conciliatory eight-point proposal in February 1995. Lee, however, rebuffed this initiative and, later that year, realized a long-desired visit to the United States.

The reconfirmation of the Japan-U.S. security alliance, which China perceives as closely related to the Taiwan matter, was the largest issue between Japan and China in the 1990s. For Japanese policy makers, what mattered most was the political significance of stabilizing the alliance with the United States. The alliance needed new meaning after the cold war. Japanese feared that economic friction with the United States and problems arising from U.S. bases in Japan, particularly those in Okinawa, could lead to stronger anti-U.S. feelings and questioning of the alliance. Cancelling the alliance would fundamentally change the status quo in Japan and in the region, something with which Japanese and most countries in the region had become rather comfortable. So the Japanese government willingly cooperated with the U.S. government in adjusting the alliance to the new post–cold war situation.

When the Japanese and U.S. governments talked about possible "circumstances surrounding Japan" in the new guidelines for defense cooperation, the main allusion was to war on the Korean peninsula, where a crisis had been overcome in 1994. With regard to China, the April 1996 Japan-U.S. Joint Declaration on Security stated, ". . . it is extremely important for the stability and prosperity of the region that China play a positive and constructive role, and, in this context, . . . the interest of both countries [is] in furthering cooperation with China."[7] Japan and the United States had to be extremely careful, lest China and other members of the region got the wrong message about the reconfirmation of the alliance. As it turned out, the declaration was signed only a month after China launched missiles off the coast of Taiwan and the United States sent two aircraft carriers to the area.

Nevertheless, many Chinese suspected that the reconfirmed Japan-U.S. alliance was an integral part of the new U.S. strategy to dominate the globe, with the North Atlantic Treaty Organization (NATO) expanding in Europe and with Japan playing a larger security role in East Asia. In addition, the Chinese official media linked a visit to Yasukuni Shrine by Japanese Prime Minister Hashimoto Ryutaro to construction of a lighthouse on the Senkaku Islands by right wing activists, seeing these as part of a plot to revitalize militarism in Japan (Funabashi 1997, 455).

The immediate question that worried the Chinese was whether or not the "circumstances surrounding Japan" included the Taiwan Strait. The Japanese government explained rather ambiguously that "circumstances surrounding Japan" was not a geographical concept, but a concept that focused on the nature of the "circumstances." Overall, Japan intended neither to encourage Taiwan's independence, nor to promote unification, but to prevent the use of force in solving the problem. Hostilities across the Strait would be a nightmare for Japan, not only because of geographical vicinity, but because the basis of regional stability and prosperity would be undermined.

In the mid-1990s, Japanese were increasingly concerned about China's future. Concern stemmed partly from friction about China's nuclear testing—over which Japan held back grant aid to China—and partly from strong anti-Japanese, patriotic propaganda around commemorations of the fiftieth anniversary of the end of the Second World War. There was also growing unease in Japan about China's staggering economic growth. Japanese generally welcomed China's economic development and its deepening economic ties with the world, even though China's success stood in stark contrast to the quagmire into which the Japanese economy had fallen. Chinese missile tests, aimed at intimidating Taiwanese on the eve of their presidential election, took place just next to Yonakuni Island, the western tip of Japanese territory. These missile tests, together with the nuclear tests, enhanced the image of a militaristic China in Japanese minds. The percentage of those Japanese who felt an affinity for China in the annual Japanese government survey declined to 45 percent in 1996, its lowest ever, while those who did not feel any rose to 51.3 percent, its highest ever.[8]

There was also a surge of nationalistic sentiment among the Chinese public, which was apparently supported by China's economic success and by a campaign on patriotism. Whatever the intent of the patriotic campaign, it imprinted a very negative image of Japan and the Japanese in the minds of Chinese, including children.[9] It seemed symbolic that an anti-U.S. and anti-Japanese book, *The China That Can Say No*, became a bestseller in 1996.[10] A vicious circle of friction and distrust seemed to characterize bilateral relations between Japan and China in the mid-1990s.

## JAPAN'S RESPONSE TO CHINA'S NEW ROLE IN THE REGION

The latter half of the 1990s saw an important strengthening of cooperation among East Asian nations. A new, constructive aspect also emerged in Japan-China relations. The catalyst for this development was the Asian financial crisis that erupted in July 1997. China, which narrowly avoided direct damage from the crisis, modified its traditional reluctance to participate in regional multilateral forums, and started acting as a strong promoter of regional cooperation and integration. For some Japanese, this was a challenge to Japan's leading role in the region.

Regionalism or regional approaches are not traditional jargon in China's diplomatic vocabulary. China typically sees international politics as a basic power game, with great powers competing for hegemony. Jiang has noted (2001, 28 and 182) that the competition for comprehensive state power includes the economy, the military, science and technology, and national integrity. So diplomacy is a struggle for survival and development. It is true that China treasures and makes good use of its status as a permanent member of the United Nations Security Council, and that Third World diplomacy has been an integral part of Chinese diplomacy. Nevertheless, China has attached greatest importance to its bilateral relationships.

China realizes that it lags behind the United States, Europe, Japan, and Russia in terms of economic, military, and scientific and technological strength. It considers itself to be a regional "developing power" in transition to becoming a global power (*Some Strategic Questions* 2000, 186). China's cautiousness about multilateralism stems partly from this complex self-perception. On the one hand, China prefers bilateral approaches since it has the upper hand over most of the states in the region, and it fears that once it is co-opted into a multilateral framework, it will lose this advantage. This type of concern is reflected in its hesitance toward the ARF. On the other hand, China does not want the initiative and leadership in multilateral frameworks to be assumed by powers stronger than itself. This seems to have been a concern behind China's cold shoulder to Japan's proposal for an Asian Monetary Fund in September 1997.

Yet several factors appear to have altered China's position and galvanized it into taking positive steps in multilateral regional frameworks in the late 1990s. First, the turnabout stemmed from understanding that globalization was the new trend in world history.[11] China regards globalization as a historic opportunity for economic growth and for developing its domestic industries, while regionalism is seen as being able to neutralize some of globalization's negative impact. This understanding is related to the adoption of the concept of economic security, which took place amidst the Asian financial crisis.

The chain of currency and financial crises in Southeast Asian countries and South Korea from July 1997 alarmed Chinese leaders, partly because of China's own serious problem with nonperforming loans.[12] Chinese analysts perceive the crisis as having contributed to a strengthened East Asian identity, as East Asian states realized that their fates were interwoven and interdependent.[13] The Chinese reaction was probably typical.

The experience of the Asian financial crisis simultaneously strengthened China's self-confidence. In the face of large Asian currency depreciations, China resolutely refrained from devaluing its currency, the yuan. At the same time, the Chinese media sharply criticized Japan for exacerbating the crisis by allowing the yen to fall. For various reasons, Asian countries were grateful to China for not devaluing the yuan.[14] That China managed to hold the Asian financial crisis at bay, coupled with its staggering economic growth since 1992, understandably boosted China's confidence, including in regional multilateral frameworks.

China's increased comfort in multilateral settings was important in advancing Chinese thinking about its dilemma of needing a peaceful international environment to pursue economic development, while simultaneously not raising a sense of a "China threat" among its neighbors. Threat perceptions about China stem from its enormous territory and population, the long history of Chinese regional dominance, and China's pursuit of power politics and its military build-up. The Chinese realized, however, that ways of dispelling neighbors' worries include promoting regionalism, contributing to the regional economy by further opening China's own economy, and providing more opportunities for others to benefit from its substantial economic growth (Hu 2000, 53).

More specifically, in November 2000, China surprised the region by proposing a free trade agreement with ASEAN. Perhaps this was stimulated by Japan's switch to a positive attitude toward bilateral free trade agreements in the late 1990s.[15] Regardless, three years later, there has been significant progress, with China and ASEAN signing a framework agreement for an economic cooperation pact. In addition, China has agreed to upgrade trilateral summits with Japan and South Korea from breakfast meetings to political dialogue, and it simultaneously proposed jointly studying a free trade treaty covering the three countries.

The shift in China's regional policy has resulted in a new approach to bilateral relations with Japan. The dominant view appears to be that joining hands with Japan is essential if China wishes for effective regional cooperation. It is true that during Jiang's visit to Tokyo in November 1998, he sharply and repeatedly reminded Japanese of their wartime deeds and the need to contain militarism. Many Japanese regarded this as unnecessary, impolite, and irritating, and felt that Japan had apologized to China on many occasions, including during the emperor's visit to Beijing in 1992. Even when the word "apology" was not uttered, the spirit had been unequivocal and had appeared to have been accepted by China's leadership at the time.[16] Also, Prime Minister Obuchi Keizo was under pressure from within the LDP not to give in to Chinese pressure that time. Despite the bickering over historical issues, the Jiang visit to Tokyo also saw a Sino-Japanese agreement on "Strengthening Cooperation toward the Twenty-first Century." This was a key agreement as it specified cooperating on international issues such as the Korean peninsula, multilateral trade, and the East Asian economy.

In the wake of the Jiang visit, Chinese policymakers adjusted their tactics in their policy toward Japan. The Obuchi visit to China in July 1999 went smoothly, with China not raising historical issues. China also chose Japan to be the first country with which it concluded bilateral negotiations for China's entry to the WTO. In May 2000, Jiang personally entertained 5,000 members of the Japan-China Tourism Exchange Mission, and spoke about developing Sino-Japanese relations in the twenty-first century. Subsequently, when historical issues have emerged, such as a textbook being drafted by some chauvinists or a visit to Yasukuni Shrine by Prime Minister Koizumi, China has responded strongly but not as aggressively as in the past.

That China was now seeing relations with Japan in the regional context became clearer when Jiang told Prime Minister Mori Yoshiro at the United Nations Millenium Summit in September 2000 that the rise of Asia was only possible with friendship and cooperation between Japan and China, and that the two countries must take a long and broad view of bilateral relations. When Prime Minister Zhu Rongji visited Japan the following month, he raised regional economic cooperation as one of the three target areas for joint cooperation, and stressed that he looked forward to strengthened coordination with Japan within the framework of cooperation in East Asia.[17]

This was precisely what Japan had been advocating. For instance, in 1997, Hashimoto had suggested that Japan and China should not only discuss bilateral issues but also regional and global issues, and that they should be tackled jointly and constructively (*Nicchu kankei kihon shiryoshu* 1998, 851-60). More recently, Koizumi has highly praised China for its active role in regional cooperation (Koizumi 2002b). In April 2002, Koizumi attended the first meeting of the Boao Asia Forum, an Asian version of the World Economic Forum in Davos, and stated that the strategic task for all was to combine individual efforts into broader, regional economic integration (Koizumi 2002a).

Yet many Japanese are annoyed that China, not Japan, is leading regional efforts in integration. Although Japan first changed its traditional trade policy of not seeking free trade arrangements and concluded a bilateral agreement with Singapore in January 2002, it is being left behind in promoting a regional framework. Japan did sign a framework agreement for a comprehensive economic partnership with ASEAN late in 2003, one year after China did so, but its content is less bold in terms of the prospects of achieving free trade.

A major reason for Japan falling behind lies in the structure of its domestic politics. There is a powerful lobby that effectively protects farmers' interests by arguing against liberalized trade in agricultural products. In 2001, quite ignorant of China's talks with ASEAN about a free trade area, Japan introduced tentative safeguard measures on three agricultural items, against which China retaliated by raising tariffs on Japanese cars and mobile phones. For Japan, the Japan-Singapore Economic Agreement was easily agreed to as Singapore hardly has an agricultural sector.[18] Opposition from Japan's agricultural sector was one of the concerns when Koizumi turned down Zhu's proposal for a joint study of free trade between China, Japan, and South Korea, saying that China had just joined the WTO and that the time was not ripe.

Another factor in Japan's hesitation, however, is that it is still uncertain about its future relationship with China. The Japanese Ministry of Foreign Affairs explains that, while possible free trade with China is in sight, the decision will only be made after taking into account factors such as China's implementation of its WTO commitments; overall relations between Japan and China, including the situation with the Chinese economy; and the results of free trade negotiations with ASEAN and South Korea.[19] But uncertainty about future relations stems largely from concerns about the security environment in East Asia.

## JAPAN'S RESPONSE TO CHINA'S NEW SECURITY CONCEPT

China's positive shift on regionalism and on its approach toward its neighbors was accompanied by a so-called new concept of security, which gradually took shape between 1996 and 1999 (Asano 2003). The new concept was reflected in two joint declarations of China and Russia, issued in April 1996 and April 1997, when Russian President Boris Yeltsin and Jiang visited each other's capital city. Subsequently, Jiang stated repeatedly that, unlike the old concept based on military alliances and the solution of conflict by military means, the core of the new security concept was mutual trust, mutual benefit, equality, and cooperation. The Asian financial crisis then added other dimensions to the concept, namely, those of comprehensive security and economic security. The new security concept provided the basis for promoting multilateral dialogue in traditional and nontraditional security in forums such as the Shanghai Cooperation Organization with Central Asian neighbors, and the ARF and ASEAN + 3 (ASEAN with China, Japan, and South Korea) in East Asia.

One factor that pushed China to promote cooperative security was the fear of being isolated in the region. This was something that China could not afford, particularly as Japan and the United States had adjusted and reinforced their alliance. China's military build-up and flexing of muscles, however, met with protests and suspicion from its neighbors. In March 1995, one month after the Philippines announced China's occupation of Mischief Reef in the South China Sea, ASEAN foreign ministers jointly urged the concerned countries to halt any action that threatened regional peace and security. In the first half of the 1990s, in fact, some ASEAN countries had welcomed an enhanced U.S. military presence in the region (Cheung 2001, 438).

Relations with the United States constituted another factor in China's policy shift. While China steadily built its military capabilities with a central focus on possible hostilities with Taiwan, it did not want confrontation with the United States. Knowing that there is a huge gap in the comprehensive state power of the two nations, China's policy toward the United States is conciliatory. Jiang maintained that the principles of China-U.S. relations should be increasing trust, decreasing trouble, developing cooperation, and no confrontation. Along with rising public confidence and nationalism in the mid-1990s, Jiang sought an equal partnership with the United States to enhance his prestige and power at home. Jiang's efforts were rewarded with a state visit to the United States in 1997, and a reciprocal visit by President Bill Clinton to China the following year.

However, a series of events in the first half of 1999 shattered China's hopes for establishing a strategic partnership with the United States. In April, NATO's new strategic concept allowed it to protect humanitarian values in out-of-area operations, on which grounds it bombed Yugoslavia. Chinese leaders severely criticized this since they are accused of "human rights violations" in Tibet and Xinjiang, and are confronting a democratized Taiwan. In April, Premier Zhu visited Washington, D.C., but failed to conclude tough negotiations with the United States for China's admission to the WTO, and was severely criticized for this at home. That

May, the Chinese embassy in Belgrade was bombed. Thereafter, Chinese leaders had no illusions about the unstable nature of relations with the United States.

Anticipating mounting pressure from the United States as it develops, China's conciliatory policies toward its neighbors and its pursuit of regional integration are also attempts to secure some room for maneuver. The view that regional cooperation should be extended to security matters is increasingly strong in China. According to Zhang Yunling, an influential academic on China's regional policy, a defense ministers' meeting and an East Asian security cooperation council are objectives that Chinese authorities envisage for ASEAN + 3 (Cheung 2001). Zhu (2001) stated at the ASEAN + 3 summit in November 2001 that efforts should be made to carry out dialogue and cooperation in the political and security fields, consistent with the principles of consensus and incremental progress.

Japanese are undecided on desirable security arrangements in the region. Japan faces an enigmatic North Korea, and many Japanese are increasingly worried about a stronger China. Some perceive Japan's reconfirmed alliance with the United States as essential to maintaining the regional power balance. An increasing number of Chinese, including military personnel, are also taking it for granted that, sooner or later, Japan will become a "normal" country, and will assume a more active role in its own defense. Meanwhile, both Japan and China agree that exchanges between security personnel should be promoted to increase confidence and transparency. During Zhu's 2000 visit to Japan, for instance, China consented to the friendly exchange of naval vessels, something that Japan had been proposing for some time.

Simultaneously, an increasing number of Japanese believe that Japan should promote the formulation of a multilateral security framework in East Asia. Such people include scholars[20] and politicians, of whom one is General Nakatani Gen, a former director of the Japan Defense Agency. Nakatani (2002) maintains that an unstable security environment in Asia negatively affects economic cooperation and integration, and that Japan should initiate a new security framework in Asia Pacific that would include Southeast Asia, China, the two Koreas, Russia, and the United States. During an official visit to South Korea in April 2002, Nakatani proposed, as a first step, joint research on a regional framework for cooperative security. He was to do the same in a visit to China later that month, but that visit was postponed after Koizumi visited Yasukuni Shrine on April 21. Nakatani subsequently lost his post in a cabinet reshuffle. The development of such thinking has, however, been helped by China's conciliatory approach toward regional security issues and bilateral historical issues.

## CONCLUSION

Since China's changed posture on regional cooperation, Japan and China's bilateral and regional policies have become quite similar. Both now promote regional integration and establishing an East Asian Community, although China envisages such a community to be based on ASEAN + 3 while Japan wishes it to include Australia and New Zealand. Both countries also agree now about adopting a multilateral approach to the nuclear crisis on the Korean peninsula, and about preventing friction over historical issues from negatively influencing other aspects of bilateral relations. In China, debate has even been allowed on whether historical issues should no longer be a diplomatic issue in China's policy toward Japan (*Tokyo Shimbun* 12 August 2003).

A major difference exists, however, in the desired pace of change. China appears ready for a free trade area in East Asia, and has been trying to persuade Japan to consider it. Meanwhile, Japan, which began proposing Japan-China cooperation for the sake of regional and global peace and prosperity, remains essentially undecided about its political response to the overtures from a rising China. There are multiple reasons for Japan's hesitance.

First, when the focus of regional cooperation is free trade, powerful vested interests in Japan's protected sectors constitute a major stumbling block in the policy process. This is not the case in China, where farmers' interests are hardly represented in the policymaking process.

Second, it cannot be denied that mounting public ill feeling toward China has hampered the Japanese government in taking bold steps. In addition to China's missile and nuclear tests, and increased crime in Japan by some Chinese, there seems to be a basic psychological problem that needs to be solved. Japanese feel superior to Chinese in terms of economic and social development, while they feel inferior vis-à-vis China's culture and civilization, and its status and role in international politics. The opposite is true for Chinese. They feel superior to the Japanese in terms of tradition, civilization, and influence in international politics, but they feel inferior about their level of economic and social development. Both sides become concerned when they perceive that their superiority is being undermined, or that the superiority of the other side is being enhanced. It is vitally important that both governments coordinate efforts to contain the rise of chauvinism in their countries. In both cases, xenophobia may increase among the public if growth rates decline, causing further unemployment.

Third, Japan's hesitation about its relationship with China reflects a lack of strategic vision about the region's future order. This is not unrelated to the mindset of many Japanese policymakers, who seem to believe that their task is to come up with policies that are immediately acceptable to the United States. True, the United States cannot be ignored in envisaging the future order of East Asia. But what Japanese need to do first is identify their long-term objectives, and then, as a matter of course, the means to achieve them, which may well include persuading the United States and China of their merit.

## Notes

1. Globalization is taken to mean the free and active circulation of goods, money, people, services, and information beyond national boundaries through the development of communications technology. Globalization is seen as qualitatively different to internationalization in that a global system is formed for the circulation of these commodities.
2. For instance, the United States does not give ODA to socialist countries, and, to this day, has never provided bilateral assistance to China.
3. Wu Xiuquan, who headed the General Staff Department of the People's Liberation Army, said that Japan's defense expenditure should be increased from 1 percent to 2 percent of gross national product.
4. The results are available at <http://www8.cao.go.jp/survey/gaikou_01/images/zu28.gif> and <http://www8.cao.go.jp/survey/gaikou_01/images/zu29.gif>.
5. See Takahara (2000) for details of Japan's position on Taiwan's status.
6. Lee expressed this position in an interview with Japanese writer Shiba Ryotaro in *Weekly Asahi*, an interview that became notorious among mainland Chinese.
7. The Joint Declaration is available at <http://www.jda.go.jp/e/policy/f_work/sengen_.htm>.
8. See note 4.

9. Chinese youth often reveal that the Japanese they meet are actually much "nicer" than the image they had of Japanese from China's media. They may be mistaken, of course, but the point about education still holds.
10. The book was promptly translated into Japanese and published in Japan. See Song et al. (1996).
11. The rest of this paragraph relies on *Huangqiu Shibao*, a report from a group discussion of scholars issued in September 2000, and *Some Strategic Questions* (2000, 184–185).
12. A reliable source regards the percentage of nonperforming loans of China's four major state-owned commercial banks as having been 24.4 percent at the end of 1996, rising to 29.2 percent at the end of June 1997. The same source suggested that the figure was 7.9 percent in Thailand and 17 percent in Indonesia. Also see Li (1998, 31–32).
13. For example, see Hu (2000, 51), Sun (2001, 25), and Zhao (2001, 32). Another common argument was that East Asian countries realized that, in such a crisis, the United States was unhelpful and that the Asia-Pacific Economic Cooperation (APEC) forum was useless.
14. Considering its frail financial situation at the time, Chinese authorities feared that even a hint of devaluation could trigger a collapse in people's confidence in the yuan and in the Chinese economy. They sold this policy very skilfully by declaring that China would sacrifice its own interest and not devalue the yuan in order to support troubled Southeast Asian economies. For details of China's response to the Asian financial crisis, see Takahara (1999, 53–79).
15. See Feng (2001, 22), and Otsuji and Shiraishi (2002, 75).
16. Otherwise it would not have been possible to normalize relations in 1972, and sign the Peace and Friendship Treaty in 1978. For instance, the 1972 Japan-China Joint Communiqué reads, "The Japanese side realizes keenly its responsibility as to the serious damage it inflicted on the Chinese people through the war, and feels deep remorse" (*Nicchu kankei kihon shiryoshu* 1998, 428).
17. The remarks by Jiang and Zhu can be read at <http://www.china-embassy.or.jp> (5 May 2002).
18. The minister for agriculture and fishery remarked then that Japan had to be cautious and prudent in considering similar agreements with other countries with which Japan had agricultural issues.
19. See "Japan's FTA Strategy" at <http://www.mofa.go.jp/mofaj/gaiko/fta/senryaku/05.html> (10 March 2003).

20. For instance, see Asahi Shimbun (2000); Takahara, Fujiwara, and Lee (2003); and Tanaka et al. (2002).

## Bibliography

Asahi Shimbun. 2000. *Asia Network Report 2000.* Tokyo: Asahi Shimbun.

Asano Ryo. 2003. "The Inherent Logic in China's Security Policy and Its Changes." *International Affairs,* no. 514 (January): 18–23.

Cheung J. Y. S. 2001. "Sino-ASEAN Relations in the Early Twenty-first Century." *Contemporary Southeast Asia* 23(3).

Feng Zhaokui. 2001. "Strategic thinking on Sino-Japanese relations."*Fuyin Baokan Ziliao* (Chinese Diplomacy) 3.

Funabashi Yoichi. 1997. *Domei hyoryu* (The drifting of an alliance). Tokyo: Iwanami Shoten.

Hu Shaocong. 2000. "The Progress and Prospects of Cooperation in East Asia." *Studies in International Affairs 5.*

Jiang Zemin. 2001. *On the "Three Represents."* Beijing: Central Documents Publishers.

Koizumi Jun'ichiro. 2002a. "Ajia no shinseiki: Chosen to kikai" (Asia's new century: Challenges and opportunities). Speech at the Boao Asia Forum. 12 April. <http://www.kantei.go.jp/jp/koizumispeech/2002/04/12boao.html> (15 April 2002).

———. 2002b. *Japan and ASEAN in East Asia—A Sincere and Open Partnership.* Speech in Singapore, 14 January. <http://www.kantei.go.jp/foreign/koizumispeech/2002/01/14speech/e.html> (15 April 2002).

Li Xinxin. 1998. "Viewing the Hidden Financial Peril of Our Country from the Viewpoint of the East Asian Financial Crisis." *Reform 3.*

Nakatani Gen. 2002. "The Defense Policy of Japan." Lecture Series No. 448. Tokyo: Naigai Josei Chosakai.

*Nicchu kankei kihon shiryoshu, 1949–1997* (Basic materials on Japan-China relations, 1949–1997). 1998. Tokyo: Kazankai Foundation.

Otsuji Yoshihiro and Shiraishi Takashi. 2002. "We Advocate an Enlarged FTA between Japan and ASEAN." *Chuo Koron* (February).

*Some Strategic Questions for China Facing the 21st Century.* 2000. Beijing: Chinese Communist Party Central Party School Press.

Song Qiang, et al. 1996. *No to ieru Chugoku* (The China that can say no). Tokyo: Nihon Keizai Shimbunsha.

Sun Cheng. 2001. "Relations between Powers and Cooperation in East Asia." *Studies in International Affairs* 4.

Takahara Akio. 1999. "The Political Economy of the Asian Financial Crisis: The Case of China." *Asian Studies* 45(2): 53–79.

———. 2000. "The Present and Future of Japan-China Relations." *Gaiko Forum English Edition* (summer).

Takahara Akio, Fujiwara Kiichi, and Lee Jongwon. 2003. "The Vision for Peace in East Asia." In Kaneko M., Fujiwara K., and Yamaguchi J., eds. *Our Future is with East Asia!* Tokyo: Iwanami Shoten.

Tanaka Akihiko et al. 2002. "The Twenty-second Policy Recommendations on Building a System of Security and Cooperation in East Asia." <http://www.jfir.or.jp/e/pr_e/e-jf-pr-22/pr22-top.html> (17 August 2003).

Zhao Jianglin. 2001. "Construct a Free Trade Area in East Asia." *World Affairs* 8.

Zhu Rongji. 2001. "Strengthening East Asian Cooperation and Promoting Common Development." Statement at the Fifth ASEAN Plus Three Summit. 5 November. <http://www.fmprc.gov.cn/eng/21861.html> (6 May 2002).

# 11

# The Impact of China's Rise on Sino-Japanese Economic Relations

## OHASHI HIDEO

The rise of China affects Japan's economy and Sino-Japanese economic relations considerably. Bilateral trade between the two countries is growing very fast, with China's rapid economic growth providing a number of opportunities for Japan, which has struggled with prolonged recession. In fact, many Japanese companies now rely on China's huge, growing market for their economic well-being. At the same time, there is unease in Japan, as some attribute Japan's economic difficulties to China's rise. Those who express this view suggest that increased Chinese imports have damaged Japan's domestic industries, that massive Japanese investment in manufacturing in China has led to rising unemployment and the hollowing out of industries in Japan, and that China is exporting deflation to Japan.

The focus of this chapter is the wide-ranging impact of China's economic emergence on Japan's economy and on Sino-Japanese economic relations. The chapter considers the influence of growing Chinese imports and expanding Chinese exports on the Japanese economy, and whether or not there is a causal relationship between China's rise and Japan's slump. It examines how China's rise has changed the nature of East Asia's economy, and how China's accession to the World Trade Organization (WTO) has affected Sino-Japanese economic relations. Finally, it looks at how China's rise has affected Japan's foreign economic policy.

## Deepening Economic Interdependence

### Increasing Imports from China

Japan's imports from China are growing very rapidly. In 2002, when Japan's overall imports dropped minus 0.6 percent from the previous year because of its sluggish economy, imports from China recorded 9.9 percent growth.[1] That year, China also became Japan's largest import partner.[2] Japan's imports from China exceeded those from the Association of Southeast Asian Nations (ASEAN) four countries of Indonesia, Malaysia, the Philippines, and Thailand in 1991; the newly industrializing economies (NIEs) of Hong Kong, Singapore, South Korea, and Taiwan in 1997; the European Union in 2000; and the United States in 2002. Japan's imports from China accounted for 18.3 percent of its total imports in 2002. Among China's major trading partners, such as members of the Organisation for Economic Co-operation and Development (OECD) and East Asian countries, with the exception of Hong Kong, Japan is most dependent on its imports from China.

Most of Japan's imports from China are manufactured goods. The ratio of manufactured goods to Japan's total imports from China rose to 84 percent from 58.1 percent during 1991–2001. The percentage of textiles and clothing remained relatively unchanged at 29.7 percent in 1991 and 29.1 percent in 2001, while the ratio of machinery rose considerably to 28.5 percent from 5.8 percent in the same period. In 2001, import items recording the highest growth rates over the previous year were mostly information technology (IT) products. These included telephone and facsimile machines (HS 8517),[3] that grew 98.2 percent; telecommunications equipment and television parts and accessories (HS 8529), that grew 81.4 percent; computers (HS 8471), 67.1 percent; game machines (HS 9504), 53.4 percent; televisions (HS 8528), 51.3 percent; and photocopy machines (HS 9009), 49.9 percent.

Textiles and clothing, footwear, and travel goods were the main imports from China in the 1990s. Among these labor-intensive products, suits for women recorded the highest import growth in 2001, yet this was only 5.8 percent. The import penetration rate[4] of clothing[5] rose to 87.7 percent from 51.8 percent during 1991–2001. In Japan's import clothing market, Chinese products increased their share to 87.3 percent from 53.8 percent in the same period. This is remarkable, since Japan's clothing market is mature, and it is very difficult for imported products to increase their market share. Chinese telephones, facsimile machines, and computers accounted for a mere 12 percent of Japanese imports of these products in 2001. There is much room for such Chinese-made products to expand their market share in Japan. In the near future, Chinese products are expected to dominate Japan's IT markets.

Increasing imports of manufactured goods from China suggest that Sino-Japanese trade is now specializing horizontally, across a wide range of industries, rather than vertically. At the same time, intra-industry trade between the two countries is on the rise. The high intra-industry trade index[6] of Japan's major imports from China—such as air-conditioners, refrigerators, and pumps (HS 841), and calculators, personal computers, and parts (HS 847)—means that imports and exports are almost evenly balanced.

Increased intra-industry trade is also reflected in China's high ratio of processing trade to total trade. According to Chinese customs statistics for 2002, the respective ratios are 55.3 percent for China's total exports and 47.6 percent for its total imports.[7] These ratios are higher for Sino-Japanese trade for 2002, with 58.2 percent in exports and 56.2 percent in imports. Most foreign-invested enterprises (FIEs) are engaged in processing trade in China. FIEs accounted for 51.7 percent of China's total exports and 54 percent of its total imports in 2002. These figures are much higher for Sino-Japanese trade in 2002, with 61.8 percent in exports and 66.9 percent in imports. Nearly two-thirds of Sino-Japanese trade is apparently in the form of intra-industry and intra-firm trade.

## Expanding Exports to China

In 2002, Japan's exports to China expanded substantially and recorded 32.3 percent growth over the previous year, mainly because of China's trade liberalization due to its WTO accession and its "positive fiscal policy" to stimulate domestic demand. In the 1980s, Japan was a major supplier of final goods, such as electronics appliances and automobiles, to China. In the 1990s, a number of Japanese manufacturers started production in China. As intra-industry trade has expanded between the two countries, Japan's exports of intermediate input goods to China are increasing steadily.

This change can also be seen in China's domestic consumer market. In the 1980s, for example, Japanese manufacturers of color televisions exported their final products to China, and they predominated in the local market. Most Japanese manufacturers had embarked on local production of color televisions in China by the early 1990s, when the Japanese subsidiary companies in China such as Shanghai Sony, Dalian Toshiba, Shangdong Matsushita (Panasonic), Shenzhen Huaqiang Sanyo, Nanjing Sharp, and Fujian Hitachi dominated the Chinese market.[8] Since 2001, however, China's color television market has been shared with major Chinese manufacturers, such as Changhong, TCL, Konka, Haixin, RGB, and Haier. Foreign subsidiary companies now try to supply differentiated products such as large flat monitor televisions. Foreign companies also supply some key components and parts of color televisions. China's top manufacturer of cathode-ray tubes (CRTs) is Caihong, a state-owned enterprise with technology-sharing relationships with Japanese manufacturers such as Hitachi, Toshiba, and Asahi Glass. Other major CRT manufacturers are all foreign companies, including Shenzhen Samsung; Beijing Matsushita; Shanghai Yongxin, a Hong Kong affiliate company using Toshiba technology; Philips (Huafei); Hitachi (Saige); and LG (Lejin).

Most Chinese manufacturers have not acquired a core technology. They seemingly have little interest in developing core technologies themselves; rather, they pay close attention to product design.[9] Chinese manufacturers and consumers generally favor low prices, so every effort is made to reduce the price of components and parts by making suppliers compete against each another. In sales promotions, after-sales and repair services for consumers are regarded as important. So foreign suppliers of components and parts have great business opportunities in China.

Japan has been a main supplier of capital and intermediate goods to East Asian manufacturers. As intra-industry trade increases between Japan and China, Japanese exports of intermediate input goods to China are also growing steadily. Asian input-output (I-O) tables compiled by the Institute of Developing Economies (IDE) and the Japan External Trade Organization (JETRO)suggest that China uses more domestically sourced intermediate goods than other East Asian countries because of its comprehensive industrial structure. An I-O table shows that 95.4 percent of intermediate input goods were domestically sourced in China in 1995 (see table 1). The machinery and transport equipment industries were, however, more dependent on imported intermediate input goods. Their domestic dependence ratios were somewhat lower, at 91.1 and 91.6 percent, respectively. In other words, their foreign dependence ratios were about 9 percent. Of this 9 percent, 5 percent reflects dependence on Japan.

With more than half of the imported intermediate input goods in these industries being made in Japan, the supply role of Japanese manufacturers can be said to be key.

### Table 1. China's Dependence on Domestic Intermediate Input Goods, 1995

|  | Whole Industry | Machinery | Transport Equipment |
|---|---|---|---|
| China | 95.4 | 91.1 | 91.6 |
| Japan | 1.8 | 5.1 | 4.8 |
| United States | 1.0 | 1.4 | 1.5 |
| Korea | 0.7 | 1.1 | 0.9 |
| Taiwan | 0.3 | 0.6 | 0.6 |
| Indonesia | 0.3 | 0.1 | 0.1 |
| Malaysia | 0.2 | 0.2 | 0.2 |
| Singapore | 0.2 | 0.3 | 0.2 |
| Thailand | 0.1 | 0.1 | 0.1 |
| Philippines | 0.0 | 0.0 | 0.0 |
| Total | 100.0 | 100.0 | 100.0 |

Source: Okamoto (2001, 14–15).

Again using the machinery and transport equipment industries as an example, for every 100 units produced by China's machinery industry in 1995, 82.2 of the units were Chinese intermediate input goods, and eight units were Japanese components and parts. Similarly, for every 100 units produced in China's transport equipment industry in 1995, 83.9 of the units were Chinese-made intermediate input goods, and 7.5 units were made in Japan (see table 2).

### Table 2. China's Dependence on Japanese Intermediate Input Goods, 1995

| Machinery (100) | | Transport Equipment (100) | |
|---|---|---|---|
| China (82.2) | Japan (8) | China (83.9) | Japan (7.5) |
| Machinery (36.3) | Machinery (5.8) | Transport | Machinery (2.9) |
| Metal (30.2) | Metal (2.2) | Equipment (26.0) | Metal (2.4) |
| Chemical (8.3) | | Metal (23.6) | Transport |
| Textile (7.4) | | Textile (8.1) | Equipment (2.2) |
| | | Chemical (6.7) | |

Source: Okamoto (2001, 15).

Since compiling an I-O table requires considerable time and effort, there is usually a time lag of several years.[10] Even the latest I-O tables cannot reflect current industrial structures. Considering the large-scale nature of Japanese manufacturers' investments in China after 1995, one could say though that China's dependence ratio on Japanese industries has, in all likelihood, only increased further.

As the local subsidiaries of Japanese companies grow in China, the role of exports is also changing. Exporting is no longer the only profitable business for many of these companies. According to financial statements of some leading Japanese companies, local sales by their Chinese subsidiaries are even larger than their exports to China. For an increasing number of Japanese companies, China is their main profit source (*Nihon Keizai Shimbun* 15 January 2003). For example, the profits of the China subsidiary of Komatsu, a construction equipment giant, increased 63 percent in the 2002–2003 financial year. The profit attributable to activities in China reportedly equaled nearly 40 percent of total profit for the whole company. For Fanuc, a top manufacturer of computer numerical control (CNC) machine tools, the profit from its Chinese subsidiary accounted for 30 percent of the profit increment for the 2001–2002 financial year. China business is contributing significantly to the performance of Japanese companies facing a sluggish domestic economy.

## JAPAN'S EXTERNAL AND INTERNAL ECONOMIC CONDITIONS

### The Fall of the Flying Geese?

The rise of China has changed the pattern of economic development in East Asia. Economic development in East Asia has often been explained as a "catch-up" process, with changes in comparative advantage among countries in the region reflecting shifts as less developed countries catch up with more developed countries in certain industries. This is also called the "flying geese" pattern of development. The rise of China has brought about a new pattern of economic development in East Asia. This new pattern is quite different to the previous pattern in which Japanese industries took the lead and to which Japanese have become accustomed.

First, the foreign investment-trade nexus has changed the development pattern. Foreign direct investment (FDI) has contributed greatly to East Asia's rapid economic development since the mid-1980s when Japan and the NIEs began investing massively in the region to cope with their highly appreciated currencies. There is also a virtuous cycle between FDI and foreign trade. Excellent economic performance in East Asia achieved through export-oriented industrialization has attracted sizable FDI from abroad. FDI increases foreign trade, which eventually accelerates economic growth in the region. This FDI-trade nexus realized the rise of China in the late 1990s.

As the traditional Ricardo and Hechscher-Ohlin foreign trade models suggest, differences in production technology or factor endowment create the international exchange of tradable goods, and FDI is a transfer of a cluster of managerial resources beyond international borders. Yet an FDI-trade nexus is not assumed in traditional foreign trade theories. FDI is fundamentally altering production technology and factor endowment in China, with new technology or production factors easily being transferred from Japan to China in the form of FDI. There seems to be little time lag now between the first goose (Japan) and the last goose (China) developing and mass-producing a new product. For example, a new-generation television with plasma or liquid-crystal display panels was developed and commercialized in Japan early in 2000. Just a year later, major manufacturers of this new-generation television started production at their Chinese plants. Due to FIEs bringing new technology and production factors into China, a giant Chinese "goose" flies high, ahead, as it were, of the NIEs and the ASEAN countries. FIEs have upgraded China's industrial and trade structure, showing that less developed countries can manufacture advanced and sophisticated products by absorbing new technology and production factors through FDI.

Second, agglomeration of industries has changed the East Asian "flying geese" development pattern because more FDI is attracted. Agglomeration of FDI undoubtedly reduces uncertainties about a host country's FDI policy, as a sizable amount of FDI testifies to an evidently favorable environment for FDI. The Pearl River Delta in China's Guangdong Province is a good example of the agglomeration of industries, especially the IT industry. In the delta, any components and parts of computers and photocopy machines are reportedly available within an hour's drive. Agglomeration of industries enables information sharing, promotes industrial linkages, and reduces transaction costs. Assemblers are motivated to invest by an aggregate of parts manufacturers, while parts manufacturers are encouraged to invest by an accumulation of assemblers. As a group of industries becomes agglomerated, effective infrastructure needs to be provided and human resources become well equipped.

Third, the fragmentation of production processes has also modified the "flying geese" development pattern. Multinational corporations (MNCs) and international production chains account for more than half of China's exports and imports. As mentioned, intra-industry trade is increasing in China's foreign trade. The "flying geese" development pattern has been argued on the basis of an international division of labor for whole industries, with most MNCs engaging in specialized production activities at particular stages in the production process. The IT and transportation revolutions have made it possible for MNCs to fragment production processes around the globe, and to utilize the best location for each individual production process in order to minimize total production costs.

FDI is now an essential factor in China's economic growth, and it has become a main determinant of its foreign trade. The massive inflow of FDI into China since the mid-1990s has led to China's rise in East Asia, and has changed the East Asian "flying geese" development pattern, as well as Sino-Japanese economic relations.


## The Hollowing Out of Industries in Japan

Increasing imports from China have put immeasurable pressure on industrial adjustment in Japan. Throughout the "lost decade" of the 1990s, bankruptcies and unemployment increased and the hollowing out of Japan's industries proceeded unabated. A deflationary spiral set in, which is considered a main cause of prolonged recession. Many also blame Japan's economic difficulties on the rise of China. Many Japanese reflect this viewpoint, partly because they have lost confidence in Japan's economy, which used to be Japan's strongest point, and partly because of some jealousy over China's current economic success.

There is concern about increasing imports from China as well as Japan's massive investments in China. Both of them are seen as having led to the hollowing out of Japanese industries. A wide range of Japanese industries, especially those long protected by the government, perceive China to be an economic "threat." These sentiments have been organized into powerful political pressure, which, in April 2001, for example, induced the Japanese government to adopt measures against a few agricultural Chinese imports. Yet, instead of seeing increasing Chinese imports as damaging to Japanese industry, the huge inflows of low-priced products from China should be recognized as providing Japanese industries with great opportunities to reform less efficient sectors and to create more value-added industries.

There is a tendency to attribute rising unemployment to the hollowing out of industries in Japan. Yet the high unemployment rate merely reflects the current economic slump in Japan. Most industries are obviously contributing to the increased unemployment rate, but, in some emerging industries such as IT, there is a serious short supply of labor. Therefore, some of these problems reflect a mismatch between supply and demand in Japan's transitional labor market.

It is difficult to discern a causal relationship between increased outward investment in China and the hollowing out of industries in Japan. A survey of the overseas activities of Japanese firms by the Ministry of Economy, Trade and Industry found that sales by foreign subsidiaries of Japanese manufacturers increased sharply in the late 1980s when their overseas investments unexpectedly expanded due to the highly appreciated Japanese yen. Their sales surpassed exports from Japan in the mid-1990s. The ratio of manufacturing industries to the total working population and to total Japanese gross domestic product had fallen drastically in the 1990s. The electric machinery and transport equipment industries, which created many jobs in Japan until the mid-1980s, began to absorb more workers abroad in the 1990s. These phenomena help explain the hollowing out of industries in Japan.

However, there is a connection between increasing outward investment and the hollowing out of industries in Japan. First, export industries in general tend to have a positive attitude toward FDI. Japan's leading companies with subsidiaries abroad are also very competitive in exporting.

Second, FDI substitutes for exports, and it increases imports from overseas plants. As a result of outward FDI, in the mid and long term, factor prices are adjusted, and factors are transferred between industries in Japan. However, there is no denying the possibility that the unemployment rate would rise, temporarily, in the process of restoring economic equilibrium.

Third, local areas in Japan compete intensely with foreign countries for investment. Most Japanese firms remain headquartered in Tokyo or other business centers in Japan, but domestic plants have been closed and transferred to foreign countries. In this way, Japanese FDI has negatively impacted the local economies of specific regions in Japan. Since local interests are overrepresented in Japan's political process, stagnant economic conditions in local areas are likely to become politicized.

An empirical study on FDI and the hollowing out of Japanese industries (Fukao and Yuan 2001) estimated the loss of domestic manufacturing jobs due to Japan's export-substitution and import-expansion type of FDI to East Asia to be 577,000 during 1987–1998. Unemployment in the textiles and clothing, electronics, and telecommunication equipment industries was particularly notable. This study also estimated that Japan's overseas resource and market-development type of FDI created 514,000 new domestic jobs in the same period. Job opportunities created by the latter almost cover job losses caused by the former.

The rising Japanese yen directly affected the increase in outward investment, although it had little direct relevance to industrial hollowing out in Japan. Fundamentally, the services economy accelerated the hollowing out of Japanese industries, with most Japanese spending less on manufactured goods and more on services. It is virtually impossible to demonstrate a causal relationship between Japanese FDI in China and the hollowing out of Japanese industries.

## China's Export of Deflation

There are also suggestions in Japan that China is "exporting" deflation. Kuroda Haruhiko and Kawai Masahiro, a former Japanese vice minister and a former deputy vice minister of international finance, have charged China with exporting deflation and have urged the Chinese government to take measures to counter domestic deflation or to appreciate the yuan (*Financial Times* 2 December 2002). Japan's Finance Minister Shiokawa Seijuro followed suit at a meeting of the Group of Seven industrialized countries in February 2003. Their remarks suggest that China's booming economic growth, driven by low-priced exports, is occurring at the expense of Japan and other neighboring economies.

It is a fact that low-priced imports from China are decreasing prices in Japan, especially those of textile and electronics products. It is also true that there is room for China's monetary authorities to better manage the Chinese currency. However, it is impossible to demonstrate that China is exporting deflation to Japan. Yes, both countries are suffering from deflation, but this is rooted in different causes in the two countries.

In Japan, deflation has its origin in the sharp drop of the assets market (real estate and stocks). After the bursting of the "bubble economy," most Japanese companies sold assets in order to reduce their heavy debt burdens. The assets market turned into a buyers' market as prices dropped drastically. As deflation swelled the debt burden, Japanese companies accelerated selling goods on hand—at a loss. In short, this has been the process of debt deflation in Japan. Another serious problem in Japan has been that of financial institutions' nonperforming loans. Once they fell into the deflationary spiral, Japanese companies had increasing difficulty funding operational costs and making long-term business decisions. In this way, the real economy became stagnant and the economic slump prolonged. Japan's deflationary problems are by no means imported from China.

In China, deflation reflects oversupply as a result of excessive investment in plants and equipment in the 1990s. There is much industrial overcapacity in China. The former State Economic and Trade Commission reckoned that, in 2002, 88 percent of the 600 types of goods it surveyed were in excess supply (*Zhongguo Jinjishibao* (China Economic Times) 26 December 2002). Furthermore, uncompetitive state-owned enterprises with little prospect of being restructured continue to manufacture and supply products to the saturated Chinese market.

Thus, oversupply worsens deflation in China, while the shrinking of domestic demand after the bursting of the assets bubble triggered deflation in Japan.

Imports from China accounted for less than 2 percent of Japan's GDP. Imported products from China, mostly labor-intensive products or processed and assembled products of high-tech components and parts, are mostly complementary to Japan's current industrial structure. The sharp drop in prices is most remarkable in domestic or non-tradable services in Japan. There is little evidence to support the idea that China is exporting deflation to Japan.

## TRADE FRICTION AND RULES-BASED SETTLEMENTS

### Friction in Sino-Japanese Trade

Deepening economic interdependence between Japan and China inevitably entails trade friction, but China's accession to the WTO has paved a new road of rules-based settlement of issues between them.

In response to a rapid surge in some agricultural imports, in April 2001 the Japanese government imposed provisional safeguard measures to curb imports of leeks, fresh shiitake mushrooms, and rush mats for tatami flooring. Since these items were mainly imported from China, the safeguard measures primarily targeted Chinese products.[11] Although Japan had imposed safeguard measures on pork imports in 1997, it had not previously invoked general safeguards or made special efforts to restrict imports of textiles. The Chinese government retaliated by imposing a 100 percent special tariff on imports of Japanese automobiles, cellular phones, car phones, and air conditioners in June 2001. At the time, China was not constrained by WTO rules as it was not yet a member, but, following its accession to the WTO in November 2001, it would not be able to adopt such measures.

After negotiations, the governments reached an agreement in December 2001. The Japanese government would not invoke full safeguard measures and the Chinese government would withdraw its countermeasures. At the same time, Japanese and Chinese nongovernmental bodies would establish a new trade council for agricultural products, and both governments would maintain orderly trade by exchanging information on the supply and demand of agricultural products, and on their price fluctuations.

The safeguard issue highlighted serious problems with Japan's trade policy. First, it became obvious that trade friction or conflict was inevitable with the broadening and deepening of Sino-Japanese economic relations. In the 1990s, Japan had undertaken protective measures against Chinese products. In February 1992, the Japanese government imposed, for the first time, an antidumping duty on imported Chinese ferroalloy. A number of Japanese firms also urged the Japanese government to take action against Chinese textile imports. The Japanese government repeatedly pressed the Chinese to adopt voluntary export restraint measures. In April 2001, under political pressure because of upcoming Upper House elections, the Japanese government took the mentioned provisional safeguard measures against the three agricultural products. Meanwhile, some industrial associations were requesting Japanese government action against other Chinese imports.

Second, adopting the safeguard measures further worsened Japan's image as a reluctant liberalizer of its agricultural sector. In another example, Japan was reportedly responsible for the unsuccessful Asia-Pacific Economic Cooperation (APEC) initiative on Early Voluntary Sectoral Liberalization (EVSL) because of its uncompromising attitude toward liberalizing its forestry and fishery markets. Agricultural trade was also shelved in negotiations with Singapore around the Japan-Singapore Economic Partnership Agreement (JSEPA), which was signed in January 2002. The JSEPA is Japan's first free trade agreement (FTA).

Third, the social costs of protecting the agricultural sector are increasing tremendously. The repercussions of safeguard measures extended from

Japanese consumers, who paid for the additional protection costs, to those industries on which the Chinese government imposed retaliatory duties. The Japan Automobile Manufacturers Association estimated that losses due to China's retaliatory measures amounted, in 2001, to ¥51.2 billion in the automobile industry alone, and that this figure would have ballooned to ¥420 billion if the retaliatory measures continued into 2002 (Honma 2002). Moreover, import restrictions on rush mats for tatami flooring caused serious damage to those domestic manufacturers who used imported Chinese rush mats.

## Rules-Based Settlements

With the invocation of safeguard measures, a new trend seemed apparent in Sino-Japanese economic relations. The Japanese government, in accordance with WTO rules, adopted safeguard measures against agricultural products imported from China, which was about to accede to the WTO. The case was finally brought to a rules-based conclusion. Previously in Sino-Japanese relations, any economic friction between the two countries became politicized. When such friction occurred, the Chinese government criticized Japan, and the Chinese media or the Beijing-supporting Hong Kong media would carry on a campaign against Japan. So-called friendly personages or business leaders with a stake in amicable relations between the countries would appear on the scene and would endeavor to resolve the dispute through their own personal contacts. Human factors dominated easing economic friction in bilateral relations. In invoking the safeguard measures and in taking retaliatory measures, the actions of both governments took on a different, more businesslike tenor.

There are considerable economic issues awaiting resolution between the two countries. One of these is infringement of intellectual property rights in China, including violations of patent, copyright, and registered design rights. A number of Japanese companies are struggling to eliminate imitation products in China and other third-country markets. Bilateral negotiations over such issues are now based on WTO rules. As China is integrating into the global economy and as Sino-Japanese economic relations mature, rules-based settlements will be the means for resolving economic conflicts.

OHASHI HIDEO

# CHANGES IN JAPAN'S TRADE POLICY:
# MULTILATERALISM AND REGIONALISM

## China's FTA Proposal

At a summit meeting in Phnom Penh in November 2002, the leaders of ASEAN and China's Premier Zhu Rongji signed a comprehensive economic framework agreement, the core of which was the establishment of an FTA.[12] Zhu had initially suggested an ASEAN-China FTA (ACFTA) at the summit in 2000, and then he formally proposed it at the 2001 summit.

By proposing the ACFTA, China, the region's political power, embarked on very active economic diplomacy. And this initiative was a significant shock to Japan, the region's economic power, because it was directed at ASEAN. Japan maintains friendly relations with ASEAN, and it regards its relations with ASEAN as the keystone of its Asia diplomacy. The Japanese perceived China's proposal as a challenge to the economic order it built in East Asia with ASEAN's cooperation, and as an irritant that highlighted Japan's inadequate foreign economic policy because of its prolonged recession, its protected agricultural sector, and its delayed structural reforms.

Regionalism in the form of FTAs dominates the world economy today. When Zhu proposed ACFTA, there were no FTAs in East Asia, home to some of the major trading countries of the world. His proposal was put forward before any of the other FTA ideas that were beginning to be considered in East Asia. Japan and South Korea had started a feasibility study for an FTA in October 1999 at the suggestion of Korea's President Kim Dae Jung, and Japan and Singapore took the same road at the suggestion of Singapore's Prime Minister Goh Chok Tong in December 1999. Zhu's proposal could be explained in terms of a "policymaking reaction function" or "not wanting to miss the bus." The concept, put forward by Horaguchi (2001), refers to attempts to minimize the limits of one's own country's policymaking by responding to other countries' policies by following suit. From the timing, China's proposal was not put forward for simple economic benefits and cooperation, but in pursuit of more comprehensive national interests in the region.

## Japan's Attitude toward the ACFTA

China's FTA proposal had considerable impact on Japan's foreign economic policy. Japan's Prime Minister Koizumi Jun'ichiro signed the JSEPA in Singapore during his ASEAN tour in January 2002. After the joint study was completed between Japan and Singapore, it took only a year of speedy negotiations to conclude the JSEPA. Japan would not have taken such quick action without China's ACFTA proposal.

As a main beneficiary of the post–World War II General Agreement on Tariffs and Trade regime, Japan has consistently favored multilateral trade liberalization based on the principle of nondiscrimination. This was so even as a number of FTAs were being concluded around the world. Hence the JSEPA marks a turning point in Japan's foreign trade policy. Japan has now embarked on a multilayered approach that includes regionalism and multilateralism, and has taken steps toward complementing WTO multilateral trade negotiations with regional FTAs (Ministry of Foreign Affairs 2002).

There are some reasons behind Japan's change of course in foreign economic policy. First, stagnant multilateral trade negotiations have changed Japan's foreign economic policy. Regionalism, as represented by FTAs, has always been viewed negatively in Japan, as it inevitably involves discriminatory treatment. It is still difficult to remove concerns that FTAs lead to the formation of trade blocs. Indeed, FTAs can create trade while simultaneously diverting trade. In practice, FTAs have a tendency to shelve opening "sensitive" sectors, to designate agricultural products as exceptions, and to leave country-of-origin rules ambiguous. FTAs involve much gray area, due to their flexibility and simplicity.

Since the WTO ministerial meeting in Seattle in late 1999, multilateral WTO negotiations have been deadlocked, and the momentum for multilateral trade liberalization has shifted. WTO consensus-based negotiations have become extremely difficult as the number of WTO members has increased and the scope of negotiations has expanded. APEC also seems to have lost its cohesive impetus after the 1997 East Asian financial crisis, and its raison d'être is being called into question. After its unsuccessful EVSL initiative, APEC handed over the task of regional trade liberalization to the WTO. After its earlier enthusiasm for trade liberalization in Asia Pacific, the United States seems to have changed course now toward a Free Trade Area of the Americas (FTAA). So Japan has embarked too on the path of FTAs, hoping to maintain momentum for trade liberalization, at least regionally.

Second, it has become disadvantageous not to participate in FTAs. As much as 90 percent of WTO members are now party to such agreements. Countries experienced in regional economic integration or FTAs are also likely to take the initiative in multilateral negotiations, and much preparatory negotiating for international agreements is based on regional economic integration or FTAs. Also, Japanese companies are increasingly at a concrete economic disadvantage by not participating in FTAs. The final report of the feasibility study for an FTA between Japan and Mexico (Ministry of Economy, Trade and Industry 2002) found that Japanese companies suffered losses as a result of the North American Free Trade Agreement (NAFTA) and the EU-Mexico FTA. First, Japanese companies lost market share to EU and U.S. companies, and ¥400 billion of export profit per year. Domestic production was reduced by ¥620 billion, and 32,000 jobs were lost. Second, Japanese firms withdrew due to import duties of about 16 percent, which made it impossible to compete with EU and U.S. firms. An example has been given of a power-generation plant that resulted in a ¥120 billion loss and over 10,000 jobs lost. Third, following country-of-origin rules, Japanese companies procured NAFTA-made parts instead of using Japanese parts. Changing suppliers for US$100 million in parts led to production losses of ¥33 billion in Japan and the loss of 1,400 jobs.

Third, FTAs are expected to provide effective external pressure for domestic structural reform. Since U.S.-Japan trade friction has abated, external pressures have not worked effectively, and it is increasingly difficult to overcome vested interests and to implement structural reforms in Japan. It is broadly anticipated that FTA negotiations will promote deregulation and competition with market-opening pressure, reflecting similar expectations to those for a "special zone for structural reform" proposed by the Koizumi administration. In the case of the JSEPA, 84 percent of trade between Japan and Singapore is already duty-free, and agricultural products are in fact excluded. So, as Japan's first FTA, the JSEPA has symbolic significance, but its trade-creating effects will be very limited. However, the JSEPA includes a variety of items that multilateral trade negotiations do not fully cover, such as investment promotion, competition, labor, migration, and environmental policies. Therefore, the JSEPA may have a significant effect on structural reform in Japan.

## Conclusion

The rise of China has greatly impacted Japan's economy. Growing low-priced imports from China increase economic welfare in Japan, while China's economic growth provides a number of opportunities for Japanese industries. Examples of these are China's machinery and transportation equipment industries. As China's machinery and transportation equipment industries develop into leading industries, they could become structurally dependent on imported intermediate input goods from Japan.

Japan's FDI in China has been found to have little relevance to the loss of jobs and the hollowing out of industries in Japan. Instead, these changes reflect Japan's recession and its increasingly services-led economy. Also, the deflationary spiral in Japan has caused the current economic slump there; deflation has not been imported from China.

China's rise has also critically impacted Japan's external economy. The rise of China has changed the traditional development pattern and catch-up process in East Asia. By acquiring new technology and production factors through huge amounts of FDI, China is manufacturing new products ahead of the NIEs and ASEAN. The "flying geese" development pattern seems to have been replaced by a "leaping frog" pattern, in terms of which China is passing rows of geese flying ahead of it. China's accession to the WTO has turned Sino-Japanese economic relations into a rules-based relationship. China's rise is also reflected in its positive attitude toward regional economic cooperation. The ACFTA has seemingly induced Japan to adjust its foreign economic policy to encompass regionalism together with multilateralism.

In a speech to the Boao Forum in April 2002, Koizumi (2002) suggested China's rise was not a threat but a challenge and opportunity, not about confrontation but about mutual benefit, and not about a hollowing out but an expansion of Japanese industries. Considering the positive impact China's rise has had on Japan's economy and Sino-Japanese economic relations, the views of Koizumi should be widely accepted.

## Notes

1. The trade statistics quoted in this chapter are Japanese customs statistics, released by the Ministry of Finance. Specifically, see the press release, "Japan's Customs Statistics 2002" <http://www.mof.go.jp> (27 January 2002).
2. From 1961—when Japan reported its trade with China for the first time in its customs statistics—until 2002, Japan's imports from China never exceeded those from the United States.
3. The figures in parentheses refer to the Harmonized Commodity Description and Coding System's four-digit definitions of trade commodities.
4. Import penetration rate = imports/(domestic production + imports − exports). The rate is calculated in terms of volume, and it is based on textile statistics from the Ministry of Economy, Trade and Industry, and customs statistics from the Ministry of Finance.
5. Cloth and knit outer and inner clothing.
6. Intra-Industry Trade (IIT) Index = [1 − (export − import)/(export + import)].
7. Processing trade mainly comprises processing and assembling (*lailiao jiagong*) and processing with imported materials (*jinliao jiagong*) in exports. It also includes equipment and materials made by foreign-invested enterprises.
8. For market surveys of color televisions in China, see "Quanqiu Caidian Zhuangye Shangwugang" (Global Color TV Special Business Network), Qinshigang <www.kitking.com.cn>.
9. Statistics of patent applications and registrations in *Zhongguo Tongji Nianjian (China Statistical Yearbook) 2001* show that more utility models and designs are registered in China than creations and inventions.
10. The latest IDE-JETRO Asian input-output tables are for 1995, yet they were only published in 2001.
11. For details of the safeguard measures, visit the websites of the Ministry of Economy, Trade and Industry <http://www.meti.go.jp/policy/trade_policy/safeguard> and the Ministry of Agriculture, Forestry and Fishery <http://www.maff.go.jp/sogo_shokuryo/sg_kanren/sg_kanren.htm>.
12. For the full text of the "Framework Agreement on Comprehensive Economic Co-operation between ASEAN and the People's Republic of China", see <http://www.aseansec.org/13196.htm>.

## BIBLIOGRAPHY

Fukao Kyoji and Yuan Tangjun. 2001. "Nihon no taigai chokusetsutoushi to kudoka" (Japan's overseas direct investment and hollowing out of industries). *Research Institute of Economy, Trade and Industry (RIETI) Discussion Paper Series* 01-J-003 (September).

Honma Masayoshi. 2002. "FTA to nogyo mondai" (FTA and agricultural problems). In Urata Shujiro and Japan Economic Research Center, eds. *Nihon no FTA senryaku* (Japan's FTA strategy). Tokyo: Nihon Keizai Shimbunsha.

Horaguchi Haruo. 2001. "Chiiki renkei no seijikeizaigaku" (Political economy of regional cooperation). In Suehiro Akira and Yamakage Susumu, eds. *Ajia seijikeizairon* (Political economy of Asia). Tokyo: NTT Shuppan.

Koizumi Jun'ichiro. 2002. "Asia in a New Century—Challenge and Opportunity." Speech at the Boao Forum for Asia. <http://www.mofa.go.jp/region/asia-pacific/China/boao0204/speech.html> (12 April).

Ministry of Economy, Trade and Industry. 2002. "Summary of the Report of the Japan-Mexico Joint Research Committee." <http://www.meti.go.jp/policy/trade_policy/l_america/mexico/j_mexico/data/jmsgreport_overviewj.pdf> (July).

Ministry of Foreign Affairs. 2002. "Japan's FTA Strategy" <http://www.mofa.go.jp/mofaj/gaiko/fta/policy.html> (October).

Okamoto Nobuhiro. 2001. "Chugoku no sangyokozo to tainichi izonkozo" (China's industrial dependence on Japan). *Ajiken Warudo Torendo* (IDE World Trend) 74 (November).

# 12

# The Rise of China and Korea's China Policy

## Lee Geun

During the cold war, the Communist East bloc not only threatened the West bloc physically, but there were also political and economic threats against liberal democracy and capitalist markets. For that reason, the security policies of the United States had both military and economic dimensions. These were oriented to deterring military attack by communist countries, while also deterring the expansion of the socialist revolution by aiding the economic development of allies, and by nurturing markets, and the ideas and institutions that supported these markets.

The Soviet Union and China rejected capitalism during the cold war. Now, having "lost" the cold war, Russia and China are both in transition toward developing more capitalistic market systems. But unlike the Soviet and eastern European regimes in the late 1980s and early 1990s, the Chinese government did not collapse. Indeed, in China today, the Communist Party still governs the country. Although the Chinese economy is now characterized as a socialist market system, after nearly 25 years of reform and opening up, China's political decision-making processes are not transparent or accountable. So the United States and the West are still unsure about whether China has passed the point of no return in its pursuit of reform. The global expansion of the market system, or globalization, is also yet to reach deep into the Chinese heartland.

At the moment, potential threats from China, particularly in terms of politics and security, stem from it becoming a powerful country that does not share the liberal democratic and free market values of its neighbors. If a country becomes powerful without sharing the political and economic values of its neighbors, conflicts of interest are inevitable, and, more often than not, resolution of such conflict might be coercive, with negative implications for regional security and the stable functioning of national and regional markets.

This chapter evaluates the rise of China from the perspective of South Korea's national interest. South Korea has to navigate a path for itself between the United States—on which Korea has depended for half a century for its security and wellbeing, and which is unsure about China—and an increasingly strong China that exerts significant military and economic influence over the Korean peninsula.

China's rise, which includes increased military and economic capabilities as well as expanded influence, simultaneously poses threats and offers opportunities to its neighbors. Can Korea take advantage of the new opportunities in China to enhance Korea's national interest while maintaining friendly relations with the United States? If China's rise includes security and economic threats to Korea, what options does Korea have either to thwart these threats or to push for Chinese policy changes more favorable to Korea? Are China and the United States mutually exclusive partners for Korea—must Korea choose between them, or can Korea partner both at the same time? Particularly considering China's influence over North Korea, it will not be easy for South Korea to maneuver between China and the United States if the two do not view the future of the Korean peninsula in the same way. On which side should South Korea then be? Could it pursue a policy of strategic ambiguity?

In order to answer these questions, the potential threats and opportunities stemming from China's rise will be assessed, followed by a discussion of Korea's options for increasing these opportunities and decreasing the threats. Given the inherent uncertainties—the extent of China's economic growth, and whether or not China will become as dominant as the United States, both qualitatively and quantitatively—the emphasis will be on the principles and norms that Korea needs to adopt. Principles and norms should govern Korea's policies and strategies in the region, rather than the distribution of capabilities, so that Korea is not shackled by inappropriate or rigid policies.

ASSESSMENT OF FUTURE THREATS FROM CHINA

## Size of the Chinese Economy

Forecasts about China's economic growth prospects are important for assessing the potential threat that China poses, as a large economy alone can threaten other countries, both militarily and economically. In Korea, the business community and China specialists generally anticipate fast growth for China's economy. Korea's Samsung Economic Research Institute (2003) expects China's economy will grow 7.8 percent between 2001 and 2005 and 8.1 percent between 2006 and 2010.

In general, there is near consensus that, with a few assumptions, the Chinese economy will grow fast enough for China to surpass some major economic powers in terms of either gross domestic product (GDP) or purchasing power parity (PPP) around 2020. A World Bank report (1997) states that China had already surpassed Germany in terms of national purchasing power, and would exceed Japan's economy in ten years. Foy and Maddison have argued (1998) that for China's GDP to equal that of the United States, an annual growth rate of some 5.5 percent would be required until about 2015—a perfectly possible scenario. Discussion in China targets 2030 as the year when China might surpass the United States in terms of economic size (Chung 2002, 388). Chinese newspapers (for example, *Renmin Ribao* 28 April 2000 and 15 November 2002) suggest that China's GDP will exceed that of Japan around 2020, with only the United States and the European Union then being larger.

However, there are also some cautious forecasts. Wayne Morrison (1998) of the Congressional Research Service calculated that, measured in U.S. dollars and using nominal exchange rates, China's GDP in 1997 was about 45 percent that of Germany's GDP, 23 percent that of Japan's, and 12 percent that of the United States's. China's nominal per capita GDP was calculated to be only 2.6 percent that of the United States. Nonetheless, if measured in terms of PPP exchange rates, China is already larger than Japan and Germany, and about half the size of the United States. Richard Cooper (2001) has argued that China may not overtake the U.S. economy in any meaningful sense by 2015 or 2020; at best, it will reach barely one quarter of U.S. GDP by 2020, if one considers higher than expected U.S. economic growth.

These forecasts show that, although there is some hyperbole about China soon surpassing the United States in size and becoming a world hegemon, China's economy will become so sizable that it will be a very significant actor on the world stage. Indeed, China is already an East Asian economic power and, assuming ongoing economic growth, it will become a formidable global economic power in the near future.

## Factors of Uncertainty

An expanding economy does not always threaten other countries. For example, a growing economy in the United Kingdom does not threaten the United States, just as enhanced economic growth in Canada does not pose a threat to Australia. This is, of course, because all four countries share the same fundamental values. Theories about power transition (Organski and Kugler 1980) and balance of threat (Walt 1987) posit that changes in a country's military and economic capabilities send threatening signals to geographically adjacent countries or to a hegemonic country. It is therefore not surprising that Korea, Japan, and the United States are concerned about certain aspects of China's rise. Having experienced China's enmity during the cold war, and still having different political and economic systems and ideologies, China's emergence could be a formidable security and economic threat to Korea.

Yet, at the same time, China's increased economic and military capabilities could also be opportunities for its neighbors, as new export and investment markets could be created, and support or security shields against other threatening powers could be provided. For example, many Koreans worry increasingly about unilateralist U.S. foreign policies, and are concerned about possible preemptive U.S. strikes against North Korea that would result in devastating retaliation by the North toward the South. Lacking credible diplomatic cards vis-à-vis the United States, some Koreans are viewing closer relations with China as providing an attractive counterweight to possible U.S. unilateralism on the Korean peninsula.

Accordingly, the rise of China does not automatically mean increasing threats to Korea. Yet regional policymakers are not sure about which direction China is headed. The most disconcerting element at the moment in assessing China is the "uncertainty" factor. The essential uncertainty about China stems from the fact that it is in transition—from a socialist economy to a capitalist economy, and from an authoritarian political system toward a more pluralistic one. Whether a trustworthy and stable China emerges from this transition will determine if China can be viewed either as a threat or as an opportunity.

Uncertainty about China stems too from its rapid economic growth with its attendant social costs. Many Chinese are becoming impoverished while wealth is being concentrated in the hands of small numbers of entrepreneurs. The income gap between the rich and the poor is growing, regional disparity between coastal plains and the inner provinces is growing, and unemployment is rising. Corruption is widespread in both the private and public sectors, and the banking sector remains quite fragile (*Newsweek* 6 November 2002). A World Bank report (1997) notes that for China to develop in a sustainable fashion, it would need to overcome problems related to employment insecurity, growing inequality, stubborn poverty, mounting environmental pressures, rising costs of food self-sufficiency, and periods of macroeconomic instability stemming from incomplete reforms. If Chinese reforms were to falter and China were to become unstable, Korea would be affected. Apart from instability in Northeast Asia, consequences could include economic vulnerabilities, radical nationalism in China, and perhaps even China's disintegration.

Uncertainty about China's course also relates to the lack of transparency and accountability in political decision-making. Even though recent Chinese leadership changes were implemented smoothly and demonstrated an institutionalized shifting of power, the whole process was obscure and unaccountable to the general public. This lack of transparent and accountable decision-making could destabilize China, and so threaten regional stability. Facing this opaque policy process, policymakers in neighboring countries frequently have to rely on guesswork in important bilateral or multilateral issues with China, and they fear manipulation of information and national sentiment by China's central authorities. This kind of uncertainty will remain until transparency in decision making is increased, and democratization in China is widened and deepened.

The absence of clear norms and values in China's foreign policy functions as another factor of uncertainty. From Korea's perspective, it is not clear on what norms and values China's North Korea policy is based. China's foreign policy principles such as preventing hegemonism are insufficient to help other countries trust and accept China as one of them in the world community. China must develop a consistent track record of normative justifications in its foreign policy.

In sum, the major threats from a rising China stem from the huge size of its economy, coupled with uncertainties derived from its transitional processes. If a country with China's size and economy were to falter, were to be taken over by a very radical nationalism, or were to continue

LEE GEUN

functioning without clear norms or transparent and accountable decision-making processes, a geographically proximate country like Korea would have good reason to feel threatened.


## OPPORTUNITIES COMING FROM CHINA

Yet it is quite likely that China will develop further into a status quo power in the future. First, for China's growth to continue, it has to continue taking advantage of the current global market system. As China's political stability and the Chinese Communist Party's legitimacy depend on continued high growth, it is highly improbable that China would try to disrupt the current global economic system. China's external conditions are the best they have been for the past 100 years, and China appears to be as interested as its neighbors in regional and global stability. Other than reunifying Taiwan with the mainland—an important, and potentially very destabilizing, exception as China has not excluded using force for this purpose—China seems to have no urgent territorial need or ambitions in the region.

In this context, China's expanding economy with its attractive export and investment markets can provide Korea with both economic and diplomatic opportunities. Already many economic opportunities are being realized. The Bank of Korea (2002) calculates that, in 2001, 12.1 percent of Korea's exports went to China, making it Korea's second largest trading partner after the United States. This trend continued in 2002. From January to October 2002, Korea's exports to China amounted to 13.9 percent of total Korean exports. Steel, machinery, semiconductors, communication equipment, and computers are Korea's main export items to China. Korea ran a trade surplus with China of US$5.7 billion in 2000, and US$4.9 billion from January to October in 2002.

China has also become Korea's most important investment market; it surpassed the United States in 2001 as the most favored destination for outbound Korean investment. Total Korean foreign direct investment (FDI) in China in 2001 was US$5.02 billion (15.5 percent of total outbound FDI), involving 5,854 investment projects (41.7 percent of all FDI projects). In 2001, the average amount of each Korean investment project in China was approximately US$400,000, which suggests strong involvement by small and medium-sized Korean companies seeking benefit from China's competitive labor costs. China is, in fact, contributing to the survival of low-value-added Korean industries. On the other hand, the average amount of investment by Korean conglomerates rose from US$11.8 million in 1997 to US$30.1 million in 2001. These conglomerates sell intermediate industrial goods to China and export technological products from China.

China could be a huge diplomatic asset to Korea, particularly if it used its influence over North Korea to help prevent adventurous policies, and to help ensure the stability of the Korean peninsula and Northeast Asia. Together, Korea, China, and Russia may also need to dissuade the United States from taking unilateral action on the North Korean nuclear issue. Also, as it is successfully reforming its own economy, China could help North Korea embark on its own market reforms. At the same time, China also shares Korea's interest in preventing Japan's remilitarization. Therefore, on many diplomatic issues, China and Korea are viable partners.

However, playing a China card against, for example, the United States could easily become a double-edged sword. For instance, if a prospective coalition forged between Korea and China is perceived as threatening to the United States, overall Korean-U.S. relations would deteriorate. China, on the other hand, would perceive very negatively open Korean participation in a missile defense project with the United States and Japan. So, although an ascendant China could be a diplomatic asset for Korea, a situation could also arise where Korea has to choose between the United States and China (Chung 2001). Such a situation is perhaps going to be one of Korea's biggest foreign policy challenges in the near future.

## CONCLUSION: BANDWAGONING THE TRANSPARENT AND THE ACCOUNTABLE

Facing a rising power such as China, diverse strategies have to be adopted to maximize one's own national interests. Suggested strategies for maximizing a country's national interests include preventive war; balance/containment; getting on the bandwagon; binding; engagement; and distancing, or "passing the buck" (Schweller 1999). Most of these strategies are, by their nature, too grand and unsuitable for a small power like Korea. Preventive war against China would be suicidal for Korea, and Korea alone does not possess the capability to bind, engage, or contain China. Getting on a bandwagon with China could seriously damage Korea's relations with the United States. Korea could also choose distancing, but this is not realistic when considering the two countries' geographical proximity and their increasing interdependence.

LEE GEUN

What then are Korea's options? An ideal strategy would be one that managed potential threats, that took advantage of the opportunities derived from relations with a rising China, and that was based on clear, accepted principles and norms. If Korea's China policy were driven purely by domestic economic interest groups, the policy would likely swing between diverse political coalitions. In dealing with major powers, unpredictable and frequent policy swings by small powers can easily backfire. So Korea's national interests could be best served by adhering to generally accepted norms and principles. In terms of containing threats and promoting opportunities, it would be desirable to gear Korea's China policy to enhancing pursuit of transparent and accountable practices and policies in China.

Uncertainties about China derive mainly from its ongoing transition. Until China reveals its political and economic choices for its future, it would be wise for Korea to be on the side of those whose policies are transparent and accountable—to their own people and to the global community. Rather than trying to hedge its interests by hypothetical calculations about the future capabilities of the region's major powers, Korea should put in its lot with those powers that are transparent and accountable—including China, if it becomes such a country.

Enhanced transparency and accountability would help China greatly as it becomes more immersed in the global economic system; indeed, it would have to increase its transparency and accountability if it wants to become a full partner in the global market system. A more transparent and accountable China would result in a more trustworthy China, and one that would care even more about regional and global stability. If China were to evolve into such a country, it would share the same interests as Korea, and there would be no reason for Korea to think about containing, balancing, or distancing itself from China.

Korea's China policy should therefore urge China to abide by globally accepted norms, values, rules, principles, and treaties. Korea should support China's smooth transition toward a market economy and democratization, as these will demand more transparency and accountability in China's political and economic governance. As China's economy grows, Korea should not see itself as having to choose between the United States and China (Chung 2001). Rather, Korea's choice is between the transparent and the accountable on the one hand, and an authoritarian black box on the other.

# Bibliography

Bank of Korea. 2002. "2001 nyonjung kukje suji donghyang" (Trend in the balance of international payments in 2001). *Monthly Bulletin*: 74–94.

Chung Jae Ho. 2001. "South Korea Between Eagle and Dragon: Perceptual Ambivalence and Strategic Dilemma." *Asian Survey* 41(5): 777–796.

———, ed. 2002. *Jungguk gaehyuk gaebang eui jeongchi dyongje 1980–2000* (Political economy of China's reform and opening: 1980–2000). Seoul: Kachi.

Cooper, Richard. 2001. Testimony of Richard N. Cooper, Public Hearing on Chinese Budget Issues and the Role of the People's Liberation Army in the Economy. 7 December. U.S.-China Economic and Security Review Commission <http://www.uscc.gov/tescpr.htm>.

Foy, Colm, and Angus Maddison. 1998. "China: A World Economic Leader?" *OECD Observer*, no. 215 (January 1999) <http://www1.oecd.org/publications/observer/215/e-foy.htm>.

Morrison, Wayne. 1998. *CRS Issue Brief*. Washington D.C.: CRS.

Organski, A. F. K., and Jack Kugler. 1980. *The War Ledger*. Chicago: The University of Chicago Press.

Samsung Economic Research Institute. 2003. *Jungguk kyongjeryuk hwaksan gasok chuse* (Trend of expansion of the Chinese economy). World Report 76.

Schweller, Randall. 1999. "Managing the Rise of Great Powers: History and Theory." In Alastair Johnston and Robert Ross, eds. *Engaging China: The Management of an Emerging Power*. London: Routledge.

Walt, Stephen. 1987. *The Origins of Alliances*. Ithaca: Cornell University Press.

World Bank. 1994. *Global Economic Prospects and the Developing Countries*. Washington, D.C.: World Bank.

———. 1997. *China 2020: Development and Challenges in the New Century*. Washington, D.C.: World Bank.

# 13

## The Rise of China's Economy: Opportunities and Threats to China-Korea Economic Relations

### Jwa Sung-Hee *and* Yoon Yong

The relationship between China and South Korea,[1] at least prior to the 1990s, centered largely on political and security issues. Much of the contact between the two neighbors was conducted secretively or with little public fanfare. This was done primarily not to offend North Korea, with whom China had 50 years of diplomatic relations, but also in order not to complicate relations with Japan, the United States, and other countries.

China's move toward a market-based economy has boosted trade and investment opportunities for Korean businesses, while also providing enormous challenges. In 2001, China surpassed the United States as Korea's number one destination for foreign investment, and, that same year, it overtook Japan as Korea's second largest trading partner. China too has recognized Korea as an important trade and investment partner. China's customs office reported, for example, that Korea was China's sixth largest trading partner in 2001, with total trade of around US$39.91 billion.[2] Two-way trade is expected to top US$100 billion by the time of the Beijing Summer Olympics in 2008. This would move the cautious Chinese-Korean relations of a decade ago further into the background, and place trade and investment issues fully at the forefront.

This chapter briefly sketches the general trends in China-Korea trade and investment relations. It then examines the pressing economic issues between the two countries in the past decade. Finally, it proposes an institutional framework for further expanding mutual trade and investment, and enhancing economic integration.

## GENERAL BACKGROUND TO CHINA-KOREA
## ECONOMIC RELATIONS

The dynamism in China-Korea bilateral trade began with the establishment of diplomatic relations in 1992. Broadly speaking, from 1992 to 2001,
exports of Korean goods to China increased at an average annual rate of
about 24 percent, while imports of Chinese goods increased at an average
annual rate of 15 percent. As conveyed in table 1, since 1992, the share of
Korean exports to China as a percentage of total Korean exports almost
quadrupled from 3.46 percent in 1992 to 12.09 percent by 2001, while the
share of Korean imports from China more than doubled from 4.56 percent to 9.43 percent.

Table 1. Shares of Korea's Trade with China (1992–2001) (US$ '000)

| Year | Total Exports | Exports China | Share (%) | Total Imports | Imports from China | Share (%) |
|------|---------------|---------------|-----------|---------------|--------------------|-----------|
| 1992 | 76,631,515 | 2,653,639 | 3.46 | 81,775,257 | 3,724,941 | 4.56 |
| 1993 | 82,235,866 | 5,150,992 | 6.26 | 83,800,142 | 3,928,741 | 4.69 |
| 1994 | 96,013,237 | 6,202,986 | 6.46 | 102,348,175 | 5,462,849 | 5.34 |
| 1995 | 125,057,988 | 9,143,588 | 7.31 | 135,118,933 | 7,401,196 | 5.48 |
| 1996 | 129,715,137 | 11,377,068 | 8.77 | 150,339,100 | 8,538,568 | 5.68 |
| 1997 | 136,164,204 | 13,572,463 | 9.96 | 144,616,374 | 10,116,861 | 7.00 |
| 1998 | 132,313,143 | 11,943,990 | 9.02 | 93,281,754 | 6,483,958 | 6.95 |
| 1999 | 143,685,459 | 13,684,599 | 9.52 | 119,752,282 | 8,866,667 | 7.40 |
| 2000 | 172,267,510 | 18,454,540 | 10.71 | 160,481,018 | 12,798,728 | 7.98 |
| 2001 | 150,439,144 | 18,190,190 | 12.09 | 141,097,821 | 13,302,675 | 9.43 |

Source: Korea Trade Information Services <http://www.kotis.net>.

Although the value of this trade has increased greatly, table 2 reflects
how the nature of Korean exports to China has remained more or less the
same in the past decade. These exports have typically been intermediate
industrial goods such as equipment and electrical machinery, and inputs
including plastics, organic chemicals, and iron and steel. But there has
been a change in the commodity structure of Chinese imports into Korea, as reflected in table 3. In 1992, for example, the main Chinese imports into Korea were primary products such as agricultural goods and
fishery products, mineral fuels, and a few consumer goods. Since 2000,
however, Korea has increasingly imported industrial goods from China,
such as equipment, electrical machinery, and iron and steel. From 1995 to
2000, the share of capital goods imported from China more than doubled

from 8.7 percent to 20.6 percent, the share of consumption goods increased from 21.3 percent to 29.4 percent, and the share of raw materials declined from 69.9 percent in 1995 to 42.1 percent in 2000 (Korea Trade Information Services <http://www.kotis.net>). Stated differently, in 1992, the top ten imported goods from China accounted for 70.8 percent of total imports, but this gradually dropped to around 62.4 percent in 1995 and 65.9 percent in 2000. Korea has become an important destination market for Chinese goods, with many of these goods—particularly textiles, household utilities, and agricultural products—having the potential to compete against Korean products at home.

Table 2. Top 10 Items of Korea's Exports to China (HS 2 digit level)
(US$mn)

| Year | 1992 | 1995 | 2000 |
|---|---|---|---|
| Total | 2,653 | 9,144 | 18,454 |
| Electrical machinery, etc.(HS 85) | 189 | 822 | 3,430 |
| Nuclear reactors, boilers, etc. (HS 84) | 158 | 998 | 2,033 |
| Plastics, etc. (HS 39) | 325 | 1.276 | 1,908 |
| Organic chemicals (HS 29) | 151 | 780 | 1,880 |
| Mineral fuels (HS 27) | 85 | 480 | 1,854 |
| Iron and steels (HS 72) | 730 | 552 | 1,203 |
| Raw hides, etc. (HS 41) | 141 | 617 | 755 |
| Man-made filaments (HS 54) | 118 | 479 | 665 |
| Man-made staple fibers (HS 55) | 175 | 590 | 508 |
| Impregnated textiles, etc. (HS 59) | 38 | 208 | 459 |

Source: Korea Trade Information Services <http://www.kotis.net>.

Table 3. Top 10 Items of Korea's Imports from China (HS 2 digit level)
(US$mn)

| Year | 1992 | 1995 | 2000 |
|---|---|---|---|
| Total | 3,724 | 7401 | 12,798 |
| Electrical machinery, etc. (HS 85) | 107 | 599 | 2,704 |
| Mineral fuels (HS 27) | 530 | 860 | 1,158 |
| Nuclear reactors, boilers, etc. (HS 84) | 60 | 184 | 1,051 |
| Iron and steel (HS 72) | 183 | 1,219 | 759 |
| Cereals (HS 10) | 648 | 13 | 700 |
| Articles of apparel, etc. (HS 62) | 39 | 226 | 560 |
| Fish (HS 03) | 30 | 108 | 468 |
| Man-made staple fibers (HS 55) | 281 | 659 | 413 |
| Optical instruments, etc. (HS 90) | 10 | 41 | 309 |
| Cotton (HS 52) | 173 | 218 | 309 |

Source: Korea Trade Information Services <http://www.kotis.net>.

Korea's foreign direct investment in China can be traced to 1988, when Jin Woong, Inc., a tent manufacturer, invested US$3 million in Xiamen, Fujian Province. Korean FDI into China continued steadily and, when Korea and China established official diplomatic relations in 1992, an investment protection treaty was signed promptly. Geographic proximity and complementary industrial structures have resulted in a remarkable increase in Korean investment in China. By 1994, Korean companies found China to be the second most attractive place for overseas investment, after the United States. Despite Korea's FDI growth stagnating drastically due to the 1997 financial crisis, China overtook the United States in 2001 to become the number one destination of outbound Korean FDI.

The majority of Korean investors in China have traditionally been small or medium-sized enterprises (SMEs), and they have focused primarily on Shanghai and Tianjin, and Shandong, Liaoning, and Jiangsu provinces. That Korean SMEs, rather than larger Korean firms, have played the dominant role in Korean FDI into China contrasts sharply with U.S. and EU investment into China (Kim 2001). Korean SME investment in China reflects a relatively low average amount of capital invested. Prior to the 1997 Asian financial crisis, the bulk of Korean FDI to China was so small in size that investments of less than US$2.5 million per project accounted for 94.4 percent of total Korean FDI to China (Export-Import Bank of Korea <http://www.koreaexim.go.kr>). With the onset of the crisis in 1997, Korean SME investment in China fell dramatically compared to that of larger firms and, since 2000, large firms have displaced SMEs in dominating Korean FDI to China.

In 2001, total Korean FDI outflows to China were distributed as follows: 83.9 percent went to manufacturing; 4.1 percent to real estate; 1.9 percent to the wholesale and retail sectors; and 10.1 percent to unspecified other sectors (Export-Import Bank of Korea <http://www. koreaexim.go.kr>). About 57 percent of total Korean FDI to China between 1991 and 1998 also went to manufacturing, reflecting an overall strong tendency for Korean FDI to China to be directed at manufacturing (Kim 2001). The cumulative number of actual Korean FDI projects in China was recorded to be 5,943 at the close of 2001, with the total investment from the actual contracts being about US$5.11 billion (Export-Import Bank of Korea <http://www.koreaexim.go.kr>). Added together, Korean FDI projects in China account for 42.3 percent of all Korean FDI projects, with the total value of these investments being 17 percent of the total of all Korean FDI (Export-Import Bank of Korea <http://www.

The Rise of China's Economy

koreaexim.go.kr>). Korean FDI into China will be pivotal to the future of bilateral economic relations between the two countries.

Telecommunications, consumer goods and electronics, and, more recently, automobiles are the three areas that Korean FDI has targeted. The telecommunications sector has undoubtedly been of greatest interest to Korean corporations, particularly since the 1997 Asian financial crisis. Mobile phone manufacturers in Korea have experienced triple-digit expansion of the domestic industry, which has encouraged them to seek export and investment opportunities in China and other parts of the world. The Korean government has also supported Korea's business interests considerably, by trying, for example, to persuade its Chinese counterpart to support Korean participation in China's code-division multiple access (CDMA) development.[3] The payoff came for Korea with an initial US$150 million contract to Samsung Electronics to develop CDMA lines in Shanghai, Tianjin, and Fujian and Hubei provinces in 2001.[4] Ambition remains strong, and Korean companies hope to capture the market in China for at least half of all CDMA handsets sold by foreign suppliers.

In addition to CDMA handset production and network management, the Korean government is also trying to expand telecommunications exports by taking advantage of Korea's own rapid adaptation of and leadership in broadband and asymmetrical digital subscriber lines technologies. The Korean Ministry of Information and Communication is promoting Korea Telecom, SK Telecom, and Hanaro Telecom as providing opportunities for China and other Asian countries interested in investing in their national communications infrastructures. These three companies have already captured the lead positions in Korea's broadband market, the number one market in the world. The ministry stated that the 2002 target for exports of information technology (IT) products to China was US$10 billion (*Korea Now* 8 February 2003).

Regarding consumer goods, the demand in China for large consumer and electronics goods such as washers, freezers, and televisions will rise drastically, and Korean companies have already gained a significant market share in the production of low-cost, dependable household consumer goods. The Korea Trade-Investment Promotion Agency reports that, in a recent study, 20 percent of Beijing consumers picked passenger cars as a product associated with Korea, while 16.7 percent and 11.8 percent respectively commended Korean mobile phones and television sets.

Since the end of 2002, Korean automobile manufacturers have rushed to invest in China to capture market share as China is projected to emerge as the world's largest automobile market within two decades. Recent predictions have suggested that Chinese automobile demand will increase by 8.8 percent per year through 2005, and by about 18 percent per year through 2010 (*Yonhap News* 4 December 2001).

## Main Issues in China-Korea Economic Relations

Despite their dynamism over the past decade or so, Chinese-Korean trade and investment relations are hardly free of controversies. This section examines specific issues that are critical to the future of China-Korea economic relations.

### Bilateral Trade Issues

When two countries at different stages of economic development trade with each other, the question of trade imbalances rises almost inevitably.[5] As shown in Figure 1, Korea developed a trade surplus with China from 1993 and this grew rather rapidly until 2000. As of 2001, Korea's trade surplus with China was US$4.9 billion, which accounted for about 53 percent of Korea's total trade surplus of US$9.3 billion. While China could be concerned about its present trade imbalance with Korea, Korea faces greater peril in the medium and long term as China's penetration of global markets has the potential to erode Korea's market shares, particularly in global manufacturing. The Korea International Trade Association has projected that Korea's bilateral trade surplus with China will widen by US$540 million per year due to China's accession to the World Trade Organization (WTO). Yet it also estimates that Korean exports to third-country markets will decrease by US$80 million per year as a result of enhanced Chinese competitiveness in global trade.

As noted, Korean exports to China over the past decade have mainly been intermediate industrial goods such as equipment and electrical machinery, and intermediate inputs such as plastics, organic chemicals, and iron and steel. These items are often used in final processing that is completed in China, with most of the finished goods then heading to third-country markets in the United States, Europe, or Southeast Asia. So the bilateral trade imbalance should not automatically suggest Korean goods invading the Chinese domestic market. Rather, the surge in Korean exports

Figure 1. Trends in Korea's Exports to and Imports from China

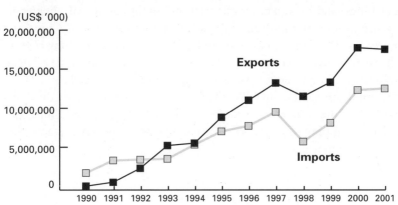

Source: Export-Import Bank of Korea <http://www.koreaexim.go.kr>.

to China contributes intermediate goods that significantly augment Chinese manufacturing for both local and international markets. Increased Korean exports to China have also helped create employment in China, which is an important precondition for successful economic reform. Hence the trade imbalance between Korea and China is hardly detrimental to China; in many cases, it is in fact quite favorable to China.

In past years, the agricultural and fishery sectors have provided contentious issues that have strained China-Korea bilateral trade relations. A dramatic example is the heated, but short-lived, dispute over Chinese garlic in mid-July 2000. Chinese garlic flooded the Korean market in 1999, with Chinese imports increasing tenfold in a year to incorporate 35 percent of Korea's garlic market. In response, Korea slapped a punitive tariff of 315 percent on Chinese garlic imports. Beijing responded by banning imports of polyethylene and mobile phone equipment, which caused losses of almost US$100 million to Korean companies during the six-week dispute. A compromise was reached, with Korea agreeing to allow continued garlic imports at a level slightly less than that permitted in 1999.[6]

The Korean Commercial Arbitration Board, which tracks trade disputes involving individual companies, finds that Koreans' biggest problems with China arise in the areas of payment, transit, and product quality. Of the 79 China-related conflict cases presented to the Board since 1998, 32 pertained to loan payments, 16 dealt with shipment problems, and 15 concerned product quality. Such trade disputes are likely to increase with the rise in China-Korea economic activities, and with China's entry into the WTO.

Managing these disputes will become an increasingly important aspect of Chinese and Korean economic relations. In the absence of a bilaterally agreed modus operandi for addressing contentious issues, China and Korea—as the number one and number two targets of dumping cases in the world—may become frequent users of WTO rules to settle bilateral trade disputes. In many ways, both Beijing and Seoul have begun to test the implications of China's WTO membership. Korea lowered dumping tariffs on Chinese lighters in conformity with WTO rules, and China considered dumping cases against Korea and Japan for polyester staple fiber and steel imports.

## China's Admission into the WTO: Implications for Korea

For Korea, enormous opportunities arise for China-Korea economic relations from China's accession to the WTO. The Korean industrial sector seems well placed to take advantage of the WTO-mandated tariff reductions that will expand access to Chinese markets for many Korean companies. The Korea Institute for Industrial Economics and Trade projects that China's WTO entry will boost bilateral trade with China by 10 percent, while the Korea Institute for International Economic Policy forecasts an increase of US$1.3 billion in exports and US$300 million in imports.

The most promising sectors for this surge in exports are seen to be fiber, clothing, plastic products, steel, automobiles and auto parts, electronics and electronic parts, and machinery equipment. China's compliance with its WTO-obligated tariff reductions is, for example, projected to boost sales in Korea's textiles sector by 5 percent. Although the electronics and apparel sectors will be hurt by Chinese competition in third-country markets, Korean exports of automobiles, petrochemicals, and high-end steel products to China may expand, as China lowers tariffs and demand increases with continued Chinese economic growth. Also, opening up the service industry and relaxing foreign ownership restrictions on a number of important capital and technology-oriented service industries, including distribution, telecommunications, and financial and professional services, would facilitate Korean firms' making inroads into the mainland market.

Finally, as an official member of the WTO, China could speak for developing countries' interests during multilateral trade negotiations, which would ultimately enhance Korea's overall foreign trade environment.

The downside for Korea of China's entry into the WTO will show itself as Korea faces stiff competition from Chinese goods in China and third-country markets, as well as from third countries in China's market. Low-cost, labor-intensive industries and labor groups in Korea are also apprehensive that China's market opening will generate further pressure to move jobs to lower-wage destinations such as China. Potential FDI to Korea may also be diverted to China, as a more attractive and less costly location.

For China, there are opportunities for China-Korea economic relations stemming from its accession to the WTO. Its entry into the WTO is commonly seen as a powerful weapon to speed up reform of its state-owned enterprises and banking structures. Reforms in these areas would facilitate strategic collaboration with Korean corporations. Competition in service areas such as finance, banking, telecommunications, distribution trade and export rights, and professional services from Korean (and other foreign) firms would foster entrepreneurship and greater private business initiatives in the economy.

The biggest challenge and threat for China from its entry into the WTO in its relations with Korea relates to unemployment. Many small and medium-sized township and village enterprises with serious structural shortcomings may not survive the influx of more competitive Korean SMEs. This may result in greater rural unemployment, in addition to ever increasing large numbers of urban unemployed. While enhancing pressure for faster economic reform, greater penetration of the Chinese market by Korean and other foreign firms will greatly increase the adjustment costs for Chinese firms.

## China's Competitiveness as a Challenge to Korea

At the macro level, the relatively stronger Korean won has helped China's export competitiveness against some traditionally strong Korean products, both within China and internationally. For instance, Korean-made televisions have been virtually shut out of the Chinese market due to low-cost competition. The Kumho Company has, however, had the opposite experience: it captured the number one position in China's tire replacement sector and topped US$100 million in sales in 2001. But its experience is the exception. In the short term, the strong Korean won will continue to hurt Korea's price competitiveness in international markets compared to its Chinese rivals. The Chinese yuan remains fixed at a constant rate to the U.S. dollar, but Korean economic researchers are paying close attention to a possible Chinese currency revaluation and the implications of such a development for Korean economic competitiveness.

The impact of China's increasing competitiveness as a low-cost producer in key third-country markets is of great concern to Korea. Chinese goods continue to erode Korea's market shares in traditional sectors in third countries where Korea had an established reputation as a leader or holder of significant market share. Recent trends illustrate the impact of China's export boom on Korea's competitiveness in such third-country markets. Figure 2 depicts how Korea's share of the U.S. market appears to have "peaked" at 3.31 percent in 2000, while China's market share in the United States continues to grow, from 8.22 percent in 2000 to over ten percent in 2002. Figure 3 illustrates a similar trend in the Japanese market vis-à-vis China and Korea.

**Figure 2. The Ratio of Chinese and Korean Exports in the U.S. Market**

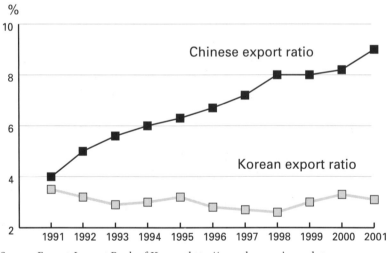

Source: Export-Import Bank of Korea <http://www.koreaexim.go.kr>.

The Federation of Korea Industries and the Ministry of Commerce, Industry, and Energy released a report in July 2002 that demonstrated the impact of increasing Chinese competitiveness on Korean exports in key industries, including electronics, steel, automobiles, textiles, petrochemicals, and shipbuilding. The study showed that China enjoyed double-digit growth in exports to the United States and Japan in these sectors (23.6

Figure 3. The Ratio of Chinese and Korean Exports in the Japanese Market

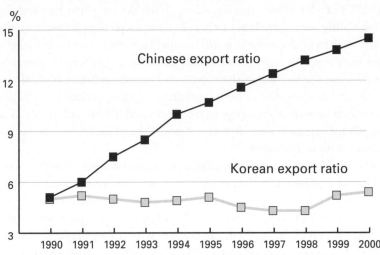

Source: Export-Import Bank of Korea <http://www.koreaexim.go.kr>.

percent and 13.1 percent, respectively), while Korea managed only single-digit growth (7.4 percent and 2.7 percent, respectively). The study projected that China would surpass Korea in the competitiveness of its auto parts and semiconductor industries by 2010, while China had largely equaled Korea already in the production of many ordinary household appliances and electronics goods. In another example, Posco was until recently the lowest-cost producer of cold-rolled steel sheets; World Steel Dynamics reports that Chinese labor costs now undercut Posco's efficiency advantages in many areas of production. Korean construction firms also are losing business to Chinese firms in international construction markets on the basis of lower Chinese labor costs. Korean firms need to develop effective higher-technology methods to help them compete overseas and in China.

Based on its labor cost advantage, China has now assumed the undisputed position as the central global hub for low-cost production of consumer goods. It is also the world's leading destination for FDI. In 2002, China received US$52.7 billion in investment, and so it surpassed the United States as the world's biggest recipient of FDI. Many Korean companies in labor-intensive industries such as textiles and parts assembly for electronic goods have joined the global trend, and have begun moving their factories to China.

Korean FDI into China also faces stiff competition from third countries' FDI in China. For example, although the Korean petrochemical and shipbuilding sectors are likely to benefit from increased Chinese demand in the near term, they will face stiff competition after 2005 from Chinese joint ventures with non-Korean partners, as well as from investments by the Chinese themselves in these sectors. From oil refining to steel and container handling, the stimulus to Korea's economy created by China's increasing demand may prove to be short lived. China's plans to build indigenous capacity, with or without non-Korean partners, may be fulfilled in three to five years.

Another aspect of China's increased price competitiveness is the growing Chinese presence in Korean domestic markets. The aforementioned "garlic war" is a clear example of this. The Korea International Trade Association reports that Korea recorded its first-ever trade deficit with China in electrical goods in 2002, and that Chinese home appliance and communications goods producers are seriously undercutting Korea's position as a low-cost supplier in key global markets. From the beginning of 2002, the Korean textile sector also suffered a trade deficit with China. As multinational companies increasingly use China as the world's low-cost production platform across industrial sectors, Korea will find itself pressed by China in ever more sectors. Korean companies will only be able to hold on to market share by advancing product quality, rather than by relying on pricing mechanisms.

## Narrowing the Technology Gap

China has benefited from Korean imports in the form of new technology, particularly in manufacturing and IT. In fact, China is the leading destination for Korean technology exports that require royalty payments; payments from China constituted half of the US$193 million Korea earned in royalty payments in 1999. Yet it is not improbable that China's rapid industrial development will eventually challenge Korea's technological superiority. The Korean Ministry of Commerce, Industry, and Energy is projecting that Korea's technological advantages in automobiles, semiconductors, and shipbuilding will be "greatly reduced" by 2010. A recent survey of major Korean conglomerates shows that 43 percent of the businessmen believe the technology gap between Korea and China has been reduced to approximately four to five years in key industrial fields, while

27 percent believe the gap is only one to three years. Most of the polled firms were nevertheless planning to expand their operations in China, mostly through FDI.[7]

## China-Korea Private-Sector Initiatives and Strategic Collaboration

Joint initiatives and strategic collaboration are becoming more prevalent between large Korean corporations and Chinese firms. This is encouraging, because deeper economic integration between the two countries in particular and regional integration in general cannot occur without private sector initiatives and collaboration. Subregional and regional agreements that support private business interests and smooth strategic alliances between individual firms are also necessary to enhance integration in Northeast Asia. Such agreements should facilitate effective risk and profit sharing, quick solutions to trade disputes, efficient allocation and use of resources, unrestricted access to markets, smooth transfer of technology, and other necessary elements for sustaining strong regional partnerships.

Collaboration between Chinese and Korean firms has, in fact, already begun. As noted previously, telecommunications, automobiles, and consumer goods and electronics are the three sectors where China-Korea private business collaboration is most active. A Korean Ministry of Information and Communication road show to Beijing and Shanghai in June 2001 to promote Korean CDMA-related exports resulted in export contracts worth US$41 million for the 30 Korean companies. This included a US$10.6 million contract in Shanghai for Withus, a venture firm producing repeaters used in CDMA mobile networks.[8] SK Telecom has provided consulting services for successful commercial launches of CDMA technology in Heilongjiang, Fujian, Liaoning, Jiangsu, and Hainan provinces, and it has reached a cooperation accord with China Unicom (a partner of Qualcomm, the leading licenser of CDMA technology) in February 2000.

In terms of the Internet specifically, there has been some noteworthy cooperation. In March 2000, Korea Telecom and China Telecom announced a comprehensive business partnership focused on the Internet and international data services. China, Japan, and Korea have been cooperating over the past three years to expand domain registration options to include non-English scripts. China is a preferred destination for expansion for Korean Internet service providers. Korean Internet and software companies have also aggressively sought Chinese partners in anticipation of expanded Chinese content development, including in online gaming, an area where Korean companies have shown success and popularity.

Several Korean automotive companies have recently announced plans to build or open factories in China in order to take advantage of Chinese labor's lower costs and to position Korean brands in China's rapidly expanding domestic automobile market.[9] Ssangyong, for example, announced a 50-50 joint venture with the Jiangling Motor Company to produce sport utility vehicles and large luxury cars (Reuters 11 December 2002). Daewoo Commercial and Baotou North-Benz Heavy-Duty Truck Co., based in Inner Mongolia, signed an agreement on joint truck manufacturing in November 2002. Hyundai Motor's joint venture launched its locally produced EF Sonata on December 23, 2002, with plans to sell 80,000 cars in 2003. The company hopes to expand production capacity to 500,000 units by 2010 through US$1.1 billion in investments. Kia Motors launched the "Qianlima" in a joint venture with Dongfeng Yueda, and aimed to sell 50,000 units in 2003.

China's economic emergence is also driving economic reforms in Korea, as Korean companies see China as both a source of growth and stiff competition. Several Korean conglomerates, including Samsung, SK Telecom, and LG Electronics, are restructuring and adopting new management strategies to prepare for expanded roles in China's domestic economy. In certain sectors, strategies have even accelerated to take advantage of new business opportunities as China entered the WTO and lowered obstacles to market entry for foreign companies. China is central, for example, to Samsung's corporate development strategy that seeks to take advantage of the rapidly expanding Chinese mobile phone market. SK Telecom claims to regard its affiliates in China as Chinese companies, rather than branches of the Korean conglomerate. Posco has sought to develop partnerships with Chinese steel producers, instead of regarding them solely as competitors.[10] To take advantage of the growing demand for consumer goods and electronics, the LG Group has invested US$1.44 billion to build 24 production bases in China, including plants in Tianjin, Changsha, and Beijing (see the side bar "LG Electronics in China"). It seeks to consolidate its position as a major provider of reasonably priced household goods for Chinese consumers. Its Shanghai VCR plant, for instance, produces and sells ten DVD models.

Initial signs are that private-sector business initiatives and strategic

## LG Electronics in China

LG Electronics (LGE) is a good example of a large Korean company that has been highly successful in China. LGE first started operating in China in 1993, yet it has established itself as a mainstay for Chinese consumers in less than five years. In 1999, LGE led the Chinese market in sales of CD-ROMs, it was second in microwave ovens, third in monitors, sixth in washing machines, and seventh in air conditioners. It is continuing to expand dramatically. In 1999, LGE completed construction of a factory capable of producing 1.2 million color picture tubes for use in 29-inch flat and 33-inch wide televisions, both of which are in high demand in China due to the rapid growth of the Internet and the digital products industry. LGE currently runs ten locally incorporated manufacturing companies with a total of 17,000 employees, most of whom are Chinese. In addition to production facilities in locations like Shanghai and Changsha, LGE has 28 marketing offices throughout China, and maintains ties with 2,000 local companies. As of 2002, LGE held 35 percent of the market for microwave ovens, 20 percent for projection television sets, 10 percent for washing machines, 8 percent for air conditioners, and 4 percent for refrigerators. LGE is confident of realizing a turnover of US$5.5 billion in 2003, US$6.8 billion in 2004, and US$8 billion in 2005.

collaboration between Chinese and Korean firms have the potential to pave the way toward broader and institutionalized China-Korea economic integration, and this could help generate momentum toward regional integration initiatives. There is little confidence though in East Asia's record of regional economic cooperation, given failures like Japan's 1967 Pacific Free Trade proposal and the 1997 Early Voluntary Sectoral Liberalization initiative of the Asia-Pacific Economic Cooperation (APEC) forum. Yet the past should not be an obstacle. In the long run, strong private sector business collaboration between China and Korea could provide the stimulus for institutionalizing economic arrangements between the two countries in particular and in the region in general. The 1997 Asian financial crisis, the failure of the WTO and APEC to make headway on trade liberalization, the positive inspiration of the European Union, and broad disquiet with U.S. and EU behavior could all motivate China and Korea, as well as Japan and other countries in the region, to come together in the cause of regional integration.

Jwa Sung-Hee

## Institutionalizing Regional Economic Cooperation

The advantages of trade liberalization and its welfare effects for both China and Korea have become more understood with increased trade and investment in the past decade. Sectors like telecommunications, automobiles, consumer durables, and electronics have already shown the benefits of mutual exchange and cooperation. This should provide inspiration for a free trade agreement (FTA) between the two countries. Yet, subregional economic integration in East Asia has proven to be rather difficult, and progress toward this goal has been extremely slow.

## Prospects for China-Korea Economic Integration

Mainly because of political, economic, and ideological differences, at least prior to 1978 when China began its economic reforms, it was impossible for China and Korea to think of an FTA. China's pursuit of economic cooperation in Northeast Asia seems to have begun after the government granted special policy privileges to areas in Shangdong and Liaoning provinces in 1987. Discussions followed about forming "economic circles" around the East China Sea or the Yellow Sea. Korea's role was almost never mentioned in such proposals, partly because of North Korea, and partly because Korea had not directly approached Chinese authorities about possibly doing business together. In the 1990s, China's attention was mainly directed toward joining the General Agreement on Tariffs and Trade and its WTO successor, and subregional trade arrangements for East Asia were somewhat ignored.

China's rapid trade liberalization and its official WTO membership in 2001 have tremendously increased the chances for further opening up, and for eventual economic integration initiatives in the region. Moves toward regional cooperation would also be a natural response to the spread of regionalism in the past decade, and to the growing number of FTAs around the world.[11] The North American Free Trade Agreement (NAFTA), the Southern Common Market (Mercosur), the Free Trade Area of the Americas (FTAA), and the European Union are important examples from both sides of the Atlantic Ocean. The Association of Southeast Asian Nations (ASEAN) Free Trade Area (AFTA) and the APEC forum have established themselves as important regional institutions guiding economic activity in Southeast Asia and the Pacific Rim, respectively. The East Asian

220

region cannot afford to miss out on the many advantages of establishing a subregional FTA, and a China-Korea FTA should also be considered.

The arguments in favor of a China-Korea FTA include the need to fill the FTA vacuum in Northeast Asia. By coming together, China and Korea could play a dominant role in Northeast Asia specifically and in Asia as a whole. Even though there are still political and ideological differences between China and Korea, bitter past experiences with Japan have made it easier for them to come together. Geographic proximity also facilitates economic integration. In terms of comparative advantage, economic integration between Korea and China would enable efficient division of labor and speed up structural reform, both of which would boost mutual international competitiveness. A preferential trade agreement could also lead to further economic cooperation, such as a free trade zone, a tariff union, a common market, or even an economic and monetary union. Deeper economic integration in the region could also result in cooperation on political and security matters.

Arguments against a China-Korea FTA include the point that such a process should be subordinate to broader East Asian economic cooperation. Since 1997, the annual summit of the leaders of ASEAN member countries and China, Japan, and Korea (ASEAN + 3) has provided an important vehicle for regional dialogue beyond just China and Korea. Another argument against forming a China-Korea FTA is that China may not have enough capability and/or political will to implement deeper economic integration with Korea (or other neighboring countries, for that matter). Without detracting from its enormous efforts in liberalizing and expanding trade over the past two decades, China still has a weak industrial sector, and it lacks a comprehensive external economic strategy. Skepticism and pessimism are widespread about the prospects for a regional FTA.

In the aftermath of the 1997 Asian financial crisis, two trends have developed in discussions on regional economic cooperation, both involving trilateral cooperation between China, Japan, and Korea. The first initiative has focused on expanding regional trade cooperation, and has led to specific proposals for a free trade zone involving Japan and Korea. The Korean proposals in this regard have emphasized Chinese participation, such as in the September 2000 proposal for a Yellow Sea Rim Free Trade Belt. The second area of potential cooperation has focused on financial sector collaboration. The 1997 financial crisis, and the accompanying dissatisfaction with IMF reform packages and recommendations, stimulated high-level discussions on financial cooperation, including the establishment of an Asian Monetary Fund. Through a mechanism called the Chiang Mai Initiative, ASEAN + 3 countries have agreed on bilateral swap arrangements, as well as regional surveillance to monitor exchange rates and macroeconomic and sectoral policies, to help reduce the risk of another financial crisis. There is little reason why China and Korea, together with Japan and other Asian countries, should not actively discuss constructing a regional monitoring system of short-term capital movements in the future. Also, in August 1997, Japan astounded the international policy community with a proposal, dubbed the New Miyazawa Initiative, to create a US$100 billion Asian Monetary Fund to stabilize exchange rates in the region. Although this proposal died due to U.S. and IMF pressure, the idea of Asian monetary cooperation persists—but a lot of hard work still lies ahead.

## Road Map to Subregional Economic Integration

Economic relations between China and Korea, as well as neighboring countries such as Japan, ebb and flow as challenges and difficulties present themselves. Despite the private sector initiatives already discussed, a road map is perhaps needed to keep the East Asia region on track toward stronger regional growth, prosperity, and cooperation. Another key element of successful regional cooperation would be Japan's involvement. Despite its current problems, Japan remains an economic powerhouse. Any regional economic cooperative arrangement would be all the stronger, more stable, and successful if Japan joined hands with China and Korea.

As the first steps toward such regional cooperation, there are three areas where strategic alliances between Chinese and Korean companies could be strengthened: Production facilities and technologies could be exchanged, to help reduce excess capacity by introducing economies of scale; management strategies and decision-making could be coordinated and consolidated; and use of natural resources, such as energy, could be coordinated. There are, of course, many other possibilities for corporate collaboration. Cooperation between companies is felt to be the best way forward. Companies know their businesses most intimately, so this is the best way to make the most of business opportunities, and they enter into partnerships voluntarily in order to enjoy mutual benefits.[12]

Three subsequent phases are perceived in the road map toward realizing deeper economic integration in East Asia. Next, bilateral investment treaties should be signed between China and Korea, and between China and Japan. (As co-hosts of the 2002 World Cup, Korea and Japan signed a bilateral investment treaty in December 2001). In this respect, the launch of the China-Korea Investment Cooperation Committee on May 11, 2002, was a milestone in China-Korea business relations. The following step in furthering regional integration would be establishing a China-Korea-Japan FTA. At a breakfast meeting of the leaders of China, Korea, and Japan at the ASEAN + 3 meetings in Manila in November 1999, there was consensus on the need for three-way collaboration leading to a China-Korea-Japan FTA.[13] The subsequent step in the road map toward regional cooperation would be establishing an AMF. China, Korea, and Japan establishing and managing a joint fund together would be most useful for regional financial stability. This would then allow for the development of an Asian Monetary Union, in terms of which member countries would coordinate monetary policy and the activities of financial institutions. With these elements in place, the momentum would then allow for the final stage of East Asian economic integration—the establishment of an Asian Economic Community, not unlike the European Union in structure.

## Conclusion

Two challenges will present themselves as China and Korea, as well as Japan, move toward closer economic cooperation and integration. The first challenge will be to set up properly defined roles for the three economies. A natural division of labor already seems to be emerging. For example, as the number one global producer in many labor-intensive industries (such as apparel, footwear, and many home electrical appliances), China would be the regional (if not global) manufacturing hub. As Korea and Japan are technologically more advanced, they would focus on high-end business in the capital sector, and the production of technology and skill-intensive goods. Korea's geographic location between China and Japan would suggest Korea becoming the region's transportation hub and the transit point for goods and services in Northeast Asia specifically. In the past years, Korea has experienced rapid growth as an intermediate transshipment point for goods into northeastern China, primarily due to the lack of capacity and quality in China's own transportation sector. Expanded air service at Korea's Incheon International Airport since March 2000 has provided a regional gateway for cargo and passenger service to many Chinese regional hubs. Pusan surpassed Kaoshiung to become the third busiest container port in the world in 2000, on the strength of its role in offloading and transshipping to smaller Chinese harbors in the East China Sea that lack large container capacity.[14] Since Japan is worried about future deflationary pressure, it could transfer its excess capacity and inject its state-of-the-art technology into both Korea and China. The enlarged market formed by the three countries would provide great economies of scale for all three countries. The benefits are obvious. But political barriers continue.

The role and influence of the United States is relevant too to the roles of China, Korea, and Japan in a future Asian Economic Community. China and the United States continue to regard each other warily, and, in many ways, the United States is not enthusiastic about China's ultimate aim of replacing it as the most influential power in East Asia. The international political climate, including the North Korean factor, will have great bearing on the prospects of deeper economic integration in East Asia.

The second challenge to fostering progress and stability in East Asia will be establishing a common Asian development model. Such a model would be influenced by Asian beliefs, values, as well as customs and traditions. Since the 1997 financial crisis and with Japan's decade-long economic malaise, Asian and Western analysts have widely criticized the Asian model. Whatever the criticisms, the unique strengths of East Asian countries that have brought them this far—together with proper coordination and commitment to economic integration and cooperation between China, Korea, and Japan—will allow a future of unprecedented economic opportunities, along with regional peace and stability. When reviving East Asia's strengths, it would also be worthwhile to examine certain features of Western governance systems. These would include its financial institutions and risk management techniques, corporate governance mechanisms, democratic and legal institutions, and so on. The new Asian model should not blindly or wholesale adopt any predefined standards or "proven" business practices (Jwa 2003). The standards defined and practiced should be put to the test of the markets; the region should define its place by the terms of the global economy, where strengths are acknowledged and weaknesses are quickly amended. The challenge for China, Korea, and Japan this century is to build an unique East Asian development model that contains its own standards, values, and business ideals, and that will truly balance power in the future tripartite world between East Asia, the European Union, and the United States.

## NOTES

1. Henceforth Korea is used to mean South Korea, unless otherwise specified.
2. Korea trailed the United States, Japan, Hong Kong, and ASEAN, but surpassed Taiwan.
3. Korean companies held 78 percent of the world's CDMA market in 2001, with exports valued at US$4,126 million. Three Korean mobile-service carriers—SK Telecom, KTF, and LG Telecom—lead the market.
4. Although LG Electronics got shut out in its bid to provide CDMA lines to four other cities, the Samsung Electronics contract is likely to bring with it sales to the Chinese market of hundreds of millions of dollars of Korean-made telephone handsets, including those from SK Telecom and other Korean mobile phone makers.
5. Bilateral trade surpluses or deficits are not universally regarded as leading indicators of economic competitiveness or macroeconomic imbalances.
6. For the first 20,000 tons of frozen or pickled Chinese garlic imports, the usual 30 percent tariff applies. Imports in excess of this quota are subject to a 315 percent tariff. Up to 11,895 tons of raw Chinese garlic imports are permitted, subject to a 50 percent tariff. The agreement essentially attempts to cap Chinese garlic imports to contain competition and future damage to Korean garlic growers, but it accepts that Chinese growers have already captured a share of the Korean market. A secret clause in the July 2000 agreement that has now become public notes that such controls were not to be extended beyond 2002. So Korean garlic growers, a significant domestic constituency representing a third of the Korean agricultural sector, were to be subjected anew to international competition from 2003.
7. This dovetails with a recent Korea Industrial Technology Foundation survey of over 1,000 Chinese business and research institutes, which revealed strong interest among Chinese firms for Korean capital and technology.
8. China's total demand for CDMA infrastructure, estimated to be over US$2.7 billion in 2001, is expected to have reached US$8.2 billion in 2003. The *Korea Economic Daily* reports that China's market for CDMA phones is projected to be 40 million users in 2003.
9. In addition to a foothold in the Chinese auto assembly market, Korean

companies are also exploring opportunities to develop high-speed railroads in China.
10. For further discussion of Korean corporate strategies in China, see Lee (2002).
11. Trade agreements have been reached at an unprecedented rate globally. A recent WTO report notes that more than two-thirds of the 144 regional trade agreements about which it was notified under Article 24 of the GATT were signed in the 1990s.
12. *The Economist* of July 13, 2000, argues that finance, rather than trade, could be the major impetus behind East Asian economic integration. Although there are merits to this, financial sectors are still underdeveloped in East Asia, so subregional integration through companies seems more realistic and viable.
13. Much needs to be done to foster trade between these three countries. According to *Korea Now* (24 August 2002), the share of intra-regional trade between China, Korea, and Japan was only 18.7 percent in 1997, in contrast with 59.7 percent for the European Union, 43.5 percent for NAFTA, and 71.1 percent for ASEAN.
14. The surge in transshipment activity at Pusan has stimulated massive expansion plans at Gwangyang. The construction of state-of-the-art port facilities in Shanghai will clearly eat into transshipment activity, raising questions about the viability of the Pusan-Gwangyang expansion plans. Korean businessmen and economic planners have focused on the short-term bottom line, despite the dangers that wait in the mid- and long-term as China builds its own capacity.

## Bibliography

Cai Penghong. 2002. "Chinese Perspectives on the Possibility of the China-Korea-Japan Free Trade Agreement." *Journal of East Asian Affairs* XVI(2): 198–224.

Cheong Inkyo. 2001. *The Impact of China's Entry to the WTO on China-Japan-Korea Trade Relations and Policy Implications for Regional Economic Cooperation.* Seoul: Korea Institute for International Economic Policy.

Jwa Sung-Hee. 2003. "In Search of 'Global Standards': The Fallacy of Korea's Corporate Policy." *Harvard Asia Quarterly* 7(2): 45–52.

Kang Jung Mo and Park Won Kyu. 2003. "The Implications of the Emerging Chinese Economy as a Manufacturing Superpower." *Comparative Economic Review.* October. Seoul: The Korea Association for Comparative Economics.

Kim Ju Young. 2001. "Korea's FDI to China: Current and Future." The Korean Bank of Exports and Imports. September.

Kim Si Joong. 2002. "Implications of China's Accession to the WTO for the Korean Economy." In Lee Kyung Tae et al., eds. *China's Integration with the World Economy: Repercussions of China's Accession to the WTO.* Seoul: Korea Institute for International Economic Policy.

Kojima Kiyoshi. 2002. "Asian Economic Integration for the 21st Century." *East Asian Economic Perspectives* 13(March): 1–38.

Korea Trade-Investment Promotion Agency. 2000. *The Recent Trend of Hong Kong's Re-export Performances and Its Implications.* Seoul: Korea Trade-Investment Promotion Agency.

Lee Jeanyoung. 2002. "Korea's East Asian Cultural Diplomacy and the Korean Wave in China." Conference paper for the Korea Advanced Institute of Science, 23–24 August.

# 14

# ASEAN and the Rise of China: Engaging, While Fearing, an Emerging Regional Power

## Noel M. Morada

Political and security relations between the Association of Southeast Asian Nations (ASEAN) and China is the focus of this chapter. The achievements of security cooperation between the two are discussed, as are the prospects for enhanced cooperation. The chapter argues that there is much room for improvement in security relations between ASEAN and China. ASEAN remains wary of Beijing's intentions in the region, despite some limited gains from the policy of engaging China. Much is expected of an emerging power like China, not only in terms of allaying fears, but also in building credibility and integrity as a responsible power in Southeast Asia.

### Exploring Mutual Interests and Building Confidence

China's political and security relations with ASEAN have improved significantly in the last ten years, in spite of concerns in the region about the security implications of China's growing economic and military capabilities. Increased ASEAN-China exchanges, even prior to a dialogue partnership being formalized in 1996, and interaction in the context of the ASEAN Regional Forum (ARF) have served as the main venues for ASEAN to engage China on security matters. China was initially uncomfortable with the ARF as a multilateral security framework in Asia Pacific, but it gradually adopted a more positive stance and a more active role in the forum. Much of this may be attributed to the "mutuality" of interests between ASEAN and China. This includes ensuring that no Western power dominates the agenda of the ARF, although China does support ASEAN being in the driver's seat in the ARF.

China's political and security ties with ASEAN were further enhanced when the ASEAN + 3 framework—that also includes Japan and South Korea—was launched in 1997. A regional approach to mutual concerns, including security matters, was envisioned with this framework, which is based on ASEAN's existing dialogue partnerships with China, Japan, and South Korea. At the sixth ASEAN-China summit in Phnom Penh in November 2002, ASEAN and China signed joint declarations on Cooperation in Non-Traditional Security Issues and on the Conduct of Parties in the South China Sea, as well as agreeing to comprehensive economic cooperation. Interestingly, ASEAN highlighted the declaration on the South China Sea as the most important achievement of the Phnom Penh summit, while China played up the economic cooperation initiative and the declaration on nontraditional security issues.

## Moving Toward a Binding Code of Conduct on the South China Sea?

For ASEAN, agreement on a regional code of conduct concerning the South China Sea would be an important yardstick. Although the Phnom Penh summit failed to produce a legally binding code of conduct,[1] the agreed-upon declaration was nevertheless viewed by many in ASEAN as a "big step" in the right direction. The Phnom Penh Declaration attempts to ensure the peaceful management of territorial conflicts, and to establish an informal code of conduct among parties based on the nonuse of force, self-restraint, and freedom of passage in the area (Emmers 2002). The declaration calls on the parties' defense officials to exchange views, on advance notice to be given voluntarily of military exercises, and on humane treatment to be extended to any person in danger or in distress in the South China Sea. The parties to the declaration also indicated their desire to cooperate in marine environmental protection and scientific research, navigational safety, and search-and-rescue operations, as well as in combating transnational crimes (Emmers 2002).

The Philippines hopes that the Phnom Penh Declaration will eventually lead to the adoption of a binding code of conduct that would also uphold pertinent international laws on navigation and on access to the

South China Sea (*Asia Pulse Pte Limited* 6 November 2002). However, this remains wishful thinking for now, given that the declaration failed to settle the issue of sovereignty over the disputed islands in the South China Sea. In Phnom Penh, parties had to make certain concessions before a watered-down version of the declaration could be finalized. Specifically, in a compromise to demands from the Philippines and Vietnam, China agreed to the stipulation that claimants must refrain from settling uninhabited islands and reefs in the disputed area (Chongkittavorn 2002a). ASEAN then agreed to include the phrase "on the basis of consensus" when referring to attaining a code of conduct on the South China Sea, and to the declaration's geographic scope being left undefined (Emmers 2002).

Overall, the Phnom Penh Declaration on the South China Sea is much more elaborate than the declaration ASEAN and China agreed to in Manila in 1992. The latter simply urged self-restraint among claimants, and peaceful resolution of territorial disputes. The former is more explicit about activities that must be avoided—such as inhabiting new islands and reefs—and those that can be pursued without exacerbating the situation in the area. It also recognizes the important role of militaries in preventing future clashes in the South China Sea, and it explicitly notes commitment and respect to the 1982 UN Convention on the Law of the Sea, particularly the freedoms of navigation and overflight. Both the Manila and Phnom Penh declarations emphasize the need for an international code of conduct among claimant states, with the later declaration, as noted, recognizing the need for parties to work toward this objective based on consensus. The progress made since the 1992 Manila Declaration indicates that ASEAN and China could overcome a number of obstacles toward achieving such a goal if they moved away from viewing their interests as mutually exclusive. In today's economically integrated world, much is expected of those that are stronger to be more responsible in their actions toward those that are weaker.

## Promoting an Alternative Framework for Nontraditional Security Issues

The events of September 11, 2001, created opportunities for ASEAN-China security cooperation, including in the fight against terrorism. China has promoted a security framework based on "five principles of peaceful coexistence" that emphasizes building mutual trust with other countries, and shuns military alliances, overseas deployment, and even military exercises. This "new security concept" was proposed at an ARF ministerial meeting in Brunei in July 2002, and was seen by some as a Chinese attempt to capitalize on strong international opposition to U.S. unilateralism in dealing with terrorism. Although there is really nothing new in China's proposal, it indicates Beijing's desire to carve a niche for itself, and to promote an alternative to the U.S. security framework anchored in military alliances (Chongkittavorn 2002b).

China's growing confidence in regional security issues stems mainly from its positive experience as a founding member of the Shanghai Cooperation Organization (SCO). The SCO security framework has contributed to reducing tensions between China and its Central Asian neighbors, including Russia.[2] So Beijing is eager to promote a similar framework in Southeast Asia. Hence the importance it attaches to the ASEAN-China Declaration on Cooperation in the Field of Non-Traditional Security Issues. This declaration covers illegal trafficking of drugs, people smuggling, sea piracy, terrorism, arms smuggling, money laundering, international economic crime, and cyber crime. It also identifies information exchange, personnel exchange and training, capacity building, and research on nontraditional security issues as the primary areas for cooperation between ASEAN and China (*Xinhua* News Agency 13 November 2002).

China's attempts at boosting bilateral security ties with some ASEAN states as part of its cooperative counterterrorism initiatives may also be aimed at countervailing similar efforts by Western powers. Australia and the United States particularly have been pushing for closer military ties with their regional allies. In a September 2002 visit to Indonesia and the Philippines, Chinese Defense Minister Chi Haotian proposed cooperating against terrorism through military training, equipment assistance, exchange of students and defense officials, and information sharing. Taiwan could also be a factor in these offers; some ASEAN states and Taiwan intermittently seek closer linkages, including cooperation in the military sphere. For example, the Armed Forces of the Philippines explored buying second-hand fighter jets from Taiwan, but had to abandon the idea following strong protests from China, complaints which were reiterated during the Chinese defense minister's visit (*Philippine Daily Inquirer* 26 September 2002). Manila bowed to Chinese pressure partly because it was courting support from Beijing for a Philippine bid for a seat in the United Nations Security Council (Kyodo News Service 14 September 2002). China also protested the planned visit of Taiwan's president to Indonesia in December 2002 to forge closer trade ties between Taiwan and Yogyakarta province. Indonesia was forced to cancel the visit due to strong pressure from China (*Jakarta Post* 13 January 2003).

## PROSPECTS FOR SECURITY COOPERATION: ISSUES AND CONCERNS

Notwithstanding significant improvements in ties at the regional level, a number of issues and concerns continue to disturb, if not undermine, ASEAN-China relations. Foremost among these is ongoing wariness in ASEAN about the security implications of China's rise as a military power. As depicted in table 1, much of this stems from the fact that China's military expenditures have increased considerably in the past decade, while those of ASEAN and other powers have remained constant or have even decreased. Despite Beijing's efforts to allay persistent fears in the region about its military posture, particularly through publication of defense white papers, some in ASEAN remain suspicious of China's intentions. Domestic politics also contributes to vacillating attitudes in ASEAN states toward China.

## Perceptions and Policies toward China: Vigilance and Guarded Optimism

A number of ASEAN countries continue to be latently suspicious of China's intentions in the region. In Indonesia, the traditional view of China as an "expansionist power" establishing a "sphere of influence" in Southeast Asia still persists, especially in standard texts of Indonesian history. The perception of most Indonesian leaders of a Chinese "threat" is anchored in the belief that, because China sees itself as the "Middle Kingdom," it will behave as an aggressive and arrogant power (Sukma 2002, 189). Even though relations between Indonesia and China were normalized in 1990, Jakarta has not abandoned its vigilant stance toward China due to the latter's more assertive policy in the South China Sea. Bilateral relations between the two countries may be complicated in the future by domestic politics in Indonesia: The consolidation of democracy in Indonesia will likely lead to a more "intrusive" foreign policy, particularly on human

Table 1. Comparative Military Expenditures between China, Japan, the
United States, and ASEAN-10, 1990–2001

| Countries | 1990 SIPRI | 1995 SIPRI | 2000 SIPRI | 2000 IISS | 2001 SIPRI | 2001 IISS |
|---|---|---|---|---|---|---|
| (US$ bn) | | | | | | |
| China | 12.0 | 13.9 | 23.1 | 42.0 | 27.0 | 46.0 |
| Japan | 34.3 | 36.9 | 38.0 | 45.3 | 38.4 | 39.5 |
| U.S. | 405.5 | 316.4 | 305.2 | 304.1 | 306.5 | 322.3 |
| ASEAN-10 | 14.1 | 17.8 | 15.6 | 15.1 | 8.1 | 15.2 |
| (US$ mn) | | | | | | |
| Brunei | 307 | 255 | - | 353 | - | 279 |
| Cambodia | 58 | 106 | 80 | 195 | 78 | 188 |
| Indonesia | 756 | 925 | 1,111 | 614 | - | 860 |
| Laos | - | - | - | 20 | - | 19 |
| Malaysia | 1,053 | 1,744 | 1,567 | 2,579 | 1766 | 3,249 |
| Myanmar | 6,146 | 8,036 | 5,727 | 1,020 | - | 1,088 |
| Philippines | 733 | 945 | 843 | 1,357 | - | 1,065 |
| Singapore | 2,284 | 3,208 | 4,523 | 4,316 | 4542 | 4,280 |
| Thailand | 1,803 | 2,598 | 1,808 | 2,419 | 1731 | 1,831 |
| Vietnam | 1,031 | - | - | 2,303 | - | 2,351 |

Sources: Stockholm International Peace Research Institute (SIPRI) 2002 Military Expenditure Database <first.sipri.org> and International Institute for Strategic Studies'
(IISS) *The Military Balance, 2002-2003*. Figures for ASEAN-10 based on an aggregate
of SIPRI and IISS data; those in brackets are based only on available SIPRI data.

rights. Islamic groups in Indonesia are likely to express solidarity with Mus-
lims in other countries, including China, as the role of Islam increases in
Indonesian politics. The Indonesian military's wariness toward China may
resurface, especially if the TNI demands that civil-military relations in the
country be anchored in an equal partnership (Sukma 2002, 197–198).

In the Philippines, perceptions about China are shaped by historical,
geographical, and domestic factors. Specifically, suspicions about Chinese
intentions spring from Manila's ideological and political differences with
Beijing, particularly during the cold war, and the uncertainties of the post–
cold war regional security environment. Also influential in concerns about
China are the Philippines' internal and external vulnerabilities following
the 1992 withdrawal of U.S. bases, and China's assertive behavior in the
South China Sea and toward Taiwan. Indeed, apprehensions about an increasingly powerful and confident China, coupled with the weakness of
the Armed Forces of the Philippines, have shaped the Philippine
government's responses vis-à-vis China in the South China Sea (San Pablo-
Baviera 2002, 260–261). Given the country's weak external defenses, the

Philippines has relied primarily on diplomatic pressure in dealing with China. Both bilateral and multilateral diplomatic approaches—the latter primarily through ASEAN—have been pursued to bring international opinion to bear on Chinese actions in the Spratlys (Morada and Collier 1998). In addition to undertaking military modernization, the Philippines also signed a visiting forces agreement with the United States in 1998. This was perceived by many as providing some kind of psychological assurance about U.S. willingness to play a stabilizing role in the region (Lamb 1999).

Vietnam's relations with China have improved considerably since 1991, particularly in the economic sphere. Yet Hanoi is still wary of Beijing's intentions in the region. While border agreements in 1999 and 2000 may have partly resolved some of the long-standing animosity on territorial issues, the South China Sea dispute is still a major irritant in bilateral relations. For instance, even though it reluctantly agreed to a declaration on conduct in the South China Sea, China rejected Vietnam's demand to include the Paracels in the scope of the declaration (Hung 2000, 105). Along with Manila, Hanoi has been pushing for a regional code of conduct on the South China Sea to which all claimant states would agree to abide.[3] Overall, Vietnam is attempting to find a balance between its economic relations with China and its territorial interests; it is also trying to have good political relations with China while maintaining a credible military deterrence (Thayer 2002, 282–283). The Vietnamese are prudently trying to avoid either confrontation with or dependence on its northern neighbor, knowing full well the disparity in power capabilities.

Malaysia has managed its dispute with China over the Spratlys quite well, even as it maintains close political ties with China. In August 1999, when Malaysia erected some structures on Erica Reef and Investigator Shoal, there were strong protests from the Philippines, but there was no reaction from China. Although the political leadership in Kuala Lumpur thus far maintains a positive perception of China, concerns about China prevail within the Malaysian defense establishment. One view maintains its concerns are mainly confined to the regional spillover effects of a potential war in the Taiwan Strait (Baginda 2002, 244–245). Another view identifies three sources of insecurity about China: the general uncertainty about the region's strategic climate; China's military buildup, in the context of the post–cold war decline of the U.S. and Russian military presence in the region; and the Spratlys dispute (Acharya 1999, 131–133).

Singapore views the rise of China more as a potential threat than as an actual threat. Just like its ASEAN neighbors, Singapore's security concerns revolve around China's emergence as a military power, its policies in the South China Sea and Taiwan disputes, and whether or not it will behave like a regional hegemonic power in the long run. Being a very small state and one that is dependent on external trade, Singapore regards managing the trilateral relationship between China, Japan, and the United States as important for ensuring peace and stability in Southeast Asia. The Singaporean leadership also believes that a strategy of engagement and integration in the East Asian community best serves the interests of both ASEAN and China over the long term (Storey 2002, 221).

## Whither Constructive Engagement?

While effective management of China-Japan-U.S. relationships has certainly been crucial to regional stability over the past decade, ASEAN's engagement strategy vis-à-vis China may have contributed too. Even so, there are still some lingering doubts within ASEAN about the long-term effectiveness of engaging China, especially if the main aim is to "socialize" the Chinese into becoming a responsible and benign regional power. Skeptics suggest that engaging China cooperatively serves, for now, the economic and, to a limited extent, security interests of ASEAN. It has been argued, for example, that Indonesia's policy of accommodation toward China is "a stratagem undertaken without any deep-seated conviction in its merits and also without much regard for its outcomes" (Leifer 1999, 105).

So there is a somewhat schizophrenic attitude in ASEAN about the merits of engaging China. A scholar from Singapore suggests "hav[ing] a fall-back position because there is no guarantee that engagement will work. Letting China know that one is not disarming or repudiating the United States while one is actively engaging China will also give the latter the extra incentive to take engagement seriously" (Khong 1999, 125).[4] The same scholar also takes to heart a lesson from European experience: "[It] is not that accommodation is an inherently flawed policy but that accommodation from strength, rather than from weakness, is a surer way to socialize peacefully a new power into an existing order" (Khong 1999). Clearly, ASEAN is both hopeful and doubtful about China's intentions in the region, which suggests that a level of comfortable mutual trust has not yet been achieved.

However, the beneficial socializing element that is implicit in ASEAN's engagement policy toward China, even within the context of the ARF, for example, may not necessarily transform Beijing's fundamental interests, even in the medium term. There is merit to the argument that institutions merely constrain noncooperative behavior, but do not alter the interests from which such behavior springs (Johnston and Evans 1999, 263–265). Indeed, unless the policy of engaging China moves beyond dialogue and confidence building to a more institutionalized and substantive way of handling security issues, China's behavior will always be subject to interpretation and ASEAN may always hold it suspect. In bilateral relations and in the larger context of the ARF, ASEAN and China must push for instruments and mechanisms that will enhance compliance with behavioral norms. Being the stronger power, much is expected of China in helping to establish and strengthen such mechanisms. China's response to these needs would contribute to allaying persistent regional fears, and to building credibility and integrity in the eyes of its smaller neighbors.

## Lessons from SARS and the Lack of Chinese Transparency

The international outbreak in early 2003 of severe acute respiratory syndrome (SARS), a disease that originated in southern China in late 2002, raised serious questions—not only in the region—about whether China could be trusted at all (Rosenthal 2003). Many saw Beijing's initial attempts to downplay the serious threat posed by the infectious disease as indicative of China's continuing political immaturity and apparent lack of transparency, despite its impressive economic gains of the last three decades. The SARS outbreak, which affected ASEAN countries too, was a serious setback in China's efforts to gain the confidence of many countries in the region. This was especially so because SARS became a national security concern for many of these countries—it did not only undermine countries' health systems, but their economies too, particularly their tourism and travel-related industries. Chinese officials ought to be commended for their belated admission about the reality of the spread of SARS in China, albeit only after much international pressure, especially from the World Health Organization. But it remains to be seen whether Beijing has learned its lessons from the SARS crisis, and, if so, whether this will lead to China being more transparent over the long run. If China wants to be taken seriously by its neighbors as an emerging and responsible power in the region, it has to learn how to acknowledge its own limitations in handling problems that could have serious implications for others. Indeed, the SARS outbreak could be a catalyst for greater cooperation and enhanced mutual trust between ASEAN and China. An initial step in this direction would be to include emerging health problems in nontraditional security cooperation.

## Conclusion

ASEAN-China political and security relations have made significant progress over the last decade. Much of this can be attributed to China being more confident in the way it deals with ASEAN as a group. Some of its recent economic and security initiatives aimed at boosting ties testify to this. However, despite the limited achievements of ASEAN's engagement policy vis-à-vis China, fears about China's true intentions still persist in the region. For many in ASEAN, the glass is still half empty, and more is expected of the stronger power. The immediate challenge for an emerging power like China, therefore, is how to harmonize its national interests with those of its neighbors and the larger Asia Pacific community. The SARS epidemic that plagued the region in the first quarter of 2003 is a case in point, and an important learning experience for both ASEAN and China. For many in ASEAN, the SARS crisis was a wake-up call. Despite its impressive economic achievements over the last three decades, China must improve its political maturity and transparency, particularly in terms of its readiness to admit its own limitations. If mutual trust and confidence are to be furthered between ASEAN and China, China must take seriously the importance of complying with regional norms. Otherwise, ASEAN member countries will continue to be suspicious of China, especially if there are disparities between what it says and what it does.

## Notes

1. Malaysia apparently convinced ASEAN members to agree to a watered-down declaration, instead of a legally binding document (Chongkittavorn 2002a).
2. The SCO was formed to foster cooperation between member states in the fight against terrorism, "splittism" and extremism, illegal drug and weapons sales, transnational organized crime, and illegal immigration.

Its six member countries are China, Kazakhstan, Kyrgyzstan, Russia, Tajikistan, and Uzbekistan. At a November 2002 meeting in Moscow of SCO members, Chinese Foreign Minister Tang Jiaxuan emphasized the need to strengthen bilateral and multilateral cooperation among SCO members through increased consultation and coordination, and stepped-up exchanges with other countries and international organizations such as ASEAN.
3. For further discussion of Vietnamese views on the South China Sea issue, see Binh (1995) and Thao (2001).
4. A similar view is expressed by Hernandez (2000, 125).

## BIBLIOGRAPHY

Acharya, Amitav. 1999. "Containment, Engagement, or Counter-Dominance: Malaysia's Response to the Rise of China." In Alastair Iain Johnston and Robert S. Ross, eds. *Engaging China: The Management of an Emerging Power.* London and New York: Routledge.

Baginda, Abdul Razak. 2002. "Malaysian Perceptions of China: From Hostility to Cordiality." In Herbert Yee and Ian Storey, eds. *The China Threat: Perceptions, Myths, and Reality.* London: RoutledgeCurzon.

Binh Nguyen Din. 1995. "Security Implications of Conflict in the South China Sea: A Vietnamese Perspective." Paper presented at the conference "Security Implications of Conflict in the South China Sea: Perspectives from Asia-Pacific." Manila (12–14 November).

Chongkittavorn, Kavi. 2002a. "ASEAN-China Ties Take Big Leap Forward." *The Nation.* <http://www.nationmultimedia.com/page.arcview.php3?clid=2&id=68585&usrsess=1> (4 November).

———. 2002b. "China challenges U.S. with New Security Idea." *The Nation.* <http://www.nationmultimedia.com/page.arcview.php3?=11&id=63972&usrsess=1> (12 August).

Emmers, Ralf. 2002. "ASEAN, China, and the South China Sea: An Opportunity Missed." *Perspectives.* Singapore: Institute of Defence and Strategic Studies, Nanyang Technological University. <http://www.ntu.edu.sg/idss/Perspective/Research_050228.htm>.

Hernandez, Carolina G. 2000. "ASEAN Responses to an Emerging China: A Philippine Perspective." In Hung-mao Tien and Tun-jen Cheng, eds. *The Security Environment in the Asia-Pacific.* London: M. E. Sharpe.

Hung Nguyen Manh. 2000. "Vietnam in 1999: The Party's Choice." *Asian Survey* 40(1): 98–111.

Johnston, Alastair Iain, and Paul Evans. 1999. "China's Engagement with Multilateral Security Institutions." In Alastair Iain Johnston and Robert S. Ross, eds. *Engaging China: The Management of an Emerging Power.* London and New York: Routledge.

Khong Yuen Foong. 1999. "Singapore: A Time for Economic and Political Engagement." In Alastair Iain Johnston and Robert S. Ross, eds. *Engaging China: The Management of an Emerging Power.* London and New York: Routledge.

Lamb, David. 1999. "Philippines Pushes for Increased US Military Cooperation." Detnews.com. <http://detnews.com/1999/nation/9904/10/04100086.htm> (10 April).

Leifer, Michael. 1999. "Indonesia's Encounters with China and the Dilemmas of Engagement." In Alastair Iain Johnston and Robert S. Ross, eds. *Engaging China: The Management of an Emerging Power.* London and New York: Routledge.

Morada, Noel M., and Christopher Collier. 1998. "The Philippines: State versus Society?" In Muthiah Alaggapa, ed. *Asian Security Practice: Material and Ideational Influences.* Stanford: Stanford University Press.

Rosenthal, Elisabeth. 2003. "From China's Provinces, a Crafty Germ Spreads." *The New York Times.* <http://www.nytimes.com/2003/04/27/health/27SARS.html?ex=1052405023&ei=1&en=7d3d3c23615779fd> (27 April).

San Pablo-Baviera, Aileen. 2002. "Perceptions of China Threat: A Philippine Perspective." In Herbert Yee and Ian Storey, eds. *The China Threat: Perceptions, Myths, and Reality.* London: RoutledgeCurzon.

Storey, Ian. 2002. "Singapore and the Rise of China: Perceptions and Policy." In Herbert Yee and Ian Storey, eds. *The China Threat: Perceptions, Myths, and Reality.* London: RoutledgeCurzon.

Sukma, Rizal. 2002. "Indonesia's Perceptions of China: The Domestic Bases of Persistent Ambiguity." In Herbert Yee and Ian Storey, eds. *The China Threat: Perceptions, Myths, and Reality.* London: RoutledgeCurzon.

Thao Nguyen Hong. 2001. "Vietnam and the Code of Conduct for the South China Sea." *Ocean Development & International Law* 32(2): 105–130.

Thayer, Carlyle E. 2002. "Vietnamese Perspectives of the 'China Threat.'" In Herbert Yee and Ian Storey, eds. *The China Threat: Perceptions, Myths, and Reality.* London: RoutledgeCurzon.

# 15

## China's Economic Rise and the Responses of ASEAN

### Mari Pangestu

The emergence of China in the last decade has been felt by the member countries of the Association of Southeast Asian Nations (ASEAN), as well as by countries in other parts of the world. China's growth and size, and its ability to sustain high levels of growth in the face of vulnerabilities such as weaknesses in the financial sector and social imbalances, is greatly debated. However, no matter how growth and size are measured, and given inevitable ups and downs in any country's development, China's future actions and reactions will have a regional as well as global impact. China's ongoing process of fulfilling its World Trade Organization (WTO) obligations will lead to the increased openness of its economy, and it will impact emerging trade and investment patterns in the region. Any discussion of China's impact on ASEAN must, therefore, take into account China's WTO accession. ASEAN companies and countries have responded in different ways to the increased competition and opportunities arising from China's emergence. China is well aware of its neighbors' consternation about its emergence and has, since 2001, pursued a "good neighbor" approach to the region, most concretely evidenced by its proposal to create a free trade area (FTA) between China and ASEAN.

The chapter has three aims. The first is to understand the impact of China's economic emergence on ASEAN to date. The second is to assess China's potential impact on ASEAN arising from its adherence to its WTO commitments. The third and final aim is to evaluate the responses that will or should be taken to anticipate these major changes in the region.

# The Present Impact of China on ASEAN

## How Big Is the Giant Next Door?

From 1990 to 2000, China experienced an average real growth rate of 10 percent per annum, and its exports quadrupled from some US$62 billion to close to US$250 billion. At the same time, investment flows increased dramatically, from some US$3 billion to US$40 billion over the same period (ASEAN-China Expert Group 2001). China has also become the second largest economy in the world in purchasing power parity (PPP) terms, comprising 11.1 percent of the world economy, while the United States accounts for 20.7 percent.

However, in terms of effective economic purchasing power or current income at present exchange rates, China is an important, but not dominant, market. The current value of China's gross domestic product is less than a quarter of Japan's and one-tenth that of the United States and the European Union. In current dollar terms, China accounts for only 3.5 percent of world GDP.

Even though China has experienced rapid growth in its international trade, it still comprises only 4 percent of world trade, and the value of its total trade is three-quarters of Japan's and half that of the Asia-7 countries (although it is almost the same when intra-trade is excluded) (see table 1). Nevertheless, it has become an important source of export growth in the region and in the world. China accounted for around 30 percent of world trade growth in 2002, with different impacts on individual countries. For instance, China accounted for 70 percent of Japan's export growth in 2002, around 40 percent of South Korea's, most of Taiwan's, and around 20 percent–30 percent for ASEAN countries (Morgan Stanley 2003).

### Table 1. Comparisons in the Region

|  | China | Japan | Asia-7* |
|---|---|---|---|
| Population | 1,260 mn | 127 mn | 483 mn |
| GDP (US$) | 1,157 bn | 4,749 bn | 1,252 bn |
| Trade (US$) | 510 bn | 748 bn | 1,197 bn** |

Source: Compiled from Anderson and Hu (2003).
* Asia-7 comprises Indonesia, Malaysia, the Philippines, Singapore, South Korea, Taiwan, and Thailand.
** $649 bn without intra-trade.

The growth in China's exports is in line with the pattern of export-oriented development that other East Asian countries experienced. In fact, China's share of global trade growth and GDP have expanded at a relatively slower rate than was the case with Japan. During its period of significant export-oriented growth, Japan's share of world GDP increased tenfold and, vis-à-vis Asia-7 (Indonesia, Malaysia, the Philippines, Singapore, South Korea, Taiwan, and Thailand), it quadrupled. In the case of China, its share of world GDP is about the same as that of Asia-7 and about half that of Japan (see table 2). In terms of percentage of world trade, all three countries/regions experienced a fourfold increase in their shares, but China's share is presently half of Japan's share and that of the Asia-7 countries.

Table 2. Comparative Changes in Shares of World GDP and Trade

|  | China (1970–2000) | Japan (1955–1985) | Asia-7 (1965–1995) |
|---|---|---|---|
| Percentage of world GDP | 2 to 3.5 | 1 to 10 | 1 to 4 |
| Percentage of world trade | 1 to 4 | 2 to 7 | 2 to 8 |

Source: Compiled from Anderson and Hu (2003).

By most measures, China is not dominating the world economy. The major markets for China and Southeast Asia remain the United States and the European Union, and, to a lesser extent, Japan. However, China's continued growth and structural changes imply competitive pressure for structural change in Southeast Asia, as well as opportunities arising out of China's demand.

## Has ASEAN Lost Trade Market Share?

China's spectacular export growth has led to suggestions that China will become, if it has not already become, the world's factory that produces everything from low-technology and labor-intensive products to higher value-added goods, and that takes market share from competing countries. At the aggregate level, trade data from major markets indicate that, as China's share of world exports has gone up, the shares of Japan and the newly industrializing economies (NIEs) of Hong Kong, Singapore, South Korea, and Taiwan have declined, while Southeast Asian countries have thus far been able to maintain market share. However, the impact of greater competition from China for ASEAN and East Asia was a fall in unit prices.

This resulted in a slight decline in the East Asian share of U.S. imports to 33 percent from 40 percent for 1987 to mid-2002 as volume growth did not offset the price declines (Xie 2002).

A detailed look at the U.S. and Japanese import markets for 1987 to mid-2002 reveals other interesting trends (see tables 3 and 4). The Chinese/Hong Kong share of the U.S. market more than doubled to 10.4 percent from 3.9 percent. In terms of the East Asian portion of the total U.S. import market, China's increased share came at Japan's expense, with its share of the U.S. market falling to 10.6 percent from 20.6 percent. Taiwan's share fell to 2.8 percent from 6 percent, and South Korea's to 3.1 percent from 4.1 percent. ASEAN's share of the market was 6.4 percent for January to June 2002, a decline from its height in 1997 of 8.1 percent, and a rise from 1987 when it was 4.2 percent. In terms of imports to the Japanese market, from 1992 to mid-2002, the East Asian share increased to 41 percent from 30 percent. China's share increased to 18 percent from 8 percent, while ASEAN's share remained stable at around 13 percent–14 percent. The NIEs experienced a slight decline in their shares, with most of the impact of increased Chinese exports to Japan being felt by Japanese suppliers (Xie 2002).

Table 3. Shares of the U.S. Import Market (percentage of total)

|  | Total | China/HK | ASEAN | Korea | Taiwan | Japan |
|---|---|---|---|---|---|---|
| 1987 | 39.0 | 3.9 | 4.2 | 4.1 | 6.0 | 20.6 |
| 1990 | 36.9 | 5.0 | 5.5 | 3.7 | 4.6 | 18.1 |
| 1993 | 40.1 | 7.1 | 7.3 | 2.9 | 4.3 | 18.5 |
| 1994 | 40.1 | 7.3 | 7.8 | 3.0 | 4.0 | 18.0 |
| 1995 | 39.6 | 7.5 | 8.3 | 3.3 | 3.9 | 16.6 |
| 1996 | 37.1 | 7.7 | 8.3 | 2.9 | 3.8 | 14.5 |
| 1997 | 36.8 | 8.4 | 8.1 | 2.7 | 3.8 | 14.0 |
| 1998 | 36.5 | 9.0 | 7.9 | 2.6 | 3.6 | 13.4 |
| 1999 | 35.7 | 9.0 | 7.4 | 3.0 | 3.4 | 12.8 |
| 2000 | 34.8 | 9.2 | 7.0 | 3.3 | 3.3 | 12.0 |
| 2001 | 33.4 | 9.8 | 6.4 | 3.1 | 2.9 | 11.1 |
| Jan.-June 2002 | 33.3 | 10.4 | 6.4 | 3.1 | 2.8 | 10.6 |

Source: Xie (2002).

## Increased Exports Mean More Imports: The Story behind Market Share

The growth in China's exports has also meant increased Chinese imports due to the changing nature of the value chain. China's central role in this

Table 4. Shares of the Japanese Import Market (percentage of total)

|  | China/HK | ASEAN | Korea | Taiwan | USA |
|---|---|---|---|---|---|
| 1992 | 8.1 | 12.9 | 5.0 | 4.1 | 22.4 |
| 1993 | 9.3 | 13.5 | 4.8 | 4.0 | 23.0 |
| 1994 | 10.8 | 13.3 | 4.9 | 3.9 | 22.9 |
| 1995 | 11.5 | 13.5 | 5.1 | 4.3 | 22.4 |
| 1996 | 12.3 | 14.0 | 4.6 | 4.3 | 22.7 |
| 1997 | 13.0 | 13.7 | 4.3 | 3.7 | 22.3 |
| 1998 | 13.8 | 13.1 | 4.3 | 3.6 | 23.9 |
| 1999 | 14.4 | 13.9 | 5.2 | 4.1 | 21,7 |
| 2000 | 15.0 | 14.5 | 5.4 | 4.7 | 18.7 |
| 2001 | 17.0 | 14.3 | 4.9 | 4.1 | 18.1 |
| Jan.-July 2002 | 18.2 | 14.1 | 4.5 | 4.3 | 18.1 |

Source: Xie (2002).

process must be understood in order to assess the impact China is having on the region. When Japanese firms first relocated to the NIEs in the 1970s and 1980s, the export of capital goods and inputs from Japan to the NIEs usually followed the initial investment. Goods were processed in the NIEs and then reexported to the U.S., European Union, and Japanese markets. As the NIEs became more expensive in the 1980s and 1990s, Japanese and then NIE firms began investing in Southeast Asia. From the 1990s, they also began investing in China. Capital goods are now exported from Japan to the NIEs and China, and capital-intensive and other inputs are then exported from the NIEs to China and Southeast Asia. Labor-intensive processing takes place in China and Southeast Asia, and is then reexported to third markets. This is the vertically integrated value chain, or "flying geese" pattern of East Asian economic development.

China is taking away market share from Japan and the NIEs in the U.S. and Japanese markets, but this is partly due to the relocation of Japanese and NIE companies to China (and Southeast Asia) for reexporting goods elsewhere. Even though China has a trade surplus with major markets like the United States, it has growing trade deficits with Japan and the NIEs. At the same time, Japan's trade deficits with the United States and the NIEs are falling. China's expanding exports also mean increased imports, with Chinese domestic sources increasingly creating the demand for these imports. The share of Chinese imports coming from Japan increased to 16 percent in 2001 from 6 percent in 1990, those from the NIEs grew to 14 percent in 2001 from 6 percent in 1990, and those from ASEAN grew to 6 percent in 2001 from 3 percent in 1990.

These general patterns of trade, relocation, and production within the value chain are also revealed by looking at export similarity indexes* between Japan and particular East Asian economies for 1965—1996. Xu and Song (2000) found three distinct phases of convergence with Japan's export structure. Japan's trade structure converged with that of the NIEs from 1971–1983, with ASEAN's from 1984–1992, and with China's from 1986–1995. Within ASEAN, Malaysia's convergence with Japan was higher than that of other ASEAN countries until the late 1980s, and Thailand's has been higher since the 1990s. China's trade structure has been converging with Japan's since the early 1980s when reform started, and the index has been higher than ASEAN's due to the capital-intensive bias of its industrialization strategy. The results show the different levels of trade specialization that existed then, with Japan leading East Asian industrialization followed respectively by the NIEs, ASEAN, and China.

This flying geese pattern was also due to differences in factor endowments, and the three distinct periods for each group of countries are also the periods when FDI, especially intra-regional FDI, accelerated. That is, when the NIEs converged most with Japan, Japan was experiencing higher costs at home. So it restructured its industries and relocated them to the NIEs. Similarly, ASEAN countries converged with the NIEs when they upgraded their industrial structures and, due to appreciating currency, labor, and other costs, relocated industries to ASEAN. China had a similar experience in attracting FDI from Japan and the NIEs. Yet it does not appear to be next in the flying geese sequence. Rather, it appears to be a lower-labor-cost alternative to ASEAN countries.

Vertical specialization and the division of production along the value chain explain much of the shift in the pattern. The industrialization gap between ASEAN and the NIEs is larger than that between ASEAN and China in their relationship with Japan, indicating that the NIEs are competing more with Japan, and ASEAN more with China in third markets. To measure this, Xu and Song calculated export similarity indexes between China and other East Asian economies. They found that China's

---

*For commodities, an export similarity index measures the extent of similarity in commodity exports of any two countries (or group of countries). For markets, an export similarity index measures the extent of similarity of export destinations of any two countries (or group of countries). The extent of similarity in the commodity exports of any two countries (or group of countries) to a third market (or world market) can be measured by combining the indexes for commodities and markets.

exports were more similar to those of the NIEs than of ASEAN from the early 1960s to early 1990s. Then the trend started reversing, with the similarity between ASEAN and Chinese exports increasing rapidly. This suggests that the NIEs have widened their scope for export specialization by continuous upgrading and restructuring, including relocating parts of the production process to China. Meanwhile, increased export similarity between ASEAN and China indicates narrowed export specialization, especially since the mid- to late 1980s. This is presumably due to similar patterns of export-oriented industrialization based on labor-intensive industries. So the NIEs and China compete less in third markets than they did previously, while China and ASEAN are competing more in third markets.

To evaluate this competition, Song and Xu looked at export similarity indexes comparing China and other Asian economies, especially ASEAN, in the U.S. and global markets for total manufactures, and textiles and clothing. The measures show that the similarity between manufactured exports from Japan and China to the U.S. market began diverging in the 1970s. The export structures of the NIEs and China in the U.S. market in the 1970s were more similar than ASEAN's; in the late 1980s, the trend began to reverse itself, with the export structure of ASEAN countries and China to the U.S. market becoming more similar. In terms of individual countries, China has been competing most with Indonesia and Thailand, and least with the NIEs, especially Singapore.

The results are similar for textiles and clothing in the U.S. market. Vis-à-vis individual countries, by the mid-1990s, China was competing most with Thailand, Indonesia, and the Philippines, and least with Japan, Taiwan, and South Korea in producing textiles and clothing in the world market. Among ASEAN economies, Malaysia competed least with China in producing and exporting these products.

The aggregate trend showing ASEAN's share of major markets to be stable does, of course, hide the effect of increased competition from lower-cost Chinese exports for some products. As can be expected, the biggest impact for Southeast Asian countries has been on labor-intensive products. James et al. (2003) also shows that China has gained Japanese market share in textiles and clothing at ASEAN's expense. For instance, from 1996 to 2001, China's share of Japan's cotton knit apparel market increased to 77.3 percent from 47.3 percent, and, for man-made fiber knit apparel, to 80.4 percent from 59.1 percent. Japan does not impose bilateral quotas, so these figures reflect more open competition. That ASEAN countries maintained, and sometimes slightly increased, their U.S. market share also reflects the effect of quota allocations, and the fact that China was ineligible for quota growth rates prior to WTO accession. Quota restraints had helped keep the competition at bay.

## China as a Competitor for Investment

In terms of absolute value, China has definitely absorbed a greater amount of foreign direct investment (FDI) than other Asian countries, although the share of FDI is comparable to that of other East Asian countries as a percentage of GDP. The large amount of FDI going to China is commensurate with its size and the fact that, during and after the Asian financial crisis, the region's economies grew sluggishly. With its higher growth, large domestic market (potential), and assumed greater stability, China looked the more attractive option.

More worrying for Southeast Asia than the huge amount of FDI going to China should be the changing nature of the FDI that China is attracting (see the "Recent Trends in FDI in China" sidebar). This investment could enable China to climb the rungs of technological capability and higher value-added faster and with more depth than Southeast Asian countries. Up to the early 1990s, relocating to a cheaper location to process exports was the motivation for FDI flowing to China. But, in the last five years, less than a third of FDI in China has been directed at export-oriented manufacturing. There has been an increase in FDI motivated by the actual and potential size of the domestic market (e.g. real estate, automotive, machinery, retail, and catering) and by the building up of infrastructure. The FDI now going to China is expected to enhance technological capabilities as China is attempting to set up regional and global production centers, including the higher value-added product development and research and development parts of the process. There is also interest in using China for regional procurement and logistical centers. Investments relocating to China are no longer just attracted by the low cost of unskilled labor and the perceived more stable and secure political environment, but FDI is increasingly attracted by the lower cost of skilled labor and by improving support infrastructure.

| Recent Trends in FDI in China |
| --- |
| A fifth of Japanese firms are considering shifting production and procurement to China to supply parts to major customers, as well as to supply the domestic market. This includes manufacturers of flat-screen televisions, DVD players, liquid-crystal display monitors, plasma-display panels, laptops, and digital cameras. |
|     Minolta stopped manufacturing in Japan and Malaysia, and moved to Shanghai late in 2002. Olympus will produce all its digital cameras in China by 2004. |
|     Intel doubled its investment in semiconductors in Shanghai. U.S. producers of telecommunications network equipment see China as the only market with substantial growth. |
| Source: Media reports. |

## Current China-ASEAN Economic Relations

Trade between China and ASEAN has increased in the last decade, with ASEAN now China's fifth largest trading partner, after the United States, Japan, the European Union, and Hong Kong. The growth rate of China's trade with ASEAN was around 20 percent for 1991–2000, compared with its overall export growth of 15 percent (see the sidebar "Summary of China-ASEAN Trade). As a result, in the same period, ASEAN's share of China's exports increased to 6.9 percent from 5.7 percent, and its share of China's imports increased to 9.9 percent from 6 percent. The structure of ASEAN's exports to China shifted away from resource-based goods—such as minerals, pulp, wood, vegetable oil, rice, and sugar—to manufactured goods, mainly final goods such as computers, machinery, and electrical goods. The structure of ASEAN's imports from China changed too, from diversified goods to a higher share of machinery and electrical components and parts. Intra-industry trade is strong in machinery and electrical components, and is linked to trade-related investments and the region's multinational production and sourcing structure (ASEAN-China Expert Group 2001). Intra-industry trade is also evident in textiles and fibers. China specializes in cotton-based fibers and a few types of synthetic fibers, while some ASEAN countries specialize in other types of synthetic fibers.

MARI PANGESTU

## Summary of China-ASEAN Trade

*Brunei*: The main export is fuel, while the primary imports are manufactured goods and food.

*Cambodia*: The major exports are processed wood.

Indonesia: Exports in 2000 amounted to US$4.8 billion, and comprised mainly resource-based goods (pulp and paper, plywood, vegetable oil, refined oil, and rubber) and some manufactured products (synthetic yarn). Imports in 2000 totaled US$2 billion, and included mainly agricultural products (rice, tobacco, maize, cotton, and sugar) and some manufactured goods (fertilizer and vehicle parts).

*Laos*: Exports in 2000, amounting to US$324 million, consisted largely of log, timber, and wood products. Imports were valued at US$540 million, and comprised construction materials, electrical appliances, machinery, motor bikes, automotive components, and textiles and garments.

*Malaysia*: Exports in 2000 were valued at US$2.3 billion, and were primarily made up of vegetable oil, plywood, electrical machinery and components, textiles, and non-cotton yarn. Imports amounted to US$1.7 billion, and included electrical goods and machinery, cement, iron and steel, and cotton fabric.

*The Philippines*: Exports in 2000 totaled US$663 million, and comprised resource-based products, some manufactured products, and food. That year, manufactured goods and some resource-based products made up imports of US$768 million.

*Singapore*: In 2000, exports amounted to US$9.3 billion, and comprised refined oil, electronic valves, data-processing machines, components, and heating and cooling equipment; imports amounting to US$12.3 billion included the parts of data-processing equipment, telecommunications equipment, petroleum, and electronic valves.

*Thailand*: In general, the primary exports are agricultural products—largely rice, fish and prawns, sugar, and fruit—and some manufactured parts and components, while typical imports are maize, fruit, and manufactured products such as electrical and computer parts and components, electric motors, and steel.

*Vietnam*: Exports amounted to US$430 million in 2000, and included minerals (crude oil and coal), vegetable oil, vegetables, and fruit. Imports were valued at US$570 million, and comprised garments and textiles, minerals, machinery, electronic and telecommunication products, and paper and paper products.

Source: ASEAN-China Expert Group (2001, Annex I).

ASEAN countries have also been competing with China and Hong Kong for FDI flows. In 2000, China and Hong Kong accounted for 80 percent of

FDI outflows, while Southeast Asia received close to 9 percent, compared with 34 percent prior to the 1997 Asian financial crisis, and around 60 percent in the early 1990s.

In addition to trade, investment relationships between ASEAN and China are also growing. Investments from ASEAN countries in China in the last decade have met with varying degrees of success. In the late 1970s, when China opened to foreign investment, Singapore was one of the first Southeast Asian countries to enter China, mainly in the form of small businesses based on ancestral links in Guangdong and Fujian provinces. In the early 1990s, the amount of Singaporean FDI increased dramatically, and, by the end of 1998, China accounted for the highest share of outbound Singaporean FDI. Most investment was in manufacturing (61 percent) and real estate (20 percent). After slowing down during the Asian financial crisis, Singaporean FDI in China increased by 9.5 percent in 2001. By the end of 2001, the cumulative amount of Singaporean FDI in China amounted to US$18.6 billion, making Singapore the fifth largest investor in China.

Recently China has been more aggressive in its outward investment drive, with the government encouraging Chinese companies to invest and contract for major foreign engineering and construction projects (*Far Eastern Economic Review* 28 March 2002). The "go abroad" policy appears to be motivated to expose Chinese firms to international business, as well as to secure access for China to resources such as fuels and minerals on which its high-growth economy depends. In terms of the latter motivation, resource-rich ASEAN countries, especially Indonesia, are especially attractive. The Chinese state-owned offshore oil company, CNOOC, recently acquired Repsol-YPF, a Spanish oil company, for US$584 million for its Indonesian oil and gas assets. This acquisition is the biggest foreign purchase of Indonesian oil and gas assets in the last decade (*Far Eastern Economic Review* 28 March 2002). Other gas purchasing deals are currently being negotiated between Indonesia and China. Generally, Chinese private enterprises have little experience with FDI.

However, given the region's sluggish growth, ASEAN only accounts for 20 percent of Chinese outward investment. It clearly is less attractive for investment, compared with Latin America, the United States, and Europe.

Surveys in Malaysia and Singapore suggest that the problems ASEAN investors have doing business in China concur with those typically experienced by other foreign investors. A survey of Malaysian businesses listed the main problems faced in China as being unpredictable laws, uncertain product standards, the weak legal infrastructure, and insufficient trade facilitation measures. A survey of Singaporean companies operating in China described the primary challenges as being inefficient bureaucracies, the low quality of work, low protection of intellectual property, financial market restrictions, and poor enforcement legislation. So an important issue for ASEAN companies wanting to take advantage of the opportunities provided by the China market is how to ensure a level playing field that complies with the multilateral rules of the game.

The other important component of the relationship between China and ASEAN is in trade in services, especially tourism, and financial and telecommunications services. China's growing prosperity means an increasing number of Chinese tourists are able to visit ASEAN countries. In 2000, 2.2 million Chinese visited ASEAN countries, with the most popular destinations being Thailand, Vietnam, Singapore, and Malaysia. ASEAN tourists have also visited China in increasing numbers. A drawback to ASEAN's attractiveness as an investment and tourist destination is the discriminatory treatment of ethnic Chinese minorities in some of these countries, especially in Indonesia. Given its sensitive nature, perceptions in this realm need to be managed carefully.

Increased economic relations and integration between China and ASEAN are due to China's dynamic growth; ASEAN's economic success, prior to the financial crisis; liberalization and reform in some countries; and geographic proximity.

## COMPETING WITH CHINA AFTER ITS WTO ACCESSION

The depreciation of ASEAN currencies due to the Asian financial crisis in 1997, and the fact that China did not then depreciate its currency, provided a temporary respite for Southeast Asia in competing with China, especially in terms of labor-intensive products. However, the longer-term structure of trade and investment patterns in the region will clearly change, especially given China's accession to the WTO in December 2001.

China's accession to the WTO means both potential opportunities and increased competition for ASEAN. The potential opportunities lie in ASEAN's ability to take advantage of China's increasing demand for imports that is implied by the growth in its exports and in its overall domestic economy. WTO accession also means that China's goods and services markets will become more open (see the sidebar "Summary of China's Obligations from its WTO Accession). Tariffs on manufactured products will decrease to 10 percent from 15 percent in the next five years. Quotas and quantitative restrictions will be removed and then replaced with tariff quotas, which will be particularly important for ASEAN agricultural products like palm oil, rice, and sugar. Other nontariff barriers and investment-related measures, such as local-content and trade balancing requirements, will also be immediately or gradually removed. Under its accession commitments, China will also have to open its services sector over the next five years. This will be significant for ASEAN economies in terms of professional services, tourism, and possibly professional labor mobility.

### Summary of China's Obligations from its WTO Accession

*Goods*: Removal of nontariff barriers, such as licensing and quotas in agriculture (rice, sugar, palm oil, rubber, wood products, and urea); tariff quotas may remain until 2004–2005, but must then be replaced with tariffs.

Further reduction in average tariffs (to 6.95 percent for manufacturing by 2005, to 17 percent for agriculture by 2005).

Full WTO membership implies the same growth in quotas as for other WTO members.

*Investment*: Removal of local-content and other restrictions.

*Services*: Liberalization of the entry, ownership, and regulatory framework over the next five years.

*Other*: Review of intellectual property laws, in line with the WTO Agreement on Trade-Related Aspects of Intellectual Property Rights (TRIPS).

*Rules*: Address antidumping, safeguards, and subsidies.

*Greater transparency and predictability*

Imports from ASEAN are likely to increase, given greater openness, growth of demand in China, and growth in labor-intensive exports dependent on raw materials and intermediate inputs. Indeed, it is crucial to ensure that products from ASEAN economies are an integral part of China's production network, in terms of benefiting from traditional multinational and intra-Asian investment in China, and from its levels of competitiveness and productivity (see the sidebar "Current Chinese Nontariff

Measures Faced by ASEAN Economies"). The goods resulting from China's production network are in turn exported to third markets. ASEAN products that stand to benefit are raw materials and agricultural products, such as oil and gas, wood, rubber, food, and other agriculturally based products, as well as intermediate manufactured products and electronic and possibly automotive components. ASEAN members must ensure they are sufficiently competitive to be able to supply such products to China.

## Current Chinese Nontariff Measures Faced by ASEAN Economies

*Import Bans*: On clothing, used motor equipment, and motorcycles; plants and plant seeds; chemicals, fertilizers, animal foods, and antibiotics to accelerate plant and animal growth; radioactive materials and waste; and magazines related to national security and morals.

*Quantitative Restrictions*: On unprocessed plastic polyester and plastic polyester-granule materials; cotton, cotton fibers, and gray cotton; and H- and L-shaped rods of iron and stainless steel.

*Quotas*: On rice and cereal; vegetable oil; rubber; and sugar.

*Nontariff Barriers*: Such barriers exist for imported vegetables, seed, chemicals, motor vehicles, and electrical and camera equipment.

Imported vegetable oil, sugar, alcohol, petrochemicals, seed, tobacco, cotton, rubber, wood, wool, steel, and acrylic have to move through Chinese state-owned enterprises.

Regulations exist on technology transfers and intellectual property rights for processing industries.

There is a minimum quantity for exports of motor vehicles, electronics, processed food, machinery, and textiles.

Local-content regulations exist for motor vehicles, telecommunications equipment, processed food, electronics, and textiles.

There are regulations for foreign investors for balancing trade and foreign exchange.

Restrictions exist on trade in services.

Source: ASEAN-China Expert Group (2001, Annex I).

Not all ASEAN economies are WTO members yet—Cambodia, Laos, Myanmar, and Vietnam are not—and, as a result, they do not have most-favored-nation (MFN) status for exporting to China. Ensuring that these four members are integrated into the WTO system as soon as possible is a priority, in order to avoid unbalanced market access.

At the same time, pressure from competition and increased efficiency will enhance China's competitiveness in global markets and in ASEAN members' domestic markets. This competition is already occurring, and it will only increase, especially for labor-intensive products, such as textiles, garments, footwear, toys, and electronics and electrical appliances produced in labor-intensive processes. Furthermore, as China now has MFN status, importers could see it is a more secure supplier. China's removal of quotas on textiles and garments by 2005 will mean that ASEAN economies will have to compete openly in importing countries' markets; it will no longer have captive markets. It is likely that ASEAN members and other South Asian developing economies will then lose market share to China in textiles and garments. However, an increase in intra-industry trade could also result if competition leads to greater specialization and more rapid shifts in comparative advantage.

In addition to greater market access, China's WTO accession will hopefully also mean greater transparency and certainty about China's laws and regulations and their implementation. The WTO also provides a mechanism for resolving disputes on dumping or other actions deemed as violating its rules. China will also face many challenges in opening its markets and removing various tariff and nontariff barriers and subsidies. Agriculture and state-owned enterprises will be negatively impacted, with, for example, increased unemployment, and the Chinese government will need to respond to these adverse welfare effects. Exacerbated uneven development between the coastal and interior areas will also need to be properly managed.

The need to better manage China-ASEAN relations, as well as recognition of anticipated greater competition between the two, has led to a number of bilateral and regional initiatives.


## Appropriate Responses by ASEAN to the Rise of China

What the apropos reaction is for ASEAN economies to the China challenge is unclear. Should ASEAN countries compete in free open markets under a multilateral framework, while unilaterally liberalizing trade and investment regimes, and implementing other reforms in anticipation of the broad structural changes China poses? Should ASEAN members instead look to regional economic cooperation, which could include regional cooperation in multilateral forums? Could both strategies be pursued complementarily? Open discussion on these questions needs to proceed between ASEAN economies and China, as well as within each economy.

Businesses from ASEAN countries are already responding to the China challenge by trying to figure out how to be part of East Asia's export engine and new production network, and how to take advantage of China's domestic consumption demands. Companies and countries have to identify market niches and advantages, and think about how to maintain them. They also have to think about how relocating production and investment would favor them, and how to source components and final products from China while specializing in other components and products.

## Regionalism as an Answer

In response to the 1997 Asian financial crisis, an East Asian consciousness emerged. The crisis led to the first ASEAN + 3 dialogue among the leaders of the ten ASEAN member countries, and China, Japan, and South Korea. An East Asia Vision Group was then set up to discuss the group's vision. By 2000, the group proposed an East Asia–wide FTA or close economic partnership. The proposal was comprehensive, in that it included liberalization of trade in all goods, services, investment, and technology, as well as mutual recognition arrangements. It was also felt there should be separate agreements and cooperation on antidumping, competition policy, investment principles, dispute settlement, and capacity building. However, nothing much has happened to implement the study's recommendations, except there was an agreement to review a possible East Asian economic zone.

In Singapore in November 2000, the fourth meeting of ASEAN + 3 leaders agreed to a task force for studying various proposals for regional cooperation, and study committees were set up, including an ASEAN-China experts group. This group produced a visionary report, which was then discussed with senior officials. This led, in November 2001, to the surprise announcement by ASEAN leaders and Chinese Premier Zhu Rongji about the establishment of an FTA between China and ASEAN economies in ten years. That China-ASEAN economic cooperation forged ahead of East Asia–wide cooperation was seen as reflecting the lack of strategic vision of Japan's leadership at that time. Resistance to opening its agriculture sector hampers Japan. This was evident in negotiations for an FTA between Japan and Singapore, even though Singapore exports only a negligible amount of agricultural products.

In addition to cooperating with ASEAN, other collaborative proposals on the table for China include China-South Korea-Japan, greater China (Hong Kong, Macau, and China, and possibly Taiwan), and ASEAN + 3. None of these proposals has gone beyond discussion and study. ASEAN members like Singapore and Thailand have approached China for bilateral FTAs, but China has indicated its preference for dealing with ASEAN as a region, rather than on a bilateral basis. Bilateral agreements signed to date have been under the ASEAN-China framework.

Entering into regional and multilateral agreements are new experiences for China, as it considers the merits of regional versus global frameworks for pursuing liberalization and reform. The expansion of regionalism in the Americas and the enlargement of Europe has also contributed to East Asia searching for an institutional identity of its own, with deepening cooperation in trade, investment, and finance in East Asia being discussed frequently over the last few years.

There is now concerted focus on, and wide acceptance of, an ASEAN-China FTA (see the sidebar "Summary of the Framework Agreement"). Initial negotiations have been completed, and the agreement will be comprehensive, comprising an FTA, as well as facilitation, capacity building, and cooperative elements. Concern has, however, been expressed in some ASEAN economies about whether they will be able to compete with China and whether an FTA will be mutually beneficial. There have been calls to strengthen ASEAN in order to maximize the benefits accruing from any regional agreement into which it enters. Thailand and Singapore are the most supportive of the ASEAN-China FTA; Indonesia and the Philippines have assumed a moderate position; and Malaysia is careful in its stance, with the CLMV economies of Cambodia, Laos, Myanmar, and Vietnam being the most concerned about the effects of such an FTA. Anxiety on the ASEAN side includes worries about agriculture, even though an "early harvest" is being granted to give ASEAN economies entry into the China market before other WTO members. Negotiations on tariff lines have also encountered concern about sensitive-product lists, exclusions, and rules of origin.

## Summary of the Framework Agreement on Comprehensive Economic Cooperation between ASEAN and the People's Republic of China

The goal is to achieve an ASEAN-China Free Trade Area within ten years.

**Scope:**

*Market Access for Goods*: To eliminate tariff and nontariff barriers for most goods (this is taken to mean a zero percent tariff target). Tariff reduction or elimination will be done on two tracks—a fast track within three years ("early harvest"), and a normal track by 2010 for ASEAN-6 and China, and 2015 for CLMV countries.* The fast track comprises goods in the categories HS 1–HS 8** (live animals, meat, fish, dairy products, other animal products, live trees, vegetables and fruits, and nuts) whose tariffs will be reduced or eliminated by both ASEAN and China within three years. The second category includes goods that will be negotiated bilaterally between each ASEAN country and China whose tariffs will be reduced within three years; the same tariff reduction will be given to other ASEAN countries after the three years.

**Tariff-reduction schedule**:

*Category 1*: Tariffs that are greater than 15 percent in 2003 fall to 10 percent in 2004, to 5 percent in 2005, and to zero in 2006.

*Category 2*: Tariffs of 5 percent–15 percent in 2003 fall to 5 percent in 2004, and to zero in 2005.

*Category 3*: Tariffs of less than 15 percent in 2003 fall to zero in 2004.

Under the normal track, tariffs will be reduced or eliminated in stages between 2005–2010 for ASEAN-6 and China, and between 2005–2015 for CLMV. Exceptions or slower tariff reductions will be allowed for sensitive products, but these tariffs will also have to come under a tariff-reduction schedule, and the number of products classified as sensitive will be limited.

Other aspects that need to be negotiated in 2003 to realize the free trade area in terms of goods include regulations regarding tariffs, rules of origin, nontariff barriers (that is, not confined to quantitative restrictions such as quotas), and import and export bans. It also includes negotiations on safeguards, discipline in using subsidy and antidumping actions, and facilitation and protection of intellectual property rights.

**Trade and Investment Facilitation**: Effective steps will be taken to enhance facilitation; these will not only be confined to customs procedures and mutual recognition agreements.

**Other Cooperation**: Priority will be given to agriculture, information technology and communication, human resource development, and investment in and development of the Mekong River Basin. Other areas for cooperation include banking, the financial sector, tourism, telecommunications, intellectual property rights, small- and medium-sized enterprises, biotechnology, forestry, mining and energy, and other steps to promote capacity building.

Source: <www.asean.sec.org>

*ASEAN-6 comprises Brunei, Indonesia, Malaysia, the Philippines, Singapore, and Thailand. The CLMV countries are ASEAN's newer members: Cambodia, Laos, Myanmar, and Vietnam.
**HS refers to the Harmonized Commodity Description and Coding System's definitions of trade commodities. An ASEAN-China FTA would comprise a market currently totaling 1.7 billion people and a GDP of US$2 trillion, which is half of Japan's GDP at present but which could surpass Japan's in the next five to ten years, given high growth rates in China and other countries. Estimates of the potential economic benefits by the ASEAN-China Expert Study Group indicate that trade on both sides could grow 50 percent, and that GDP could increase 0.9 percent for ASEAN countries, and 3 percent for China.

Whatever the outcome of negotiations, agricultural products, especially those of interest to ASEAN, must be included for the FTA to have a meaningful beginning. The timetable for implementation should be clear, exclusions should be kept to a minimum, and the rules of origin should be as liberal as the ones used in AFTA, the FTA between ASEAN member countries. There should also be a clear signal that other crucial areas, like nontariff barriers, services, investment, and facilitation, will be addressed.

## Assessing ASEAN's Options in the Region

China has been most proactive in formalizing regional cooperation with ASEAN, and it is revealing that this push for collaboration has come ahead of East Asia–wide cooperation between ASEAN, China, Japan, and South Korea. China's initiative has propelled Japan into extending its own initiative to ASEAN, and South Korea has indicated some interest in moving in the same direction.

By default rather than by design, ASEAN has become a focal point, and, since AFTA is the formal ASEAN FTA, it too has come under scrutiny. Yet AFTA is facing problems and shortcomings of its own. So there are now calls for strengthening intra-ASEAN economic cooperation under the umbrella of an ASEAN Economic Community.

MARI PANGESTU

If ASEAN enters into further regional agreements, it needs to be clear on its objectives and must assess whether regionalism is the best way to realize these objectives. Entering into various regional agreements represents a departure from the current ASEAN approach—which has been encouraged, among other things, by regional peer pressure and WTO commitments—of opening their economies by undertaking unilateral liberalization on an MFN basis. AFTA had been perceived as a training ground for larger and wider trade liberalization; in fact, it even incorporates specific provisions for transferring regional preferences to multilateral forums. Also, the AFTA tariff-reduction schedule of most ASEAN countries mirrors a similar or identical MFN schedule, and the preferences that will be given to ASEAN members in 2010 under the ASEAN Investment Area will operate multilaterally by 2020. AFTA's rules of origin are also considered very liberal.

The stated objectives of the ASEAN-China FTA initiative are to take advantage of their complementarities and to build on existing strengths in order to make the region collectively more efficient and competitive, and also to attract investment. The additional aims are to use enhanced efficiency to compete in third markets, as well as to provide preferential entry to the markets of its members (of which China is obviously the largest).

If increasing efficiency and attractiveness for investment is the objective of forming an FTA, then ASEAN economies need to consider what they need to do in terms of unilateral reforms and to ensure that the multilateral processes continue. The latter is very important for securing China's implementation of its WTO commitments and for keeping global export markets open. Certainly, the trends discussed in this chapter indicate that ASEAN economies can benefit from being integrated into China's production network that targets the global export market and increasingly its own domestic market. It is definitely in the interest of ASEAN economies that China's markets and those of the world remain open—and, in fact, become progressively more open. If regionalism remains an option—which it may, for political reasons—then regional agreements should optimize gains for ASEAN, and minimize the resulting risks from unbalanced hub-and-spoke structures, cumbersome proliferation of administrative regulations (like rules of origin), and different schedules of elimination of barriers.

This would mean, first of all, large membership, as studies have shown that welfare gains are greater with larger numbers of members. So converging to an East Asia level of integration would make sense. Second, the type of agreement needs to be in line with deep integration and the new-age regional trade agreements that truly eliminate barriers to integration. On paper, the ASEAN-China FTA is relatively comprehensive and goes beyond removing tariffs and nontariff barriers to address trade in goods, trade facilitation measures such as conformity of standards and procedures, and trade in services. The ASEAN-Japan Comprehensive Economic Partnership may be more comprehensive, however, as its preliminary proposals include elements of cooperation in human resources, promotion, and other areas. At the moment, ASEAN is on the recipient end, and it needs to decide what kind of regional agreements are best for ASEAN. Otherwise, it could end up with different agreements with different partners that, in turn, create tensions in its relations with other trading partners, and lead to increased costs for business transactions. A two-hub world of Japan and China is disadvantageous for ASEAN; the hub should be ASEAN.

Other than these dimensions of economic integration, regional cooperation can enhance the sense of community within the region, reduce tensions, and contribute to stability. It can also enhance cooperation on external issues of common interest. At the end of the day, these dimensions may be more important.

## Conclusion

For ASEAN, its homework is, first, to continue its unilateral reform and restructuring process so that its competitiveness and attractiveness as an investment location are maintained. In this way, it would also be part of China's production network, and it would become more specialized and more flexible at shifting production processes. Some ASEAN countries will, of course, be able to exploit their natural comparative advantage in natural resources and agriculture, and they need to ensure sustainable policies on these fronts. Ensuring an open and fair multilateral trading system also remains crucial for ASEAN, given the importance of market access in third markets and in China's markets to maintain export growth. The potential for regional consensus building on issues of mutual external interest—such as the global trading system and issues within the Doha Round Agenda—should also be explored. In the past, such cooperation was more successful for ASEAN than intra-ASEAN economic cooperation, where national interests have typically dominated regional interests.

Regional agreements could be considered an option, but the scope of membership, the comprehensiveness of sector and instrument coverage, the time lines, and the downside risks of the cumbersome proliferation of these agreements need to be weighed. All sides need to assess the options carefully, to understand the potential net benefits and costs, and to evaluate whether the regional approach is the appropriate response for the stated objectives, and whether it is complementary to a multilateral approach. Broader liberalization on a multilateral basis would lead to greater net benefits. But, if regional approaches can be complementary, then there should still be net gains to adopting both approaches. An informed decision on the optimality and potential benefits of any particular type or combination of regional approaches needs to be made.

Given its growing regional economic weight, and that it will eventually surpass Japan in being the region's economic powerhouse, China will need to weigh the impact on East Asia of any options it takes. Indeed, a Chinese decision to opt for regional economic integration would be crucial for the region.

## BIBLIOGRAPHY

Anderson, Jonathan, and Fred Hu. 2003. *The Five Great Myths About China and the World.* Goldman Sachs.

ASEAN and China. 2001. Framework Agreement on Comprehensive Economic Cooperation between ASEAN and the People's Republic of China. <http://www.asean.sec.org>.

ASEAN-China Expert Group on Economic Cooperation. 2001. "Forging Closer ASEAN-China Economic Relations in the 21st Century." Report submitted to the ASEAN SEOM-MOFTEC. (October).

Findlay, Christopher, and Mari Pangestu. 2001. "Regional Trade Arrangements in East Asia: Where Are They Taking Us?" APEC Roundtable, Institute of Southeast Asian Studies. (June).

James, William E, David J. Ray, and Peter J. Minor. 2003. "Indonesia's Textiles and Apparel: The Challenge Ahead." *Bulletin of Indonesian Ecnomic Studies* 39(1).

Morgan Stanley. 2003. "Global Rebalancing."Morgan Stanley *Global Investment Research* (November).

Pangestu, Mari. 2002. "China and Southeast Asian Regional Trade

Cooperation: Trends and Perspectives." Paper presented at a conference on "East Asian Cooperation: Progress and the Future Agenda," Institute of Asia Pacific Studies and the Research Center for APEC and East Asian Cooperation, Chinese Academy for Social Sciences, Beijing. (22–23 August).

Pangestu, Mari, and Robert Scollay. 2001. "Regional Trading Arrangements: Stock Take and Next Steps." *PECC Issues* (October).

Soesastro, Hadi. 2001. "Whither ASEAN Plus Three?" Paper presented at the PECC Trade Policy Forum Seminar on Regional Trading Arrangements, Bangkok. 12–13 June.

Xie, Andy. 2002. "ASEAN and China: Partners or Competitors." Presentation for Morgan Stanley at the "ASEAN China Partnership Forum," Kuala Lumpur. 30 August.

Xu Xingeng and Song Ligang. 2000. "Export Similarity and the Pattern of East Asia Development." In P. Lloyd and Xiaoguang Zhang, eds. *China in the Global Economy*. Cheltenham: Edward Elgar.

# 16

# Reactions in Australia and New Zealand to a Rising China

## Greg Austin

In Australia and New Zealand, images of China and responses to it have been largely consonant for most of the past 150 years. Before 1949, both countries saw China as culturally exotic and intellectually rich, as well as inspiring as a civilization. In economic terms, both countries viewed China as a target of commercial interest, and in strategic terms as a victim of the Japanese aggression that was also directed against the interests of the British empire, and then directly against Australia. Neither Australia nor New Zealand had foreign policies independent of the United Kingdom until the fall of Singapore to Japanese forces in the Second World War.

After 1949, the milestones in Australian and New Zealand perceptions are, not surprisingly, the milestones in China's own political development and international policy. In 1949, the Communist victory in the Chinese civil war and subsequent upheavals—the Korean War, the Great Leap Forward, the 1958 Taiwan crisis, China's export of revolution, and the Cultural Revolution—put Australia and New Zealand in direct hostility toward China. This posture persisted until 1971–1972, with the advent of Labour Party governments in both countries, their withdrawal of support for the Vietnam War, and U.S. rapprochement with China. Growing economic interest by both Australia and New Zealand in China in the 1970s coincided with China relinquishing the export of revolution, abandoning Cultural Revolution polices, and launching reform and open-door policies in 1978 and 1979. The trans-Tasman interest in good relations with China after 1978 also coincided with the Vietnamese invasion of Cambodia and growing Soviet military or political power in areas such as Southeast Asia and even the South Pacific. Such areas were of direct strategic interest to both Australia and New Zealand.

The process of change in recognition policies of both Australia and New Zealand toward the People's Republic in the 1970s has also had a profound influence. Neither Australia nor New Zealand followed the British example in 1950 of granting diplomatic recognition to China, but instead for the most part followed the U.S. lead in this area, until 1971–1972, and recognized the government on Taiwan. This pattern of Australia and New Zealand following the U.S. posture was premised on an awareness that the security of the trans-Tasman partners could only be secured against a great power threat through close alliance with the United States. This tendency to follow the U.S. lead continued to be a key reference point for the reaction of both to China's rise in the 1990s and beyond.

There have been three notable divergences between Australia and New Zealand with respect to China in the last century. The first difference, which has persisted from most of the last century, concerns immigration and population issues. At Federation in 1901, Australia pursued a discriminatory policy toward Asians and deported most of its Chinese immigrant community. This "White Australia" policy was based on blind prejudice and was fed by fears that the largely uninhabited continent of Australia, so close by boat to Indonesia and Asia, could be overrun by "yellow hordes," an historical allusion to the Mongol invasion of Europe six centuries earlier. This policy persisted officially until the late 1960s. New Zealand did not have such an explicit policy. This was partly because it did not have large Chinese communities in the nineteenth century, and partly because it was geographically more remote. The irony is that Australia's fastest growing source of immigration in the last decade has been China. Indeed, Australia now has a large and growing number of citizens who can trace some origins to China. In this sense, Australia which was once institutionally more hostile to Chinese people than New Zealand is now much closer to them than its trans-Tasman counterpart.

The second dimension concerns the U.S. alliance relationship, and how the stance that Australia and New Zealand take to it has affected their positioning on a possible military confrontation between the United States and China over Taiwan. New Zealand has not been as visible as Australia in signaling its intention to stand beside the United States in such circumstances. But the governments and communities of both countries remain opposed to China's use of force against Taiwan, and even to the threat of the use of force.

The third dimension is that Australia has a much larger community of China specialists and China "hands" of various sorts than New Zealand.

This can be seen in many areas, but three stand out. First, Australian academics took a strong lead in the 1970s and 1980s in shaping Asia Pacific regionalism, based in part on the need to integrate China into a mutually beneficial regional order. Second, several Australian academics were among the first in the world, in the second half of the 1980s, to identify many practical measures that need to be taken to break through bottlenecks in the Chinese economy. To this day, these academics remain respected confidants and advisors of Chinese leaders. In a third example, a number of former senior Australian officials from Australia's Ministry of Foreign Affairs who managed the Sydney Olympic Committee are now assisting the Beijing Olympic Committee.

With these differences in mind, this chapter identifies four themes with respect to Australia and New Zealand. They are: their perspectives on a rising China, domestic influences on these perspectives, whether these perceptions match the likely reality of a rising China, and recommended appropriate responses to a rising China. Each section addresses these themes in terms of China's political conditions, its economic power, its strategic and military power, and its approach to Taiwan. Responding to a rising China by taking into account the question of Taiwan was a big part of the responses of Australia and New Zealand until the 1970s, and has again become central to their positions since 1995.

For the purposes of analysis, this chapter concentrates on the period from 1992 until now. In 1992, Deng Xiaoping bolstered the faltering political fortunes of economic reform, and rebooted China's stalling economy by making his famous southern tour. Foreign direct investment in China also took off in 1992, and earlier startling forecasts of China's rising economic power (especially by the World Bank in 1991) began to be linked more often with its military modernization program. This linkage no doubt arose in large part because of the collapse of the Soviet Union and international preoccupations with possible emerging challengers to U.S. hegemony.

## PERSPECTIVES ON A RISING CHINA

### Political Conditions

Between 1985 and 1989, Australia and New Zealand had responded with considerable good will and high hopes to the rapid opening up of a still-Communist China to the outside world. They were encouraged by the gradual easing of restrictions on the lives of Chinese citizens, and in 1988 and 1989 by the promise of a revolutionary embrace of humanism and liberal pluralism. The events of June 1989 and the subsequent retrenchment of political reform until 1992 meant that both Australia and New Zealand started the decade under review with a critical eye toward China, and with the somewhat jaundiced feelings of a rejected friend. China's retrenchment of political reform—and its use of force to do so—stood in strong contrast to the successful, if erratic, emergence of liberal pluralism in Russia and Eastern Europe, and was seen by many in Australia as a failure. This was the old Red China: brutal, ruthlessly dictatorial, and subject to wild political swings. In the popular imagination, this vision of China began to revive memories of the 1960s, and fuelled concerns about China returning to the international stage with an erratic or confrontational posture. The picture was very confusing, with contradictory signals.

Political reform returned to the political agenda of China's leaders after 1992. Attention was now paid to the legal and constitutional foundations of political power. Reforms included greater professionalization of China's police and court system, and a massive effort to regularize the legal framework through a raft of new legislation and public supervision of government work. The reforms also included experiments with village-level elections of village heads. A particularly important change was the recognition by China's leaders of torture in its prison and police systems, and a public campaign to eliminate it. By 2002, there was a large degree of freedom of expression that had not been imaginable in 1989. Yet continuing suppression of some types of dissent and of unofficial religion, the maintenance of the prison camp system for political prisoners, and pervasive brutality in the legal system—evidenced by the widespread use of the death penalty (even for economic crimes)—overshadowed the liberalizations.

It became quite difficult for most in Australia and New Zealand to reconcile these competing images, and to identify which was the dominant trend or characteristic. Was China reforming and moving inevitably toward a more benign and pluralistic system, or was it a nasty, brutish country captured by its authoritarian system and incapable of transforming its essence? This confusion has not been fully resolved today in the popular imagination or among many opinion leaders in Australia and New Zealand.

## Economic Power

China's potential as a source of commercial opportunity and economic gain for both Australia and New Zealand was a constant feature of popular perceptions in the decade after 1992. And the figures for the growing economic relationships with China bear this out. Even the least educated in the two countries probably viewed China's national economic power as rapidly on the increase. But few among the general public or even among opinion leaders took seriously the full implications of what the growing internationalization of an economy as large as China's actually meant in the economic councils of the world, and as a factor for change in most countries' trading and investment relations. There were two camps in the small number of professionals who did think about these things: One group viewed China as a powerful force that would substantially disturb existing relationships and economic patterns, but could be successfully integrated. The other camp was intimidated by China, and was uncertain how to think about it. China's membership of the World Trade Organization (WTO) has in one sense resolved this contradiction, yet in another sense the contradiction remains. There are some in both Australia and New Zealand who are basically skeptical about whether China can ever be a force for good in the world economic order, and who feel that the West should even begin to think strategically about how to limit and constrain China's economic influence. This is a minority view, but it is an underlying sentiment, even among some of the better informed in the community.

## Strategic and Military Power

The ambivalence about how to view China's political conditions and economic power is even more visible when it comes to perceptions of its military power. Since 1992, Australian and New Zealand newspapers have repeatedly carried the same sensationalist reports exaggerating this or that aspect of China's military capability. From time to time, some of Australia's leading academic specialists in strategic studies join this chorus of "threat mongers." Rarely have stories with such a theme been on the front pages in any Australian or New Zealand newspapers, but an underlying suspicion about China's military power is the dominant, if sometimes dormant, sentiment. The perception has even surfaced in official government assessments in both countries, as an issue of concern for the future, though

GREG AUSTIN

with lower levels of apprehension in the more remote New Zealand. The most important aspect of this perception is that there is no powerful public constituency in either country pressing a consistent "China threat" thesis.

There is, at least in Australia, the same sort of questioning going on as in the United States about whether an increase in China's power will lead to a change in the balance of power in Asia. While this question is not yet regarded as urgent in Australia, it should be noted that Australia strongly backs the existing balance of power arrangements centered on the U.S.-Japan axis, and it would not view kindly any act that looked like disturbing that arrangement.


## Taiwan

Regardless of whether or not one views Taiwan as part of China, the attitudes of both Australia and New Zealand toward their own relations with Taiwan, and toward China's relations with Taiwan, have in the past decade had a negative influence in both places on perceptions of China. Unless and until China and Taiwan reach an amicable settlement of their differences, this negative influence on perceptions of China will continue to increase. When China and Taiwan agreed in 1992 to hold formal talks, both Australia and New Zealand had every reason to believe that their formula—indeed, the world's formula—for good economic relations with both sides could be effectively pursued without any major political obstacle. Relevant statistics show that Taiwan is an important economic partner for both Australia and New Zealand. It is less important to both than China is, but it is not that far behind. For Australia in particular, China's military pressure on Taiwan changed these perceptions. Australia basically lines up with the United States on Taiwan Strait issues, not just in a declaratory position of opposing the use of force by China, but more significantly in accepting that if war arose, Australia would fight on the same side as the United States. Australian warships have conducted freedom of navigation exercises in the Taiwan Strait at the request of the U.S. government.

It is almost impossible to imagine New Zealand joining Australia at the side of the United States in any military confrontation over Taiwan.

## Domestic Influences on These Perceptions

### Political Conditions

Within the major political parties, views on China are not differentiated by party affiliation. Human rights groups do have some weight, but the Australian and New Zealand parliaments are not preoccupied with China's domestic political environment the way that the U.S. Congress is. The Australian public is not impressed with what most see as either the unremitting brutality of the Chinese political system or its unforgiving repression of particular dissidents and unofficial religious leaders. The views of academics and specialists do not influence popular views of China. There is by and large a swirling morass of views and opinions, and it would probably take some crisis to act as a lightning rod to channel these views in one direction or another. A significant China lobby is active at this general level, with group members including former political leaders such as Paul Keating and Bob Hawke. While these people also pursue commercial interests in China, they have a genuine affection for and close understanding of China, which lends them to a more positive view. These people would be influential in shaping public and elite opinion if negative sentiment about China started to become unjustifiably strong. The Australian population and the media are very poorly informed about China beyond the headline coverage that most of the world sees.

### Economic Power

All major political parties support strong economic engagement with China. But the current Liberal-National coalition is more comfortable dealing with the United States and Europe than with Asia. Big business in Australia and New Zealand, and even some medium-sized businesses, are fully committed to and strongly supportive of good economic relations with China. The state economic departments are also fully committed. The knowledge base about China's economic and commercial conditions needs to be improved substantially across the board though. There is little constituency in the Australian business community for the institutional processes that are integrating China into the world economy, though the peak industry associations pay close attention to the commercial ramifications of this process, and are active in it.

GREG AUSTIN

## Strategic and Military Power

Within the major political parties, policy positions and views are not differentiated by party affiliation. Australia and New Zealand are both weak in terms of institutional capacity—in government, academia, and non-governmental organizations—to assess appropriately all the dimensions of China's strategic and military power. One notable Australian exception is the Labor Shadow Minister for Foreign Affairs, Kevin Rudd, who served as a diplomat in China and has a good intuitive grasp of the issues. In Australia, specialists who see China's armed forces as relatively backward, and therefore China's strategic power as being quite limited, are viewed as "soft" on China in the eyes of some government officials. Talk of "panda huggers" and "panda bashers" to describe opposing views of China's strategic power parallels elements in the U.S. climate of opinion. But the degree of political activism on these strategic issues in Australia and New Zealand is small when compared to that taking place in the United States.

## Taiwan

Key constituencies on this issue in Australia and New Zealand are not yet really mobilized. At present, it is more a question of managing the matter politically so that it does not seriously impinge on other big political issues. There is one notable exception to this. As in other countries, Taiwan has conducted a vigorous and effective diplomacy, which has resulted in the formation of a Taiwan caucus in the Australian parliament. In Australia, the trend in public opinion is positive toward Taiwan, and negative toward China over its threats vis-à-vis Taiwan. In a crisis, public opinion would quickly support "democratic" Taiwan.

## DO PERCEPTIONS MATCH THE LIKELY REALITY OF A RISING CHINA?

Again, there are four aspects to the answer to this question.

*Political conditions:* The political reality inside China and perceptions of it inside the broader body politic in both Australia and New Zealand do not really match. The main problem is lack of nuance. Most perceptions are too black and white, and are also not up to date.

*Economic power:* In this case, views are generally closer to reality, espe-cially among the policymakers who count, although not necessarily among the general public. Economic and commercial necessity drives percep-tions. Institutionalizing China's integration into the world economy seems to be regarded more as a chore or necessity than an inspired act of policy.

*Strategic and military power:* There is a major gap here between percep-tion and reality. Very few people in both countries, including in the gov-ernments and in the intelligence communities, understand with any depth the dimensions of and constraints on China's military power. When put to the test, the two governments do not necessarily hold the more nega-tive or hostile views of China's military power that are seen in the United States.

*Taiwan:* If few people in Australia and New Zealand have good appre-ciation of Chinese military and strategic power, even fewer understand what is happening between China and Taiwan. There are important ex-ceptions. Yet most political leaders and officials would not credit Taiwan's political evolution in the last decade as having impacted postures adopted more than two decades ago. The old "one China" policy is disintegrating, and Australia and New Zealand are not seriously engaged in thinking about the consequences of this. Both governments have also been too uncritical of the evolving U.S. position, especially as the Bush Administration seems to be seeking to restore the U.S. military alliance with Taiwan.

## Appropriate Responses to a Rising China

This author believes that the appropriate policy responses to China's rise in the four areas should be as follows:

*Political conditions:* Australia and New Zealand should continue to en-gage China's leaders at all levels. Both countries should continue to pro-vide technical support for China's legal and institutional reforms. They should also continue to advocate greater respect for human rights and the abolition of the death penalty. The governments of both countries should also begin to engage nonofficial elite circles more effectively. Con-sideration should also be given to upgrading diplomatic and trade repre-sentation. In terms of activities in Australia and New Zealand, both governments should give leadership to wider public debate on China, with a greater emphasis on quality and specialist knowledge, to help foster improved public awareness.

*Economic power:* Both Australia and New Zealand should continue supporting Asia Pacific regionalism, and working for China's integration into the regional and global economy in ways that recognize and deal with the inevitable negative impact of China's competitive capacities. Both governments also need to help build and broaden the public information base.

*Strategic and military power:* Expanding military-to-military ties and educational opportunities in Australia for People's Liberation Army officers would be good examples of the types of confidence-building measures that should be supported. The governments in Australia and New Zealand should also prepare better and more public strategies for preventing tension between China and the United States due to the latter's robust posturing over the need to prevent the rise of a "competitor" great power. As with the other areas of policy, both governments should lead an expansion of the public debate in Australia and New Zealand, with a greater emphasis on quality and specialist knowledge.

*Taiwan:* Australia and New Zealand need to engage actively on this crisis-in-waiting. Both need to continue to oppose China's use of force on the issue of Taiwan, while moderating U.S. impulses to over-militarize the situation. Increasing the information base of the public in both countries would also be key.

In summary, much work needs to be done in Australia and New Zealand to bring perceptions in line with reality, and to shape the contours of China's emergent relationships in the region. Both countries need to study China more closely, and on a more sustained basis.

But, from the perspective of Australia and New Zealand, China also has work to do on a number of fronts. In global security, China needs to be clearer about the responsibilities that arise from permanent membership of the United Nations Security Council. China needs to stake out more clearly its own positions, and stop hiding behind the skirts of Russia and France, or the all-too-frequent "abstention." Unless China begins to act more like a responsible leader of the international community in the body where it has great influence, most will not treat it as one. In this regard, China's recent appointment of its first ever special envoy on Middle East affairs was a major and important innovation. It does represent progress toward active and constructive Chinese leadership in global policy.

Australians and New Zealanders also want greater transparency from China about its strategic policy. This would help bridge the gulf between misguided perceptions and reality. And it is a bigger issue than knowing the detail of China's military budget or its force deployments. Both countries want to know, for example, how China is viewing the new implicit threat against it contained in the U.S. National Security Strategy that was released in September 2002. This report stated, somewhat ominously, that: "China's leaders have not yet made the next series of fundamental choices about the character of their state." While noting the "historic opportunity to preserve peace" among the great powers, the report comments that the United States will encourage the advancement of democracy in China (and Russia), and "strongly resist aggression from great powers," an unmistakable reference to China. The document also notes that the United States has a "profound disagreement" with China over its Taiwan policy. What is the reaction of China's leaders to the new U.S. policy, outlined in the document, that one role of the U.S. armed forces henceforth is to "dissuade future military competition"? People in Australia and New Zealand need to know more precisely what China's leaders are thinking. Knowing this would help the Asian region to persuade the United States to walk away from its slowly escalating pressure on China that flows from the realist conviction that the United States must prevent China's emergence as a possible competitor.

Perceptions of China in Australia and New Zealand in the coming three to five years will be shaped by how China reacts to U.S. power, and by its much delayed agenda of political pluralization and democratization. If China continues to maintain its current authoritarian system, and continues to threaten Taiwan with the use of force, then it will not win many new friends in Australia or New Zealand. The positive images of China as a strong, valuable, and even indispensable economic partner, and the great admiration we all have for its rapid economic growth, would evaporate relatively quickly under the pressure of strategic alignments.

On the other hand, if China does at last "let a hundred flowers bloom" and a "thousand schools of thought contend," then the aims of the revolutionary founders of new China, including Sun Yatsen, will have been achieved. When China is "rich, powerful, civilized, and *democratic*," as Tian Jiyun, former Politburo member and former vice chairman of the National People's Congress, used to say, then people in Australia and New Zealand will again regard it with the awe that once held sway. Until that time, leading realist writers on international relations and their powerful contemporary exponents, such as Condoleezza Rice, Donald Rumsfeld, and Paul Wolfowitz, will script perceptions.

# About the Contributors

Kokubun Ryosei, Director, Center for Area Studies, Keio University

Wang Jisi, Director, Institute of American Studies, Chinese Academy of Social Science

Greg Austin, Visiting Senior Research Fellow, European Institute for Asian Studies, Brussels; Visiting Fellow, Contemporary China Centre, Australian National University

Chia Siow Yue, Senior Research Fellow, Singapore Institute of International Affairs,

Jwa Sung-Hee, President, Korea Economic Research Institute

Lee Geun, Assistant Professor, School of International and Area Studies, Seoul National University

Men Honghua, Associate Professor, Institute for International Strategic Studies, Central Party School; Research Fellow, Center for Chinese Studies, Tsinghua University

Noel M. Morada, Executive Director, Institute for Strategic and Development Studies, Philippines

Ni Feng, Associate Researcher, Deputy Director, U.S. Politics Department, Institute of American Studies, Chinese Academy of Social Science

Ohashi Hideo, Professor, Department of Economics, Senshu University

Mari Pangestu, Director, Center for Strategic and International Studies, Jakarta

Takahara Akio, Professor, Department of Politics, Rikkyo University

Jusuf Wanandi, Co-founder and Member of the Board of Trustees, Center for Strategic and International Studies, Jakarta

Wang Gungwu, Director, East Asian Institute, Singapore

Wang Rongjun, Research Fellow and Deputy Chief, Department of Economic Studies, Institute of American Studies, Chinese Academy of Social Science

Yang Guangbin, Professor, School of International Studies, Renmin University

Yoon Yong, Research Associate, Korea Economic Research Institute; Ph.D. Candidate, Seoul National University

# The Japan Center for International Exchange

FOUNDED IN 1970, the Japan Center for International Exchange (JCIE) is an independent, nonprofit, and nonpartisan organization dedicated to strengthening Japan's role in international affairs. JCIE believes that Japan faces a major challenge in augmenting its positive contributions to the international community, in keeping with its position as one of the world's largest industrial democracies. Operating in a country where policy making has traditionally been dominated by the government bureaucracy, JCIE has played an important role in broadening debate on Japan's international responsibilities by conducting international and cross-sectional programs of exchange, research, and discussion.

JCIE creates opportunities for informed policy discussions; it does not take policy positions. JCIE programs are carried out with the collaboration and cosponsorship of many organizations. The contacts developed through these working relationships are crucial to JCIE's efforts to increase the number of Japanese from the private sector engaged in meaningful policy research and dialogue with overseas counterparts.

JCIE receives no government subsidies; rather, funding comes from private foundation grants, corporate contributions, and contracts.